CONTENTS

KT-435-993

AS and A2 Level
English

Acknowledgements

The author and publisher would like to thank the following for permission to reproduce material in this book.

Bedbugs by Clive Sinclair, from *Penguin Book of Modern British Short Stories*, edited by Ray Bradbury. Reproduced with permission c/o Rogers, Coleridge & White Limited, 20 Powis Mews, London W11 1JN;
Kidspoem/Bairnsong by Liz Lochhead from *Penguin Modern Poets* published by Penguin Books;
Some regional accents spell social death copyright © Paul Goggle first published in *The Sunday Times*, 6 August 1995;
If Only Every School Taught Pidgin English, copyright © Ken Campbell, first published in *The Guardian* 20 December 1996;
Blinking Hell reproduced with the permission of Sight Savers International;
Army turns to crime to find new recruits by Michael Evans, copyright © Times Newspapers Limited, 8 November 1999;
Army targets lags in recruiting drive by Paul Gilfeather, copyright © News International Newspapers Limited, 8 November 1999;
The Army is right to recruit where it can copyright © Daily Mail, 8 November 1999;
Black English is a Language by Richard Thomas, copyright © *The Guardian*, 21 December 1996;
Purists take new dictionary to task for 'dreadful' words by Katherine Knight, copyright © Times Newspapers Limited, 5 June 1995;
A Nursery Rhyme by Wendy Cope from *Making Cocoa for Kingsley Amis* published by Faber & Faber, 1999;
Curse of the Rudest Women in London by Henry Porter, copyright © Evening Standard, October 1999;
The Penguin Book of Twentieth Century Speeches edited by Brian MacArthur published by Penguin Books, 1999. Extract from Winston Churchill's speech reproduced with permission of the Estate of Winston Churchill, c/o Curtis Brown, 4th Floor, 28-29 Haymarket House, Haymarket, London SW1Y 4SP. Extract from Gideon Hausner's speech reproduced with permission of Longman Group UK, Addison Wesley Longman Group, Edinburgh Gate, Harlow, Essex CM20 2JE.
[p. 42] from *In Search of Our Mothers' Gardens* by Alice Walker published in Great Britain by The Women's Press Limited, 1984, 34 Great Sutton Street, London EC1V 0LQ;
Fractured Fairytales from *Diana Princess of Wales 1961–1997* by J. John. First published in Great Britain by Kingsway Publications, co-published in South Africa by SCB Publishers, copyright © J. John;

In Her Own Words by Andrew Morton, copyright © Michael O'Mara Books Limited, 1997;
Don't You Want Me by Julie Burchill, copyright © Orion, 1998;
Sugar Daddy by Angela Carter, copyright © Angela Carter, 1983. Reproduced by permission of the Estate of Angela Carter c/o Rogers, Coleridge & White Limited., 20 Powis Mews, London W11 1JN;
And When Did You Last See Your Father by Blake Morrison published by Granta Books, 1993;
Look At Me by Anita Brookner published by Triad/Panther Books, 1993;
Birdsong by Sebastian Faulks published by Hutchinson, 1994;
[pp 61–62] from *The Dickies* from *The Sidmouth Letters* by Jane Gardam, published in Great Britain by Sphere Books Limited, 3032 Grays Inn Road, London WC1X 8JL;
Mrs Dalloway by Virginia Woolf published by Penguin Books, 1996. Reproduced with permission of Society of Authors, 84 Drayton Gardens, London SW10 9SB;
The Robber Bride by Margaret Atwood first published by Bloomsbury 1993, paperback edition by Virago Press, 1994;
Enduring Love by Ian McEwan published by Jonathon Cape, 1997;
Look Back in Anger by John Osborne published by Faber & Faber, 1957;
A Streetcar Named Desire by Tennessee Williams published by Methuen Publishing Company, 1984;
As I Walked Out One Evening by W. H. Auden from *W. H. Auden Selected Poems*, published by Faber & Faber, 1979;
The Silken Tent by Robert Frost from *Selected Poems* published by Jonathon Cape;

The following titles are in the public domain but the publisher acknowledges the use of extracts from the following material: *The Return of the Native* by Thomas Hardy published by Macmillan Publishers Limited; *The Catcher in the Rye* by J. D. Salinger published by Macmillan Publishers Limited, 1951; *The Man He Killed* and *The Puzzled Game Birds* by Thomas Hardy taken from *Selected Shorter Poems of Thomas Hardy* published by Macmillan Publishers Limited.

Every effort has been made to trace and acknowledge ownership of copyright material but if any have been inadvertently overlooked, the publisher will be pleased to make the necessary alterations at the first opportunity.

First published 2000
exclusively for WHSmith by

Hodder & Stoughton Educational
338 Euston Road
LONDON NW1 3BH

Text © Steve Eddy and Mary Hartley 2000

A CIP record for this book is available from the British Library.

Text: Steve Eddy and Mary Hartley, with Tony Buzan
Mind Maps: The Buzan Centres

ISBN 0-340-74330-1

10	9	8	7	6	5	4	3	2	1	
Year	2005	2004	2003	2002	2001	2000				

Typeset by Wearset, Boldon, Tyne and Wear

Printed and bound in Great Britain for Hodder & Stoughton Educational by The Bath Press, Bath

You are now in the most important educational stage of your life and are soon to take exams that may have a major impact on your future career and goals. As one A Level student put it: 'It's crunch time!'

At this crucial stage of your life, the thing you need even more than subject knowledge is the knowledge of **how** to remember, **how** to read faster, **how** to comprehend, **how** to study, **how** to take notes and **how** to organise your thoughts. You need to know how to **think**; you need a basic introduction on how to use that super computer inside your head – your brain.

The next few pages contain a goldmine of information on how you can achieve success, both at school and in your A Level exams, as well as in your professional or university career. These pages will give you information on memory, thinking skills, speed reading and study that will enable you to be successful in all your academic pursuits. You will learn:

1 How to remember more *while* you are learning.

2 How to remember more *after* you have finished a class or a study period.

3 How to use special techniques to improve your memory.

4 How to use a revolutionary note-taking technique called Mind Maps that will double your memory and help you to write essays and answer exam questions.

5 How to read everything faster, while at the same time improving comprehension and concentration.

6 How to zap your revision.

How to understand, improve and master your memory

Your memory really is like a muscle. Don't exercise it and it will grow weaker; do exercise it and it will grow incredibly more powerful. There are really only four main things you need to understand about your memory in order to increase its power dramatically:

1 Recall during learning – you must take breaks!

When you are studying, your memory can concentrate, understand and remember well for between 20 and 45 minutes at a time. Then it needs a break. If you carry on for longer than this without one, your memory starts to break down. If you study for hours non-stop, you will remember only a fraction of what you have been trying to learn and you will have wasted valuable revision time.

So, ideally, *study for less than an hour*, then take a five- to ten-minute break. During this break, listen to music, go for a walk, do some exercise or just daydream. (Daydreaming is a necessary brainpower booster – geniuses do it regularly.)

During the break your brain will be sorting out what it has been learning and you will go back to your study with the new information safely stored and organised in your memory banks.

Make sure you take breaks at regular intervals as you work through your *Revise AS and A Level* book.

2 Recall after learning – surfing the waves of your memory

What do you think begins to happen to your memory straight after you have finished learning something? Does it immediately start forgetting? No! Your brain actually *increases* its power and carries on remembering. For a short time after your study session, your brain integrates the information making a more complete picture of everything it has just learnt. Only then does the rapid decline in memory begin, and as much as 80% of what you have learnt can be forgotten in a day.

However, if you catch the top of the wave of your memory, and briefly review back what you have been revising at the correct time, the memory is stamped in far more strongly and stays at the crest of the wave for much longer. To maximise your brain's power to remember, take a few minutes and use a Mind Map to review what you have learnt at the end of a day. Then review it at the end of a week, again at the end of a month and, finally, a week before the exams. That way you'll surf-ride your memory wave all the way to your exam, success, and beyond!

3 The memory principle of association

The muscle of your memory becomes stronger when it can **associate** – when it can link things together.

Think about your best friend and all the things your mind automatically links with that person. Think about your favourite hobby and all the associations your mind has when you think about (remember) that hobby.

When you are studying, use this memory principle to make associations between the elements in your subjects and to thus improve both your memory and your chances of success.

4 The memory principle of imagination

The muscle of your memory will improve significantly if you can produce big **images** in your mind. Rather than just memorising the name of an historical character, **imagine** that character as if you were a video producer filming that person's life.

In *all* your subjects, use the **imagination** memory principle.

Your new success formula: Mind Maps®

You have noticed that when people go on holidays or travels they take maps. Why? To give them a general picture of where they are going, to help them locate places of special interest and importance, to help them find things more easily and to help them remember distances, locations and so on.

It is exactly the same with your mind and with study.

If you have a 'map of the territory' of what you have to learn, then everything is easier. In learning and study, the Mind Map is that special tool.

As well as helping you with all areas of study, the Mind Map actually *mirrors the way your brain works*. Your Mind Maps can be used for taking notes from your study books, taking notes in class, preparing

How to draw a Mind Map

1 Start in the middle of the page with the paper turned sideways. This gives your brain more radiant freedom for its thoughts.

2 Always start by drawing a picture or symbol. Why? Because **a picture is worth a thousand words to your brain**. Try to use at least three colours, as colour helps your memory even more.

3 Let your thoughts flow, and write or draw your ideas on coloured branching lines connected to your central image. These key symbols and words are the headings for your topic.

4 Next, add facts and ideas by drawing more, smaller, branches on to the appropriate main branches, just like a tree.

5 Always print each word clearly on its line. Use only one word per line.

6 To link ideas and thoughts on different branches, use arrows, colours, underlining and boxes.

How to read a Mind Map

1 Begin in the centre, the focus of your topic.
2 The words/images attached to the centre are like chapter headings; read them next.
3 Always read out from the centre, in every direction (even on the left-hand side, where you will have to read from right to left; instead of the usual left to right).

your homework, presenting your homework, reviewing your tests, checking your and your friends' knowledge in any subject, and for *helping you understand anything you learn*.

As you will see, Mind Maps use, throughout, Imagination and Association. As such, they automatically strengthen your memory muscle every time you use them. Throughout this *Revise AS and A2 Level* book you will find Mind Maps that summarise the most important areas of the subject you are studying. Study them, add some colour, personalise them, and then have a go at drawing your own – you will remember them far better! Put them on your walls and in your files for a quick and easy review of the topic.

Using Mind Maps

Mind Maps are a versatile tool – use them for taking notes in class or from books, for solving problems, for brainstorming with friends, and for reviewing and revising for exams – their uses are infinite! You will find them invaluable for planning essays for coursework and exams. Number your main branches in the order in which you want to use them and off you go – the main headings for your essay are done *and* all your ideas are logically organised.

Super speed reading and study

What happens to your comprehension as your reading speed rises? 'It goes down.' Wrong! It seems incredible, but it has been proved that the faster you read, the more you comprehend and remember.

So here are some tips to help you to practise reading faster – you'll cover the ground much more quickly, remember more *and* have more time for revision and leisure activities.

How to make study easy for your brain

When you are going somewhere, is it easier to know beforehand where you are going, or not? Obviously it is easier if you do know. It is the same for your brain and a book. When you get a new book, there are seven things you can do to help your brain get to 'know the territory' faster.

1 Scan through the whole book in less than 20 minutes, as you would do if you were in a shop thinking whether or not to buy it. This gives your brain control.

2 Think about what you already know about the subject. You'll often find out it's a lot more than you thought. A good way of doing this is to draw a quick Mind Map on everything you know after you have skimmed through it.

3 Ask who, what, why, where, when and how questions about what is in the book. Questions help your brain 'fish' the knowledge out.

4 Ask your friends what they know about the subject. This helps them review the knowledge in their own brains and helps your brain get new knowledge about what you are studying.

5 Have another quick speed through the book, this time looking for any diagrams, pictures and illustrations, and also at the beginnings and ends of chapters. Most information is contained in the beginnings and ends.

6 Build up a Mind Map as you study the book. This helps your brain organise and hold (remember) information as you study.

7 If you come across any difficult parts in your book, mark them and move on. Your brain *will* be able to solve the problems when you come back to them a little bit later, much like saving the difficult bits of a jigsaw puzzle for later. When you have finished the book, quickly review it one more time and then discuss it with friends. This will lodge it permanently in your memory banks.

Super speed reading

1 First read the whole text (whether it's a lengthy book or an exam paper) very quickly, to give your brain an overall idea of what's ahead and get it working. (It's like sending out a scout to look at the territory you have to cover – it's much easier when you know what to expect.) Then read the text again for more detailed information.

2 Have the text a reasonable distance away from your eyes. In this way your eye/brain system will be able to see more at a glance and will naturally begin to read faster.

3 Take in groups of words at a time. Rather than reading 'slowly and carefully', read faster, more enthusiastically. Your comprehension will rocket!

4 Take in phrases rather than single words while you read.

5 Use a guide. Your eyes are designed to follow movement, so a thin pencil underneath the lines you are reading, moved smoothly along, will 'pull' your eyes to faster speeds.

Helpful hints for exam revision

To avoid exam panic, cram at the start of your course, not the end. It takes the same amount of time, so you may as well use it where it is best placed!

Use Mind Maps throughout your course and build a Master Mind Map for each subject – a giant Mind Map that summarises everything you know about the subject.

Use memory techniques, such as mnemonics (verses or systems for remembering things like dates and events or lists).

Get together with one or two friends to revise, compare Mind Maps and discuss topics.

And finally . . .

- *Have fun while you learn* – studies show that those people who enjoy what they are doing understand and remember it more and generally do better.

- *Use your teachers* as resource centres. Ask them for help with specific topics and with more general advice on how you can improve your all-round performance.

- *Personalise your* **Revise AS and A2 Level** *book* by underlining and highlighting, by adding notes and pictures. Allow your brain to have a conversation with it!

Your amazing brain and its amazing cells

Your brain is like a super computer. The world's best computers have only a few thousand or hundred thousand computer chips. Your brain has 'computer chips' too; they are called brain cells. Unlike the computer, you do not have only a few thousand computer chips – the number of brain cells in your head is a *million million*! This means you are a genius just waiting to discover yourself! All you have to do is learn how to get those brain cells working together, and you'll not only become more smart, you'll have more free time to pursue your other fun activities.

The more you understand your amazing brain, the more it will repay and amaze you!

PREVIEW

This chapter will tell you about:

- **key differences between studying English at GCSE and at Advanced level**
- **how your course is organised**
- **what you will have to do**
- **how to prepare for the open book exam**
- **how to prepare for the closed book exam**
- **how to prepare for coursework**
- **what makes a good grade**

Moving on

Whatever your reasons for studying English at an advanced level, it is likely that you have already achieved good grades in the subject at GCSE. This is an excellent start, and you should feel proud of your achievement and secure in the knowledge that you have a sound basis from which to proceed. Some of your valuable skills will be further developed through advanced study, and you will also learn new skills, techniques and approaches.

CHECKLIST

You will almost certainly have the following experiences at points during your course:

- ✓ **challenge**
- ✓ **stimulus**
- ✓ **annoyance**
- ✓ **puzzlement**
- ✓ **frustration**
- ✓ **satisfaction**
- ✓ **pleasure**
- ✓ **excitement**
- ✓ **irritation**
- ✓ **insight**

Copy out this checklist. Annotate it and add to it as you navigate your voyage through the thrilling and rewarding seas of English studies!

TRY THIS

1   **Can you give the meanings of these terms and use them in sentences?**
    diction, lexis, connotation, ambiguity, style, structure

2   **Two of the critical approaches you will come across are:**

   a) **Marxist – a view that sees texts in terms of the conflict between social classes and the economic structure of society.**

   b) **Feminist – a view that sees texts in terms of the place of women in a male-dominated society.**

Read this beginning of a traditional story:

   Red Riding Hood was walking through the woods towards her grandmother's cottage. She was taking her sick grandmother a basket of food. Suddenly a wolf appeared from behind a clump of trees, and asked where she was going.

What kind of interpretation is represented by each of these statements?

Red Riding Hood is seen in a traditional female role, nurturing and caring for the sick.

The wolf is outside the social and economic structure of society.

What's different?

Be prepared for some key differences in the nature of the work you do and in the way that you approach it. Some important criteria that distinguish advanced level work are:

- becoming an independent, critical reader of a range of texts
- understanding and using a range of critical and analytical terminology
- understanding the significance of a range of contexts such as social, political and cultural
- understanding and evaluating different interpretations of texts
- working independently.

In practice it means that you will study texts which you may find challenging in their subject matter, meanings and language, and your spoken and written discussion of them will reflect your knowledge and understanding of critical interpretation.

Sorting out your syllabus

Whether you are studying English Literature, English Language or English Language and Literature, your course will be organised in a similar way. You may be taking AS level as a final qualification, to broaden your studies before specialising in other subjects, or you may be taking it as the first half of an A level qualification. Whatever your situation, your course will consist of self-contained, free-standing modules or units, some of which will be externally assessed and some of which will be internally assessed through coursework. Find out as much information as you can about the modules you will be taking.

CHECKLIST

Gather this information:

✓ **the name of your exam board**

✓ **the title and description of each module you will be taking**

✓ **how each module will be assessed**

✓ **when each module will be completed**

✓ **what you need to know and to do for each module**

✓ **the length of written papers**

✓ **what percentage of the total marks each module carries**

FACTFILE

There are three examining boards for AS and A level:

Assessment and Qualifications Alliance (AQA): Stag Hill House, Guildford, Surrey GU2 5XJ or Aldon House, 39 Heald Grove, Rusholme, Manchester M14 4PB

Edexcel Foundation: Stewart House, 32 Russell Square, London WC18 5DN

OCR: 1 Hills Road, Cambridge CB1 2EU

Getting to grips with assessment

Overview of objectives

It is helpful for you to know the assessment objectives for your course, but do remember that to a large extent they overlap and link, and that in each module or unit of study you may be assessed in a number of areas.

English Literature AS level

You should be able to:

1 communicate knowledge, understanding and insight appropriate to literary study

2 communicate clearly, coherently and accurately, using appropriate terminology

3 show knowledge and understanding of texts of different types and different periods

4 show understanding of how a writer uses language, form and structure

5 express your own ideas and judgements of literary texts, informed by other interpretations

6 show understanding of the contexts in which literary texts are written and understood.

English Literature A level

When you move on to A level, further assessments will take into account the greater breadth and depth of your study. In addition to what you have shown you can do at AS level, you will also show that you can:

1 explore and comment on relationships and comparisons between literary texts of different types and periods

2 evaluate the significance of contextual influences (such as historical or cultural) upon literary texts and the study of literature.

TRY THIS

- Read the objectives listed opposite and underline key words. Think of examples of how you show your ability in the different areas. You could include the texts you read and the ways you interpret and write about them. Start a Mind Map of the key words and your associated ideas. You could add to it as you go through the course, or complete it as a revision exercise when you have finished.

- Make a Mind Map of the information you have collected. The ones below show some of the options offered by the different boards. You could use one of them as a basis for your own Mind Map.

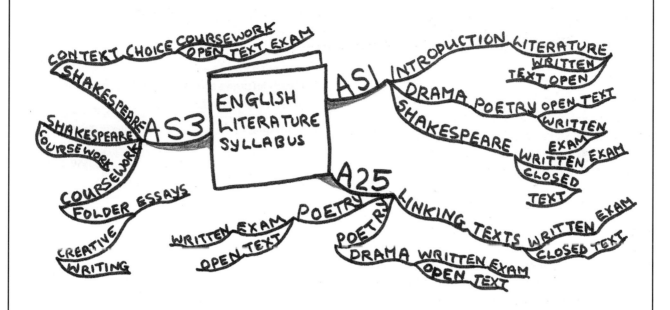

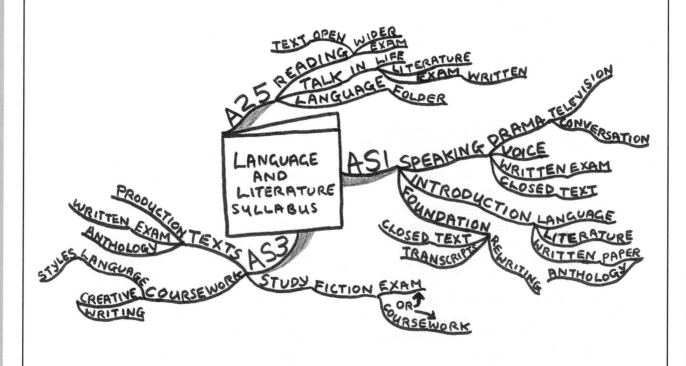

English Language/Literature AS level

You should be able to:

1 communicate knowledge, understanding and insight appropriate to linguistic or combined literary and linguistic study

2 communicate clearly, coherently and accurately, using appropriate terminology

3 in responding to appropriate texts, distinguish, describe and interpret variation in meaning and form

4 show understanding of the way contextual variation and choices of form, style and vocabulary shape the meanings of texts

5 discuss the ways attitudes and values are expressed in speech and writing

6 write expertly and accurately for a variety of specific audiences and purposes, drawing on your knowledge of appropriate texts and features of language to explain and comment on your choices.

English Language/Literature A level

When you move on to A level, further assessments will take into account the greater breadth and depth of your study. In addition to what you have shown you can do at AS level, you will also show that you can:

1 explore and comment on relationships and comparisons between texts of different types and periods

2 use and evaluate different approaches (literary/linguistic) to the study of written and spoken language, and show how these approaches inform your reading.

TRY THIS

1 **Go through your texts and read your marginal notes and underlinings. Decide what purpose they are fulfilling. Rub out any marks that are no longer useful. For your final marked text, use devices such as colour, codes, arrows and mnemonics to help you select information speedily.**

2 **For each of your texts, choose three passages that you think are significant. Make a Mind Map of the passages' features and the kind of question that could be asked about them.**

Open book exam

You may have the option of taking your text in with you to your exam. Usually, you will be able to make marginal notes and comments in the copy you are using – but do find out if there are any limits on the amount and kind of textual annotation that is allowed. You need to prepare as carefully for the open book exam as you do for any other type of test – so put some time in now thinking about how to approach this exam, and make the system work for you!

TRY THIS

There are benefits and drawbacks to having your text with you in an exam. Some advantages and disadvantages are shown below. Add your own ideas to the chart.

advantages	disadvantages
You feel more confident.	You may rely too much on having the text available.
You can quote accurately.	You may copy out quotations that are too long or irrelevant.
You may be asked a wider range of questions.	You may refer inappropriately to the critical introduction or notes in your edition.

Making notes

You may be tempted to cram as many notes as you can on to every page. Resist this temptation. Instead, make notes in the margin or underline passages **as you explore and discuss the text**. The reason you make notes is to enable you to understand the text's themes and issues. As you go through your course, make your notes in pencil. Helpful notes are those made for specific purposes – to help you to understand and remember vocabulary, for example, or to prepare for a particular assignment. Erase notes that have served their purpose, and take into the exam a text that is annotated for the purposes of the exam. At this stage you should have an overall appreciation of the text and of the type of question you may be asked; an appropriately annotated text will help you to collate and present your response.

Open questions

In an open book exam you will be asked questions that direct you to a particular passage or section of your text, or questions that require you to select certain passages. It is absolutely essential to know your text thoroughly – the given passage should not look unfamiliar, nor should you have to leaf desperately through your text looking for an appropriate selection!

of ways. You will be expected to use quotation appropriately; this means that you must memorise **short** quotations to illustrate particular points.

HINT

Get to know the different kinds of open text questions. Find examples for each of your texts.

HINT

Don't learn by heart huge chunks of quotations. Short, well-chosen quotations and close reference will gain you credit.

CHECKLIST

Some tips for the open book exam:

✓ Check that your notes are within the guidelines set by your exam board.

✓ Make sure your notes are useful and specific.

✓ Don't copy out chunks of the text.

✓ Don't copy out material from your text's introduction or notes.

✓ Know your text thoroughly.

CHECKLIST

Some ideas for learning quotations:

✓ Choose appropriate examples – know what the quotations will illustrate.

✓ Say them out loud.

✓ Sing or chant them out loud.

✓ Write them on cards and put the cards where you will see them.

Closed book exam

In a closed book exam, you do not have a copy of the text to refer to. Since you will know your text thoroughly in any case, this need not be a drawback. Prepare for the exam as you do for an open book paper: annotate your text in the same way, become familiar with the kind of question you may be asked, and prepare suitable material and responses.

Closed questions

You are unlikely to be asked to select passages to illustrate points when you do not have the text for reference. You may be given a passage on your exam paper and asked to comment on it in a variety

We could ask about the way the character is presented in this extract.

Yes and we may be asked to relate this passage to other parts of the text.

Making notes

Whatever kind of exam you take, and whenever in your course you take it, you will benefit from active, involved preparation of your texts and materials. As well as marking up your texts, you will be making notes on sessions in class and on your own reading.

> ### HINT
>
> **Make a note of everything you hear and read that could be useful. Always have a pen or pencil in your hand when you read a text.**

> ### CHECKLIST
>
> **When making notes, try using:**
> - ✓ **Mind Maps**
> - ✓ **diagrams**
> - ✓ **colour**
> - ✓ **drawings and illustrations**
> - ✓ **space**
> - ✓ **cards**

Preparing coursework

Coursework assignments give you an opportunity to explore your own choices of text and approach. Without the constraints of exam conditions, you are free to structure and develop your own tasks, and to plan and draft them carefully.

The topic/title

It is essential to get this right. Of course, you may find that as you start to research your topic your ideas change and you develop a different focus. However, inappropriate wording of an assignment or an inappropriate choice of texts or approach will limit your success. Keep your title clear and focused. Make sure that the nature of the assignment will enable you to meet the criteria for assessment. Check these in the syllabus, or ask your teacher.

Good timing

Plan your time carefully, working backwards from the deadline and leaving enough extra time for hitches that may occur. Allow time for reading, research, planning and drafting. Keep your notes and Mind Maps in good order – this will save you time.

Drafting

You will probably be submitting a first draft for comment. At this point, check the **word count** of your piece, and make adjustments if it is too short or too long. You won't get extra credit for length. Show your ability to write succinctly and to the point!

Critics and other sources

When you quote from a secondary source – this is the term for materials other than the text itself, such as critical studies and articles – you must acknowledge the source. This means that you must identify where the words or ideas originated. You must use quotation marks when you quote directly from a source. If you download material from the Internet, identify the website. All sources should be listed in a **bibliography**.

> ### FACTFILE
>
> **A bibliography is a list of the works referred to in the process of writing an article, essay, book etc.**

Oral coursework

You might present an oral assignment as part of your coursework. The Mind Map below gives you some ideas about preparing for an oral assignment. You could copy it and add your own observations and references.

> ### TRY THIS
>
> **Choose one of your texts and select one of its themes. Think of:**
> - a) **a title that could be set as an exam question**
> - b) **a title that could be set as a coursework assignment.**
>
> **Explain the differences between the exam question and the coursework assignment**

> ### CHECKLIST
>
> **When you are preparing a coursework assignment:**
> - ✓ **choose an appropriate subject and title**
> - ✓ **allow plenty of time**
> - ✓ **write a first draft**
> - ✓ **check your word count**
> - ✓ **identify all sources**

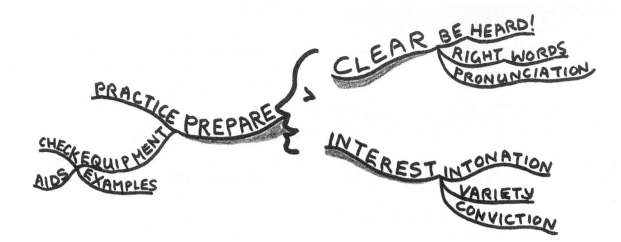

Grade A

Aim for the very best you can do, and add a bit extra. Here are some of the characteristics of a Grade A:

- a comprehensive, detailed knowledge and understanding of a wide range of literary texts
- a detailed, wide-ranging understanding of the concepts and frameworks relevant to English language and literature
- ability to analyse and evaluate
- ability to make distinctions and judgements
- answers show depth
- independent response
- thoughtful, convincing arguments
- awareness of contexts – cultural, social, historical
- convincing and significant comparisons and connections
- critical and sensitive awareness of interpretations and approaches
- well-organised material
- fluent, accurate, well-structured writing
- confident use of appropriate terminology

TRY THIS

Underline the key words in the list left. For each one, give yourself a star rating out of ten to show your level of attainment at the moment. Fix a target of a higher star rating for each area. Make a plan of action, showing how you will reach your target. Start by working through this book!

Summary

This chapter has told you about:

- **what to expect in studying English at an advanced level**
- **how your work will be assessed**
- **how to prepare for exams**
- **how to prepare coursework**
- **what makes a Grade A**

PREVIEW

This chapter will tell you about:

- **reasons for studying English language**
- **how the language developed**
- **forms and structures**
- **choice of words**
- **speech and written language**
- **the media and advertising**
- **issues in language**

Introduction

This chapter will be of use whether or not your course focuses on English language rather than literature. It will be especially helpful if you are studying English language, but most of the principles covered also apply to literature. The main difference is that language study focuses more closely on the actual words used, rather than on plot, themes or characters. There is also an emphasis on real-life everyday language use. But after all, literature draws on this, even though it does not copy it.

Take to heart two guiding principles:

1 There are **variations** in English.

2 Good English use takes account of **purpose** and **audience**.

Variations are determined by **time**, **place**, **social group** and **context**.

- **Time.** Language use constantly evolves, so that the English spoken by our grandparents is significantly different from ours, and the English written by Chaucer very different indeed. There is more on this under 'The history of English', on page 9.

- **Place.** English varies from one region to another in terms of accent and dialect. This is dealt with later in this chapter under 'Spoken and written English' (see page 21).

- **Social group.** Social groups take many forms. Class is still a major factor, and linked to this is level of education. Age is also important: if your 50-year-old teacher started using teen-slang it would sound silly. Ethnic grouping is also a factor linked to dialect. There are also gender differences; for example, it is claimed that men swear more than women.

- **Context.** People alter the way they speak according to the situation in which they find themselves.

This mention of context links to our second guiding principle – namely that all effective use of language takes account of **purpose** and **audience**.

- **Purpose.** A speaker or writer may want to entertain, warn, inform, impress, persuade, encourage, or almost any combination of these. The precise use of language will reflect this, though some users will be more effective than others.

- **Audience.** Spoken language has a known audience – friends, a shop assistant, your doctor etc. Written language has an imagined audience, which in some cases can be very precise – for example, a magazine might be aimed at 'educated, single, childless career women aged 21–25'.

Remember: PAL – Purpose + Audience → Language

In order to analyse the variations in English, and the ways in which a speaker or writer adapts language use to purpose and audience, you need a system of analysis, which is provided later in this chapter. You also need some basic terms and concepts to use as tools. The list below serves as a preview: the concepts are dealt with more fully later in the chapter. There is some variation in the precise way in which some of these terms are used. The definitions below show how we use them in this book.

Grammar: the system of rules whereby words are organised together to make mutually agreed sense.
Syntax: the aspect of grammar focusing on word order within a sentence.
Lexis: vocabulary, or choice of words.
Word classes: the different types of word, according to function, e.g. noun.
Semantics: the meaning of words, including their **connotations** (the ideas you connect to them) and **subtext** (what a speaker or writer is suggesting beneath the more obvious, literal sense of the words).
Phonetics: the sounds of words, and how those sounds are made.
Morphology: relating to **morphemes**, the smallest parts of words, which may be smaller than a syllable; the prefix *un-* (as in *un*done) is a morpheme, and so is *s* when used to make plurals.

CHECKLIST

✓ **English usage *varies* according to time, place, social group and context.**

✓ **PAL – Purpose + Audience → Language**

✓ **Terms with which you should be familiar: grammar, syntax, lexis, word classes, semantics, connotations, subtext, phonetics, morphology, morphemes.**

The history of English

English owes much of its richness and variety to the multiplicity of peoples whose separate languages have been stirred into its melting pot. Here are the main groups making up these ingredients, together with their languages:

- Celts (Gaelic and Welsh)
- Romans (Latin)
- Anglo-Saxons (Old English)
- Vikings (Old Norse)
- Normans (French)

The Celts

At the time of the Roman invasion of AD43 the whole of Britain was occupied by Celtic tribes. Those in Scotland communicated in the language spoken in Ireland – Gaelic – while those further south spoke a related language that has now evolved into modern Welsh. The last Roman troops left Britain in AD436, leaving the land vulnerable to attack. Even before this time, Germanic tribes – Angles, Saxons and Jutes – had started to invade Britain from the south-east. Now they came in waves, gradually driving the Celts into Wales, Cornwall and Scotland.

Few general Celtic words survive in modern English – *brock* (badger) and *dun* (brown) are two – though there are dialect words in the north and especially in Scotland. There are also numerous place names and river names; Thames, Exe, Dee, Derwent, Avon and Severn, for example, are all Celtic.

The Anglo-Saxons

The early Anglo-Saxons were pagan and largely illiterate. They did have a runic alphabet, but this was largely replaced by the Roman alphabet when Christian missionaries started to arrive at the end of the sixth century. Our *w* and the combination *th* survive from the runic alphabet.

Old English (Anglo-Saxon) is the backbone of modern English. Less than a thousand modern English words have Old English roots, but they are much-used everyday words. Some examples are:

earth fire water house door dog
man woman husband wife eat
drink speak work build and he

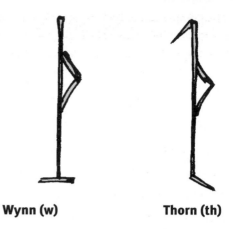

Wynn (w)   **Thorn (th)**

What classes of words (nouns, verbs, adjectives, adverbs etc.) are most of these? (There is more on word classes later in the chapter.)

It is also worth noting that the Anglo-Saxons loved wordplay and riddles, and this has remained a distinguishing feature of English (Shakespeare's puns are included in Chapter 7).

Old English was a grammatically complex language – although, strangely, it had no future tense. Its nouns had genders – masculine, feminine and neuter – and changed their endings according to their grammatical status in a sentence. For example, 'the king' is *se cyning*, but 'to the king' is *thaem cyninge* (notice the extra *e*). In addition, adjectives changed form according to the gender of the noun they described. However, a new influence was to change all this.

The Vikings

The Vikings, or Norsemen, began to invade Britain in AD793. Coming from Scandinavia, they focused particularly on the north-east, and their influence is strongly felt in northern dialects and accents to this day, as well as being obvious in place names such as Scunthorpe and Weatherby. The Vikings clashed with the Anglo-Saxons, and in fact the probable reason for Harold being defeated by William the Conqueror in 1066 is that his armies had just marched back from fighting the Vikings in the north. However, once initial conflicts had settled down, the Vikings and the Anglo-Saxons mingled. Their languages, already similar, also mingled, so that modern English contains about as many words of Old Norse origin as of Old English. Here are some:

call take law egg root window
get hit leg low root same want
wrong skin sky skein skill

The important grammatical influence of the Vikings on English was to simplify it. When the Vikings and Anglo-Saxons met, mingled and attempted to trade, they understood each other just enough to get totally confused. Hence English grammar, with its complex noun endings and agreements, became simplified. This makes it a relatively easy language to learn, and if English ever becomes the official world language, we will have the Vikings to thank!

The Norman Conquest

With the arrival of the Normans, starting in 1066, the official language of Britain became French. At first this was just the language of the ruling class – ordinary people spoke Old English – but gradually French filtered down into the mainstream of English.

The main area of influence was in the replacement of numerous Old English nouns with French ones. These particularly relate to (1) rulership; (2) the new rulers' relatively luxurious way of life; (3) the new power balance between rulers and ruled. Examples are:

advise	art	baron	beauty
castle	command	commons	counsellor
country	court	cushion	feat
flower	glory	govern	judge
jury	mercy	miserable	painting
parliament	peer	people	poor
poverty	prince	prison	realm
reign	royal	rule	sausage
sculpture	sovereign	spaniel	victory

? See if you can divide these words up into the three categories suggested.

This split between Old English and French still plays a major part in English style today. Words derived from Old English tend to have a simpler, more down-to-earth quality than those stemming from French. They tend to be used more in colloquial (informal) speech. Words derived from French – which in turn are often derived from Latin – are more likely to suggest sophistication, formality and education.

Latin and Greek

As noted above, Latin was a major influence on Norman French, and therefore on the English that developed after 1066. It was the language of the Church, which of course had a huge influence on daily life, and later on it became the language of law. Some Latin legal phrases have passed into wider use, still in their Latin form; for example, *bona fide* (good faith) and *caveat emptor* (buyer beware).

Latinate words are often **polysyllabic** (composed of several syllables), and tend to sound impressive. They are also particularly associated with abstract concepts, and therefore with education and intellect. Examples are:

justice   consolation   constitution   honour civilisation   society

Many more Latin words entered the English of the educated class during the Renaissance (fourteenth to seventeenth centuries), since education was based on reading and translating classical authors. For example, we find *arena*, *dexterity*, *genius*, *specimen* and *stimulus*.

It remains a feature of English that there is often a choice of two words meaning more or less the same thing, or with subtle differences, one stemming from Old English, and one from Latin via French. The main difference is in degree of formality; for example, *buy* and *purchase* – which sounds more formal?

Greek words also entered the language or became popular during the Renaissance, often via Latin, particularly for philosophical, political and scientific concepts. Examples are:

atom   democracy   physics   mathematics theology   thermal

Caxton and spelling

With the invention of the printing press, introduced to England by William Caxton in 1476, English spelling became more consistent in terms of individual words, but no more rational than before overall. Caxton favoured the south-eastern dialect of English, which has helped to give it a special status in modern times.

He also introduced some unnecessarily odd spellings, for example adding the *h* in *ghost* and *ghastly*. Some spellings that look very odd today remained into the seventeenth century, in particular the interchange-ability of *v* and *u* and of *i* and *j*: *God in heauen be my iudge*. Some *ick* spellings, such as *publick* and *rhetorick*, survived into the eighteenth century. One of these, *magick*, is enjoying a popular revival in the present day.

After Caxton

Several important developments occurred after 1476.

- Most nouns that formed plurals with *n* or *en* began to take *s* instead; thus Chaucer's *eyen*, *housen* and *shoon* became Shakespeare's *eyes*, *houses* and *shoes*. A few of the old forms remain, for example *children*.

- The possessive form of *it* – *its* – came into use in the 1590s. Before that it was necessary to use *his* or *her*, or to reword.

- Use of *thou* (pural *ye*), *thee* and *thy*, for *you* and *your*, and *art* for *are*, all used by Shakespeare, became limited to special contexts, and then only used in dialect.

- Many verbs that previously formed their past tense by changing their central vowel started to take *-ed* endings instead. Thus the past tense of *reap*, formerly *rope*, as in 'I rope my harvest', became *reaped*. Again, a few old forms remain, for example *strive/strove/striven*.

English after Shakespeare

English has continued to develop since then, more in terms of lexis (vocabulary) and style than in grammar. Many new words have been formed using **prefixes** (units of meaning that come at the beginning of a word).

> a- de- extra- intro- meta- micro- multi- neo- non- tele-

Take, for example: asymmetrical, dematerialise, extramarital, introspective, metabolism, microscope, multiplex, neo-Fascist, non-profitable, telephone.

? What is the meaning of the prefixes in each of the words above?

Suffixes (coming at the end of a word) have also accounted for many new words.

? Think of at least one modern word for each of these suffixes.

> -ise -less -like -ness -some -y

Another creative source of new words is the combining of old ones. For example: *chortle* (chuckle-snort, 1872); *brunch* (breakfast-lunch, 1896); *smog* (smoke-haze, 1903).

Perhaps the biggest source of new English words, however, has been borrowing from other languages:

- Arabic: coffee, caravan
- Danish: ski
- Hindustani: shampoo, bungalow, juggernaut, pundit
- Italian: balcony, confetti, opera, graffiti, gazebo
- Native American and Inuit: moccasin, moose, anorak, igloo
- Persian and Turkish: bazaar, kiosk
- Spanish: cannibal, sherry, potato, aficionado
- Urdu: pyjamas

Closely related to this is the introduction of American words, and especially of Black American words. Slang words, such as *homeboy* or *homey*, may eventually become generally accepted, just as native English slang words have gradually taken their place in standard English: *mob* is one example.

A continuing grammatical change is the use of nouns in place of adjectives, for example in a phrase such as 'School student exam nerves torment!'.

Finally, now that most English speakers are literate, written English has come closer to spoken English in style, becoming less formal and tending towards shorter, less complex sentences. Some people would call this a 'dumbing-down' of the language (to use a recently imported Americanism!). What do you think?

CHECKLIST

✓ **The main *ingredients* of English are Old English (Anglo-Saxon), Old Norse (Viking), Norman French, Latin.**

✓ ***Distinctions* between words with Anglo-Saxon and Latin roots remain to this day.**

✓ **English has *borrowed* and assimilated many words from other languages.**

✓ ***Caxton* influenced English spelling by introducing the printing press.**

✓ ***Grammar*, *lexis* and *style* have continued to evolve.**

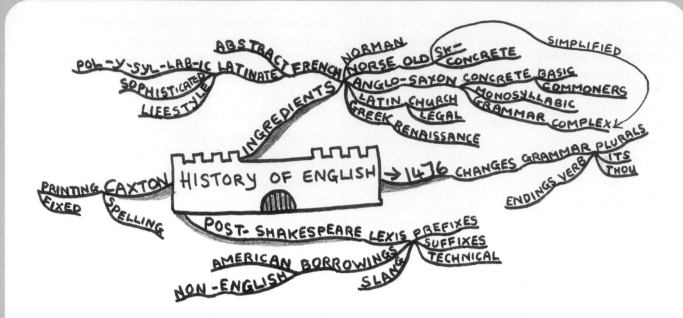

TRY THIS

Read the two passages below. One was written by a Puritan, Philip Stubbes, condemning May Day festivities. The Puritans scorned frills and frippery, and this shows in the down-to-earth style of the passage. They also tended to be commoners rather than nobles. The second passage is written by the scholarly King James I (reigned 1603–25) on the subject of kingship. (Spellings involving _u_, _v_, _i_ and _j_ have been modernised.) Highlight and compare the use of:

1 **archaic lexis and grammar**

2 **words that seem to derive from either Old English or Latin**

3 **abstract and concrete nouns**

How do you explain the differences between the passages? Mind Map them.

... their chiefest jewel they bring from thence is their May-pole, which they bring home with great veneration, as thus. They have twenty or forty yoke of oxen, every ox having a sweet nose-gay of flowers placed on the tip of his horns: and these oxen draw home this May-pole (this stinking idol, rather) which is covered all over with flowers and herbs, bound round about with strings from the top to the bottom, and sometime painted with variable colours, with two or three hundred men, women and children following it with great devotion. And thus being reared up with handkerchiefs and flags streaming on the top, they straw the ground about, bind green boughs about it, set up summer-halls, bowers, and arbours hard by it; and then they fall to banquet and feast, to leap and dance about it, as the heathen people did at the dedication of their idols, whereof this is a perfect pattern, or rather the thing itself.

Stubbes, _The Anatomie of Abuses_ (1583)

For a good King (after a happie and famous reigne) dieth in peace, lamented by his subjects, and admired by his neighbours; and leaving a reverent renowne behinde him in earth, obtaineth the Crowne of eternall felicitie in heaven. And although some of them (which falleth out very rarelie) may be cut off by the treason of some unnaturall subjects, yet liveth their fame after them, and some notable plague faileth never to overtake the committers in this life, besides their infamie to all posterities hereafter: Where by the contrarie, a Tyrannes miserable and infamous life, armeth in end his owne Subjects to become his burreaux: and although that rebellion be ever unlawfull on their part, yet is the world so wearied of him, that his fall is little meaned by the rest of his Subjects, and but smiled at by his neighbours. And besides the infamous memorie he leaveth behind him here, and the endlesse paine hee sustaineth hereafter, it oft falleth out, that the commiters not onely escape unpunished, but further, the fact will remaine as allowed by the Law in divers aages thereafter.

James I, _Basikilon Doron_

Forms and structures

It is useful to think of the **sentence** as a basic grammatical unit, even though much of our verbal communication is not in sentences. For the sentence to work, we need grammatical rules. The starting point for these – and a very useful one if you are analysing how a speech or written passage achieves its effects – is **word classes**.

Word classes

You may know the term 'word classes' as 'parts of speech'. It refers to the fact that different types of word do different jobs in a sentence, as different workers might do in a factory. You should already have learned these, but every year many AS and A2 students show in their exams that they are not quite sure of these important distinctions.

Nouns are the 'thing' words. The first ones that children learn – and interestingly the ones that have survived in greatest numbers from Old English – are **concrete nouns**, like *bread*, *dog*, *drink*, *floor*, *teddy*, *bed*. These are all labels, and perhaps they are learnt first because having a label for a thing somehow seems to bring it within our power. In a practical sense, too, we can use concrete nouns to get what we want: 'Drink!' 'Sweet!' 'Crisps!'

It is often the case that simple nouns can be replaced by more precise ones: 'Juice!' 'Toffee!' 'Beef!' More subtly, many nouns have alternatives that carry different **connotations** (associations), which speakers may exploit to make a particular impression. For example, we could call ourselves *authors* or, more humbly, *writers*; likewise *educators* or *teachers*.

Unlike concrete nouns, **abstract nouns** label things that cannot be picked up, thrown around or put in boxes. They are used for ideas. Examples are *love*, *honour*, *freedom*, *anxiety* and *wisdom*. A passage containing a number of these will have a very different tone from one employing only concrete nouns. If there are no concrete nouns or images to help us relate to the abstract ideas, it may sound impressive, but it may also be rather dry and difficult to read. We may warm more easily to a politician who offers us 'blood, sweat and tears' than one who vaguely promises 'determination, fortitude and integrity'.

Proper nouns are those used for people, places, political parties, ships and so on. In literature, names can suggest character. For example, in Hardy's *Far from the Madding Crowd*, 'Gabriel Oak' sounds virtuous and reliable; 'Francis Troy' sounds more exotic. Nicknames can imply familiarity, affection or contempt. Singer and film star Frank Sinatra was 'Old Blue Eyes' to his fans, and 'Old Black Eyes' to journalists reporting his involvement in a brawl. Name-dropping is used not only by people who want to impress us at parties, but also by journalists who want to impress or flatter by being seen to know who these people are.

Adjectives are 'describing words', but you need to remember that they describe *things*, not how something is done. In other words, they are used with nouns. To use the technical term, they **modify** nouns: the dog is *large*, *hairy*, *friendly* and *hungry*; the sausages are *plump*, *pink*, *sleek* and *fragrant*. Many adjectives are relative: they do not give precise information. This is a quality often exploited in persuasive language.

? Colour-code the relative and the more precise adjectives in the following description:

> The upper rooms are large, spacious, airy and rectangular. They look out onto a pleasant Georgian courtyard featuring a shallow, circular pond bordered by mature, evergreen shrubs. Elegant red and white flagstones add an air of sophisticated charm.

A more neutral way of modifying a noun is using another noun – or several.

> This summer holiday home boasts a stone wine cellar, breakfast room, master bedroom, guest room, and clothes cupboards throughout – and all at a budget price!

? Underline the modifying nouns in the passage above. If in doubt, they are the ones that come before the essential nouns. You should find nine.

So far we have looked at **pre-modification**. Adjectives almost always come before the noun they describe (unlike in French); very rarely they may be placed after the noun for literary emphasis, especially in archaic writing: the *siege perilous*. We have to assume that where one noun modifies another it is the second that is modified. Hence a *chocolate egg* is an egg made of chocolate, not a chocolate made of egg.

? What would you expect a *crocodile handbag* to look like?

However, nouns can also be **post-modified**.

> Brinkley Rovers, tired and discouraged, slouched off the pitch. The referee, never their greatest fan, grimly watched them go.

The nouns being modified here are *Brinkley Rovers* and *referee*.

? What are the modifying phrases? (Hint: they are separated off by commas!) Write two similar sentences of your own.

A crocodile handbag

Note that, as with other classes of words, adjectives with broadly similar meanings can have very different effects, resulting from their connotations and degree of formality. Look at this list of adjectives.

> filthy soiled grubby dirty manky stained
> mucky grimy unclean grotty

Which of these do you feel is the most formal? Which is the least formal? Which expresses the most disgust? Which is the most emotionally neutral? Compare your responses with someone else's. What does this comparison tell you?

Verbs, as you will probably know, are the 'doing words'. They are essential to any language. In fact there are even some Native American languages in which there are verbs but no nouns: everything is thought of in terms of action. As with other word classes, many verbs can be replaced by alternatives that mean broadly the same thing, but which subtly alter meaning. For example:

> push shove propel guide force get
>
> *Defendant:* He shoved me into the van.
> *Police witness:* I guided him into the van.
> *Press report:* When push comes to shove . . .

The use of a number of verbs of a particular kind can have an overall effect in a passage.

? Assess the mood of the sentence below, focusing on the verbs.

> I rushed upstairs, raced out of the house, and sprinted to the bus stop, arriving just in time to throw myself on a Number 36 as it started to pull away.

Verbs can appear in **non-finite** or **finite** form. The question 'To flee, or to fight?' contains two non-finite verbs. A collection of these in a passage might suggest indecision or inaction. Think of Hamlet's 'To be, or not to be . . .' speech. When you have a finite verb with a **subject**, you have a **clause** or **simple sentence** (more on these later): 'He fought.'

Verbs also come in two basic varieties: **stative** and **dynamic**. Stative verbs describe a *state* of being or becoming:

> I appear (sad, happy...) He seems...
> You are... I feel...

Dynamic verbs describe what a subject does:

> I swim. You imagine. He works. We play.

The repeated use of stative verbs to describe a person or situation can suggest inaction. Using a lot of dynamic verbs can have the opposite effect.

? Write two sentences describing yourself, one using stative verbs, the other using dynamic verbs. Which impression of yourself do you prefer?

Some dynamic verbs can also be used **transitively** or **intransitively**. Compare:

> The gerbil plays; the cat watches. (intransitive)
> The cat eats the gerbil. (transitive)

In the second sentence the cat is the **subject** and the gerbil is the **direct object**.

Verbs also have **tenses**. If you are a native speaker of English you probably use these correctly without thinking about it, even though some are quite complicated. For example, consider:

> By the time Dan leaves home we will have lived here for ten years.
>
> To have left blood on the carpet she must have already decided that she was never coming back.

? What kind of fiction might the second example come from, in which someone looks back in time to contemplate someone else looking forward?

Choice of tense influences the effect made by a passage. It is normal to use the past tense in narrative fiction, but occasionally the present is used. This can create a sense of immediacy, or of dreamlike timelessness. Peter Røeg's novel, *Miss Smilla's Feeling for Snow* is written entirely in the present tense. In the extract on the following page, how does the use of tense make you respond to it? What effect is made by the particular choice of verbs? (You may wish to highlight them to make this easier to assess.)

Bedbugs

The booth is already occupied by three small boys. We can see their legs, and hear their excited giggling. Then as the first flash fades we hear, above their laughter, the screech of a creature in terror. Inge tears back the curtain and exposes the boys, including one who is dangling a kitten by its tail in front of the camera. The kitten flails about uselessly, tensing and squealing with horror at each flash, only to redouble its efforts in the lacuna. 'You monsters,' cries Inge, 'stop torturing that poor animal.' The boys grin. The kitten swings. Faster and faster. Until the boy lets go. The kitten lands on Inge's shoulder. Seeking to steady itself it raises its paw and sinks its claw into her ear. Inge gently lifts the kitten so her ear is not torn although the lobe is pierced and bleeding profusely, staining her tee-shirt a deeper red.

Clive Sinclair

One also hears the present tense used in everyday conversational anecdotes, as in the illustration below.

A final feature of verb use is that dynamic verbs can be **active** or **passive** according to the way they are used in a sentence. Compare the effects of:

Adam had kissed her like she'd never been kissed before.

She had been kissed like she'd never been kissed before.

In the first, the emphasis is on Adam; in the second it is on the kiss. Now try:

I should not have taken the goat to the party.

The goat should not have been taken to the party.

? Which of these is a more direct admission of responsibility?

You will find that politicians and newspapers use the passive form of verbs in order to shift emphasis or to disguise responsibility. However, it can also be used when the full facts are not known.

Sir Jasper's statue was daubed in red paint at about 3.00 a.m. this morning: the paint was found to be still slightly tacky when the prank was discovered by commuters.

It also produces a more formal, distant tone than the active tense.

Enquiries have been made, and measures taken to remedy the situation.

Adverbs are *added* to a verb. As with adjectives, most adverbs convey only a relative truth.

Fatimah walked quickly towards the man, who was smiling happily.

Just how quick is *quickly*? How happy is *happily*? We can only relate these to our own standards. It can be argued that most adverbs are unnecessary, since English has so many subtle verb alternatives. For example, for the sentence above, we could have written:

Fatimah strode towards the man, who was grinning.

Which do you prefer, and why? What do you think of the view that some adverbs are unnecessary?

One special class of adverbs is made up of **adverbs of frequency**:

rarely seldom infrequently occasionally sometimes often frequently always

There are also adverbs that place events in time. These are useful in narrative. For example:

First it was just an itching sensation. *Then* I noticed my body hair growing. *Soon* I developed a taste for ripe bananas, and started to catch hold of scaffold

This horse walks into a bar and the landlord says, 'Why the long face?'

CHECKLIST

Before we look at the *function words* that help us string sentences together, check your recall of the four main word classes.

✓ *Nouns* are 'thing' words. *Concrete* nouns label tangible things; *abstract* nouns label ideas, qualities, emotions etc. *Proper* nouns label people and places.

✓ *Adjectives* modify nouns. Coming before a noun, they *pre-modify*; after a noun they *post-modify*.

✓ *Verbs*, 'doing words', can be *dynamic* or *stative*.

✓ Dynamic verbs can be used *transitively* with a *direct object* or *intransitively* without one.

✓ Verbs can also be used *actively* or *passively* in a sentence.

✓ *Adverbs* add the 'how', 'what' and 'when' to a verb, though they can sometimes be avoided by verb choice.

bars as I passed beneath them. *Next* I began to whoop excitedly at mealtimes. *Eventually* I had to face it: I was a gorilla.

Determiners are the first of the **function words**. The most common ones are the **definite** and **indefinite articles**: *the* and *a*. If we say, 'Give me *the* box,' it means a particular box; 'Give me *a* box,' means any box.

Plural nouns do not need an article. It makes perfect sense to say: 'Children love sweets.' This has a more general sense than: 'The children love sweets.' This might mean 'the children in this school' or 'our children'.

Other determiners can be used to modify a noun, replacing *a* or *the*. Used with discrimination your writing can become more precise and varied. How would you use the following?

all	either	enough	every	few	least
less	little	many	more	most	much
neither	several	some	such	that	these
this	those	what	whatever	which	whichever

Pronouns are words that can be used instead of nouns, providing we know what the noun referred to is: I, you, he, she, one, me, you, him/her/it. The **possessive pronouns** are my/mine, you/yours, his/her(s)/its – and their plurals. Pronouns can help avoid having to repeat a name.

Don't be deceived: these may be short, common-place words, but they can make a lot of difference to a sentence. Imagine an advertisement for beans.

> Bonzo Beans Ltd know that the people who eat Bonzo beans are gourmets but have little time to cook. That's why Bonzo Beans Ltd make Bonzo beans so tasty and easy for customers to open. Take it from Bonzo.

Compare this with:

> We at Bonzo know that you're a gourmet but have little time to cook. That's why we make our beans so tasty and easy for you to open. Take it from us.

The pronouns *We*, *you*, *our* and *us* make the appeal so much more personal. Look out for this in advertisements.

This book is written by two authors, so *we* occasionally address *you* directly using *we*. The tone would change if we said, 'The authors feel that students should…'.

? What emotional use is being made of pronouns in the following advertisement?

> We've all done it – upset someone without meaning to. What can you do? You're tired, you've had a hard day, you're human… Before you know it, you've snapped at your nearest and dearest and they've gone off in a sulk. Solution? Make them a nice mug of soothing Soupy Soup. We know you're a warm, caring person. Show it with Soupy Soup!

This advertisement, incidentally, also demonstrates a slight problem with pronouns: there are no neuter, gender-free third person pronouns. For a strict grammarian, the above example should read, '… he or she has gone off in a sulk… make him or her a nice mug…' In an informal context, as in conversation, it is widely acceptable to use plurals, as is done above, in order to avoid the clumsiness of he/she, him/her. Ask your teacher what his or her (!) policy is on this, and what your exam board's preference is likely to be.

Another issue is over the use of *one* and *you*. Consider the sentence 'One returns to the places of one's youth.' You may think it sounds too formal, or 'posh', and prefer 'You return…', but sometimes using *you* can create confusion. In terms of analysis, the key thing is that *you* sounds informal, *one* sounds formal.

Relative pronouns can be used to ask questions, and to introduce clauses in a sentence.

> **Who**'s that lady? **What** is her name? **Which** table is she sitting at?
> There's a boy called Amir. He comes from Hounslow: *There's a boy called Amir **who** comes from Hounslow.*

Prepositions are words that relate one thing or action to another.

> in into on onto to of during against beside across

For such ordinary words, they can be surprisingly evocative, as in the title of a Hemingway short story, *Across the River and into the Trees*, or in Tennyson's famous line: 'Into the valley of death rode the six hundred.'

Repetition of prepositions in a text can also have a particular effect.

> We stand against poverty, against oppression, against corruption. Stand beside us as we march into battle and you will sit beside us on the throne of truth. Across a sea of lies, across a desert of neglect...

Conjunctions are 'joining words': a 'junction' is where two roads or lines meet. The commonest conjunction is *and*, and this is usually the first to be learned by a child.

> ...and then Daddy said, 'Would you like to go to the swings?' and I said, 'Yes, I would,' and we went to the swings and we saw Finn and Scarlet and then...

The word *and* is a **coordinating conjunction**· the others are *but*, *either*, *neither*, *nor*, *or*. **Subordinating conjunctions** establish relationships between ideas.

I like you *because* you make me feel special. I will kill you *if* I must.

? Spot the conjunctions in the following:

If the rain holds off, we can swim for it when the water level drops below the arch, but if it doesn't we're doomed – unless someone raises the alarm.

CHECKLIST

✓ **Determiners** modify nouns and specify their significance or quantity, the commonest being the *articles*. Others replace the articles, e.g. *these*, *such*.

✓ **Pronouns** are used in place of nouns, e.g. *he, she, it*.

✓ **Possessive pronouns** denote ownership, e.g. *my, your, mine*.

✓ **Relative pronouns** ask questions or introduce relative clauses, e.g. *which, who*.

✓ **Prepositions** relate one thing or action to another, e.g. *in, on, beside*.

✓ **Conjunctions** join phrases or clauses, e.g. *and, beneath*.

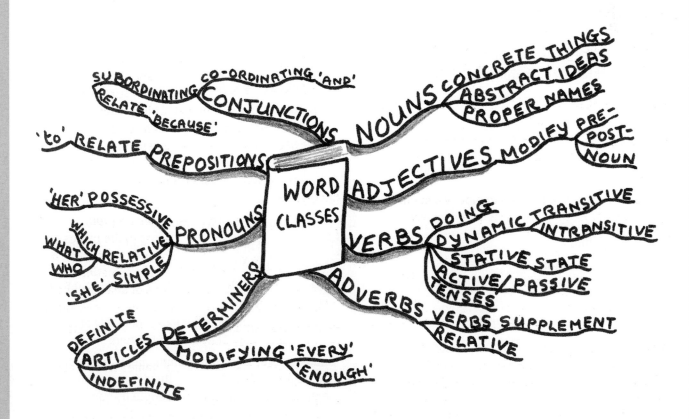

TRY THIS

1 **Read the passage below, which is a naval officer's report used in *The Times* in 1798. Colour-code the four main word classes. Mind Map your impressions of the way in which they contribute to the largely matter-of-fact tone of the report.**

27 July, a hanging offence. Two friends, Lt Edward Dawson of the *Grace* gunboat, and Lt John Matthew Miller, the commander of the *New Betsy* gun-vessel, dined with their families and other officers on board the *New Betsy*, at Sheerness on the evening of 10 July when they imbibed too freely of the wine. A Lt Forth fell asleep and Dawson picked up a speaking trumpet to blow into Forth's ear. Miller objected and an argument ensued. Dawson left the ship and made his way to the beach. About 10 p.m. the party came ashore and Miller stepped off the boat to assist the ladies. Dawson, already on the beach, incensed by the supposed insult, immediately drew his hanger [long slashing and thrusting sword] and ran it through Miller's body, which occasioned his death.

On 25 July, at Maidstone, Dawson was tried before Mr Justice Buller for the wilful murder of Miller. The jury, out for a quarter of an hour, returned a verdict of guilty. Just two days later Dawson was hanged on Pennenden Heath.

2 **Write a more descriptive version of this report using more adjectives and adverbs, and more expressive verbs.**

HINT

Look especially at the kind of verbs used, how many adjectives and adverbs are used, and what these are. Also find at least one example of each of the other word classes. Make notes on what interests you about the lexis of the passage overall. Remember to think of PAL – Purpose + Audience → Language.

The sentence

We suggested earlier that the sentence was the basic grammatical unit of English. However, this is not an absolute truth. If we compare grammar with time, the sentence is like a week. Just as the week is made up of days, hours and minutes, the sentence is made up of **clauses**, **phrases** and **morphemes**.

We have already discussed **morphemes**. They are the smallest units of language, and may be smaller than a syllable (which is a **phonetic** unit rather than a **semantic** one – i.e. related to sound, not meaning). A **phrase** is any group of words not containing a subject and verb.

lovely bunch of coconuts
mad, bad and dangerous
the hungry bird

These are phrases. Add subjects and verbs – 'I've got', 'Max is' and 'Julie fed' – and we have three sentences.

A **clause** can constitute a sentence in itself.

Julie fed the hungry sparrow, which was barely three days old.

Here, *Julie fed the hungry bird* is a sentence in itself, but in the context of the whole sentence given here, it is the **main clause**. The words *which was barely three days old* do not make sense in themselves, but they contain a relative pronoun and a verb. They could therefore be rephrased as a separate sentence.

It was barely three days old.

As they stand, using *which*, they form a **subordinate clause**.

A complete sentence must have two things:

1 A **subject** – e.g. *Julie*

2 A **predicate** – what the subject is, or is doing. This may consist of a verb on its own, e.g. *sleeps* (*Julie sleeps*) or a verb plus another element, e.g. *Julie sleeps with the sparrow*.

If we enlarge our view of bird-loving Julie a little, we might say:

Kind-hearted, caring, ornithologist Julie…

This is all part of the subject. If we add '…found the sparrow on the street,' then this is the predicate.

? Try to divide the following sentences into subject and predicate:

Cecil the marmalade cat looks longingly at the bird.
The tiny bundle of down and feathers shivered.

Subject, verb, object and complement. These terms can help you to analyse how the different parts of a sentence work together. You should by now understand the first two. In the first sentence above, *Cecil* is the subject and *looks* is the verb.

Try writing a similar sentence of your own, just to be sure you understand it. This sentence, however, also has an **object** – the thing that the subject is doing something to.

The word **complement** in ordinary use means something that goes well with, or enhances, something else. You might say that fish and chips *complement* each other, or that two colours in a room are *complementary*. Notice the spelling: it's not *compliment* – that's what you get when someone likes your haircut. In sentence analysis the complement gives information about a subject, but only when used with an intransitive verb. Examples will help you to understand this:

> Luigi seemed baffled. (The complement is *baffled* – an adjective.)
> Lisa was an usherette. (The complement is *an usherette* – article and noun.)

A single sentence might contain two types of **object**: **direct** and **indirect**.

> Lisa handed Luigi an ice cream.

Here *Lisa* is the subject, *an ice cream* is the direct object, and lucky *Luigi* is the indirect object.

Simple, compound and **complex** are three types of sentence. A **simple** sentence has just one subject and one verb: 'I like ducks.' This is one clause. A **compound** sentence has two clauses linked by a conjunction: 'I like ducks but not geese.' A **complex** sentence has two or more clauses, but with one independent clause and one or more dependent (or *subordinate*) clauses. The sentence you just read is an example of a complex sentence. Another is:

> I like chickens, which is fortunate because I live on a poultry farm.

The independent clause could also go at the end of the sentence.

> Having been to one of Sam's parties before, I took a book to read.

Note that you cannot judge simple, compound and complex by length.

> I like chickens, ducks, pigeons, albatrosses, dodos and ostriches.

This is still a simple sentence, unlike 'I was alone until you came,' which is complex.

In stylistic terms, a piece that has a great many complex sentences will normally be more sophisticated than one that does not.

Now that you know this, look back to the passages by Philip Stubbes and King James I on page 12 and compare their complexity.

Sentence purpose. A final categorisation is according to purpose. A sentence can be **declarative** (making a statement), **interrogative** (asking a question), **imperative** (giving an order) or **exclamatory**.

> Ferdinand is the Duke's heir.
> Is Ferdinand fit to govern?
> Listen to me.
> Oi – Ferdie!

These will also prove to be key concepts in your language analysis. For example, a serious, informative news report will probably be made up entirely of declaratives.

What would you expect to find in a *Sun* or *Daily Star* 'Minister in sizzling sex romps' story?

CHECKLIST

✓ A *sentence* must have a *subject* and a *predicate*.

✓ A *clause* must have a *subject* and a *verb*.

✓ *Sentences* can be broken up into *subject*, *verb*, *object* and *complement* (but not all have an object or complement).

✓ An *object* can be *direct* or *indirect*.

✓ A *sentence* can be *simple*, *compound* or *complex*.

Questions

1 For each of the following sentences identify how they are made up in terms of subject (S), verb (V), direct object (DO), indirect object (IO) and complement (C).

a) Romeo drinks the poison.

b) Juliet is just a girl.

c) The Friar gives Juliet a potion.

d) Both lovers die.

2 Identify each of the following sentences as simple, compound or complex.

a) Macbeth is a soldier and Banquo is his friend.

b) Banquo's ghost appears.

c) She removes the daggers, which are dripping with blood.

d) Malcolm becomes King.

(Answers on page 145.)

Lexis – vocabulary

We have already introduced the idea that a writer or speaker must choose words to suit audience and purpose. Sentence structures and forms will go a long way to suit purpose, but the choice of individual words is perhaps even more important. If you have read and absorbed the whole of this chapter so far, you should remember the difference in tone of Anglo-Saxon-derived and Latinate words. But words also vary in other ways.

One obvious variation is in degree of formality. Consider:

It's a right laugh… a real scream… a hoot.
It's really funny… a great night out.
It is a source of considerable amusement.

Which would you expect to find in a magazine? A letter to a friend? A court report?

Words also develop subtle shades of meaning which change over time. This happens partly according to how they come to be used. One example of a quite radical change of meaning is in the use of *gay*, which can now no longer be easily used for 'cheerful'. However, one reason for the word being used in its new sense is that it has positive connotations, which were reinforced by the slogan 'glad to be gay'.

This is where lexis becomes closely involved with **semantics** – the precise meaning of words. Words have **connotations** – some more than others. This means that they suggest certain ideas or moods to us, rather than just having a simple, easily definable meaning. Take Keats' line:

Season of mists and mellow fruitfulness.

The word 'Season' is relatively neutral. But what about 'mists'? An excellent way to test your personal connotations for a word is to do a *quick* Mind Map of whatever it makes you think of. Try one now with *mists*.

Here is a connotation Mind Map for *mellow*. How far does it include the words and ideas that you would expect? You should find some agreement, but not total agreement – because word connotations are, to some extent, personal.

Semantic fields

The concept of **semantic fields** is a useful one when analysing style and intent in a piece of writing. When a number of words have related meanings, they are said to be in the same semantic field. If several words or phrases in the same semantic field are used in a piece of writing, they can have an accumulative effect on the meaning, rather than just their separate individual meanings. Take, for example:

- Well, I'll put my cards on the table. It's a bit of a gamble. You might take a chance on her coming back to you, and you might be in luck, but if the tables are turned for good and she throws in her lot with him, you might as well try another spin of the wheel. After all, when the chips are down...

- I have a great passion for Italian watercolours, but I positively adore Matisse. I'm very fond of Monet, but if my heart's set on any one artist it's Matisse. Of course the real love of my life is Beethoven!

- My wife and I agree entirely on everything, except for a slight clash over colour schemes. I had to wage a one-man campaign to get her to back down over the purple and scarlet breakfast room – she really dug her heels in over that one. It was a cold war quite frankly. Still, we soldier on...

How would you sum up the semantic fields in each of these examples? What could you deduce about the speakers? You won't find such obvious examples in literature or non-fiction writing, but look out for them, especially in tabloid newspapers and in advertising.

Spoken and written English

The examples of semantic fields above might have been spoken or written. They are in a fairly informal **register**. This refers to the style and form of English used, determined by the situation, or context – in turn determined by intended audience and purpose. Register is largely about degree of formality. Written English tends to be more formal in style than spoken English. However, one finds formal spoken language – for example in court, or in a political speech; and one finds informal written language – for example in a magazine feature whose main purpose is to entertain.

Which of the following sounds more like spoken language, and why?

> Unless a suitable offer of reparation is made to my client within fourteen days, appropriate action will be taken.

> You'd better cough up pretty damn quick. Else I'll be round your house with a couple of lads. Get my drift?

The first example is from a solicitor's letter. Notice the Latinate lexis, the longer, complex sentence, the use of abstract nouns and the vague but impressive-sounding adjectives. Also notice the passive verbs, conveying detachment and a hint of menacing anonymity. Legal language attempts to inspire respect, and, as in this case, even to intimidate.

The second sentence uses contractions (*You'd... I'll*), slang (*cough up*), a mild swearword (*damn*), a colloquialism (*couple of lads*), and dialect (London: *be round your house*). It also features a sentence beginning with a shortened conjunction (*Else*), and an incomplete sentence (*Get my drift?*). These are all common features in speech. In particular, note that we often speak in incomplete sentences. Try using nothing but complete sentences for five minutes with a friend or family member, and you will see how stilted it sounds – even more so if you avoid contractions as well.

Standard English and dialect

The solicitor's letter is in **standard English**; the Cockney threat includes some **dialect**. Standard English is the particular form of English, originally based on East Midlands dialect, most often used by educated speakers in formal situations. It is normally used by anyone needing to be understood by a wide number of strangers. Hence it is the language of newsreaders and politicians. It is also more likely to be used in published writing.

Dialect is any systematic variation of English based on region or social group. Dialects differ from standard English in three ways.

1 **grammar**

2 **lexis** (vocabulary)

3 **idioms**

Dialect grammar can differ from standard grammar in several ways, especially:

- Use of **pronouns**. A Bristolian, or someone of Afro-Caribbean descent, might say, 'Give I the money.' A Somerset person might say, 'Er's not coming,' (instead of 'She's not coming.') Jamaican Bob Marley sang, 'Them belly full but we hungry.'

- **Word order** (often referred to as **syntax**). This is most likely to vary in a dialect influenced by a language other than English. For example, you might hear in Wales, 'Tired it is that he'll be tonight.'

- **Subject–verb agreements**, for example 'So I goes . . .' (West country), 'She were angry . . .' (Yorkshire).

TRY THIS

Suggest what might be said in each of the illustrations above. Write possible speeches, using an appropriate register.

Dialectical lexis is the easiest part of dialect to grasp, but it is also a part that is falling away as local speech is influenced by the standard English of the media. It refers to words or short phrases that exist only in a particular dialect, or which are used differently from the way in which they are used in standard English. Examples are:

- Cornish: *emmet* – tourist (also an ant!)
- Liverpudlian: *made up* – pleased
- Nottingham: *mash* – make or brew (the tea)
- Scots: *thrang* – full
- Newcastle: *wench* – an effeminate young man
- Yorkshire: *fettle* – mend
- Sussex: *twitten* – path or alley

Idioms are the characteristic expressions of a language or dialect. Often their origins have been lost, although their current meanings are clear and colourful:

- West Midlands: *Well, I'll go to the foot of our stair!* – I'm amazed!
- Northern Ireland: *fit to be tied* – very angry
- Yorkshire: *Where there's muck there's brass* – Where there's dirt there's money
- London: *Leave it out!* – Stop it!

If you are conducting a study of dialect look out for variations of this sort.

Note that dialect is not bad English, just non-standard English. At the same time, you should write in standard English, unless writing regional dialogue in a story, as that will be easily understood by any English speaker.

Accent

Accent differs from dialect, although someone may speak dialect in an accent – in fact it would be hard to speak a regional dialect without the appropriate accent. Standard English, on the other hand, can be spoken in any accent, although it is often spoken in **Received Pronunciation (RP)**. This is the kind of accent used by many – but not all – national newsreaders. Accent is a **phonetic** phenomenon, not a grammatical or lexical one.

TRY THIS

An excellent example of dialect compared with standard English is to be found in the following poem by Liz Lockhead.

1 **Read it aloud and look for the kinds of features described above.**

2 **Make a list of Scots words and phrases used and their standard English equivalents.**

3 **What does the poet seem to be saying about dialect and standard English?**

Kidspoem/Bairnsang

It wis January
and a gey dreich day
the first day I went to the school
so
ma Mum happed me up in ma good navyblue
    nap coat
wi the rid tartan hood
birled a scarf aroon ma neck
pu'ed on ma pixie and ma pawkies
it wis that bitter
said
'noo ye'll no slaive'
gied me a week kiss and a kidoan skelp on the
    bum
and sent me off across the playground
to the place I'd learn to say
'It was January
and a really dismal day
the first day I went to school

so
my Mother wrapped me up in my best navyblue
    top coat
with the red tartan hood
twirled a scarf around my neck
pulled on my bobble-hat and mittens
it was so bitterly cold
said
"now you won't freeze to death"
gave me a little kiss and a pretend slap on the
    bottom
and sent me off across the playground
to the place I'd learn to forget to say
"It wis January
and a gey dreich day
the first day I went to the school
so
ma Mum happed me up in ma good navyblue
    nap coat
wi the rid tartan hood
birled a scarf aroon ma neck
pu'ed on ma pixie and ma pawkies
it was that bitter." '

Oh,
saying it was one thing
but when it came to writing it
in black and white
the way it had to be said
was as if
you were grown up, posh, male, English and
    dead.

Some regional accents spell social death

Broadly speaking, many people dislike Brummie, Scouse and Geordie accents, while they find Scottish, Irish and some rural accents appealing, no matter how strong they are. Sean Connery, for example, who grew up in Edinburgh, is considered to have one of the sexiest voices in the world; but how many people find Derek Hatton's Liverpool accent a turn-on?

Since so many British speakers agree on which accents fall into which category, this must be a straightforward fact of life, like it or not. If you happen to be born in Newcastle or Middlesborough, too bad. You will have to lose your accent before you can achieve even the most modest of ambitions. If, however, your accent is from Dublin or Edinburgh, then you are likely to be considered charming and engaging and no modification will be necessary.

But can it be sheer coincidence that those accents that most often come under fire for their supposed 'ugliness' belong to heavily industrialised cities and are traditionally associated with the ordinary working people of those areas? And if accents are intrinsically ugly or attractive, how is it that North American speakers of English do not agree with our reactions here in the UK?

Paul Goggle, *The Times*

? How do *you* react to accents? Can you explain your preferences?

Pidgin

An interesting relative of dialect, at the extreme edge of English, is Pidgin – known to Pidgin-speakers as *Bislama*. It demonstrates some of the features of dialect in extreme form.

Pidgin evolved largely from English in the Pacific islands as a language in which islanders could communicate with British sailors and traders, and with each other – different islands spoke different indigenous languages. It is now the first language of a great many people. It has a limited vocabulary of about 1,500 words, but its simple, flexible grammar enables them to express a wide range of meanings. For example, *scru* means 'screw' and 'joint', so *scru blong arm* (the screw belonging to the arm) is Pidgin for 'elbow'. The word *ars* has come to mean foundation or cause, in the sense of 'that on which all things sit'. Therefore Christian missionaries wishing to communicate the message that God was the source of all things were obliged to preach that *God i-ars blong olgedar samting*.

> ### TRY THIS
>
> **Try to decipher this unusual news feature from the *Vanuatu Weekly*, written in Pidgin.**
>
> MAN BLONG 8 YIA LONG TUDAK
> Long las wik, yumi ridim se hemi go blong lukaot koknat crab mo afta we hemi saenem 'wan sainting', devel o Setan mi no save.
> Wan bigfoela boela I kamaot long baksaed blong hem mo boela ia I gat seven tut.
>
> **This loosely translates as:**
>
> A MAN WAS EIGHT YEARS IN TOTAL DARKNESS
> Last week you and I read how this guy went to look at a coconut crab which has been signing that it 'wanted something', whether it was just some devil or Satan himself I don't know.
> One enormous boil came out of his backside, and moreover this here boil had seven teeth.
>
> **Leaving aside your philosophical speculations about this man's fate, attempt to match up the translation with the original. Then suggest what grammatical features you can spot.**

The media

The media are composed of newspapers, magazines, broadcasting (television and radio), film, and increasingly, the Internet. Newspapers and magazines are an excellent source of written language material, and television and film provide interesting examples

> ### CHECKLIST
>
> ✓ *Lexis* refers to choice of words. Words have *connotations* in addition to their basic meanings. Words with similar connotations are said to be in the same *semantic field*.
>
> ✓ *Spoken* English differs from written. It tends to be in a less formal *register*, and features incomplete sentences. It may also include slang and dialect.
>
> ✓ *Standard English* is that used by educated speakers wishing to communicate with a wide range of people. It can be spoken in an accent.
>
> ✓ *Non-standard English* includes *dialect* and *slang*.
>
> ✓ *Dialect* differs from standard English in *grammar*, *lexis* and *idioms*.
>
> ✓ *Accent* is a phonetic feature, not a semantic one.

of dialogue and persuasive English in the form of advertising.

The ostensible purpose of newspapers is to **inform**, but they have also developed two other major purposes – to **persuade** and to **entertain**. They present facts (information), but they may be deliberately or unconsciously **biased** in their reporting. Moreover the popular papers – **tabloids**, especially – are likely to be highly selective in their reporting and to try harder to entertain than to inform. After all, they have to sell copies, and they have to persuade their advertisers – who are a major source of their income – that they are able to 'pull in the punters'.

Facts and opinions

In order to analyse media articles it is essential that you understand the difference between **fact** and **opinion**.

Here are some factual statements.

- Ducks like water.
- Fish can swim.
- Not all humans can swim.

Here are some opinions.

- Wildfowl sanctuaries are of national importance.
- Angling is more acceptable than hunting.
- Every child should learn to swim.

If we say 'Ducks hate water,' this is still a factual statement – albeit an incorrect one. If we say 'a study has shown that 80 per cent of Londoners think learning to swim is more important than learning the violin,' this is a fact: the study *has* shown this.

Bias

Bias is an understanding or reporting of facts that misrepresents them in favour of one view or argument rather than another. Bias can be deliberate or unconscious. In a newspaper you may find both, and the indications will be similar. Sometimes, however, techniques have been used so effectively that it is almost certainly deliberate.

One simple technique could be called the 'Half full or half empty?' trick.

> Labour has only been in power for eleven months, yet has already fulfilled half of its election promises.

Compare this with:

> Labour has now been in power for almost a year, yet has so far failed to fulfil half of its election promises.

Another is to report facts and figures selectively.

> The President, after a vigorous game of tennis [which he lost], went on to address a 400-strong crowd of people who had been keenly anticipating his arrival [he was two hours late; they pelted him with eggs]. After this he returned to the White House to work on the peace plan [but developed a migraine and had to go to bed].

A third technique is to quote out of context, or to quote only one side. A careless politician might say something in jest that is taken as serious statement and splashed across the headlines the next day.

? What effect do you think this has on what politicians say in public?

Emotive language

One of the most powerful techniques of bias, used in all kinds of persuasive writing, from propaganda to advertising, and from newspaper editorials to charity appeals, is **emotive language**. This is language in which the lexis is chosen to play on the audience's emotions.

Compare these three statements.

1 The government has adjusted nursery school spending to meet budget targets.

2 The government has cut nursery schools' budgets to save its own skin.

3 Government bully-boys have slashed nursery budgets in a desperate bid to keep the fat cats happy.

? In emotional terms, what are the key words in each statement? Look especially at verbs in all three statements, at the colloquial expression in (2), and at the adjectives introduced in (3).

Emotive language can be used to promote worthy causes as well as more partisan political ones. An environmental appeal might, for example, make use of emotive verbs and nouns.

> Global warming will *drown* thousands, as valleys become watery *graves*.
> The new road will *gouge* a deep *wound* in this area of natural beauty.
> Factory *filth* threatens to *ruin* our rivers, *degrading* them into a *chemical soup*.

Comparing news features

A very useful exercise in style analysis is to buy several newspapers for one day and then compare how each deals with the same news story. The fact that what is front-page news in one may get half an inch in another – or no coverage at all – will show you how selective the newspapers are. However, assuming that you find the same story in more than one paper, compare coverage, looking particularly for how each paper's style is geared towards its audience. (Remember **PAL**!)

Blinking Hell

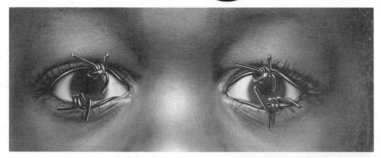

At first it's not too bad.

And it's easy to see how it's spread. Just watch a child for five minutes. They don't sit still for a moment. They're always poking their fingers into something they shouldn't, then rubbing their eyes with grubby fingers.

And that's all it takes to spread trachoma.

You only notice there's something wrong when the child's eye starts to itch and swell up

It's not terribly nice but it's bearable, and the infection will 'burn' itself out after a few weeks, leaving just a small scar on the eyelid.

The trouble is, it'll be back. And it won't just come back once. It will strike over and over again, with every reinfection burning and scarring the child's eyelid's a little bit more.

In the end, after years of suffering, the eyelids become so scarred and disfigured that the eyelashes turn inwards, into the eye. Until, agonisingly slowly, you go blind.

Imagine, every time you blink, you scratch your eyes

Think about it. You've probably blinked a dozen times since you started reading this. What if you'd scratched your eyes every time? You'd be in agony and you'd be desperately trying to stop. But how do you stop blinking?

You may never even have heard of trachoma before, but 6 million people in the developing world are blind because of it. And millions more are carrying the infection. It makes life impossible for young mothers trying to raise children. Fathers and husbands can't work to support themselves, let alone their families. So the whole family suffers.

The utterly horrifying thing is, this suffering is totally unnecessary, because trachoma can be treated very quickly and cheaply in its early stages with Tetracycline ointment.

It costs as little as £1.20 to treat one person

But this is still <u>far</u> too much for many people in the developing world, which is why Sight Savers is asking you to help.

With £12 you can help relieve the suffering of ten young people with trachoma.

You can even help with the more advanced cases. £5 is all we need for the operation to turn back the ingrowing eyelashes, so they stop scratching the eye. A donation of £50 will help save the sight and relieve the suffering of ten more people.

Delivery Guaranteed
WE PROMISE YOUR GIFT WILL SAVE SIGHT

YES, I want to help:

My gift is ☐ £10   ☐ £20   ☐ £50
          ☐ £100   ☐ £250   ☐ Other £_____

Please make your cheque payable to Sight Savers International, or if you wish to pay by Access, Visa, Amex or CAF charity card enter your card number in the boxes below.

Card expiry date _____ / _____   GU49

Signature _____

Mr/Mrs/Miss/Ms _____ Initials _____
                                    (BLOCK CAPITALS PLEASE)

Address _____

_____

_____ Postcode _____

Reg. Charity No. 207544
Please return this coupon with your donation to:
Sight Savers International,
FREEPOST, Haywards Heath, West Sussex, RH16 3ZA

Wouldn't you pay a hundred or a thousand times that if it were your eyes at stake? Please help by sending a donation with the coupon to:

Sight Savers International,
FREEPOST, Haywards Heath,
West Sussex, RH16 3ZA

Or you can call our credit card hotline (Access/Visa/Amex/CAF charity card) on 0700 01 42020

Registered Charity No 207544

Read the news feature that follows. Mark and Mind Map any grammatical or lexical features that you think contribute to its overall effect on the reader. Apply everything you have learnt so far in this chapter.

October, press gang violence

'James Fair the master of a press gang was indicted for a violent assault upon Mrs Anne Harvey, the owner of a public house in East Smithfield, on the night of 4th October.

'Mrs Harvey proved that the defendant, accompanied by his gang, came to her house in quest of seamen. There were two men sitting in the bar; one the mate of a merchant vessel, the other an old man, formerly a sailor. The prisoner upon inquiry from them learning they were seafaring men, insisted on their going along with him; they refused. The prisoner and his gang endeavoured to force them; a tussle ensued and the prosecutrix, rather alarmed for the security of those rather fragile utensils of glass and china, in which the honour and interest of her bar were so materially involved, ventured to step between them and danger; in which effort she happened to get in the way of the prisoner, who not very punctilious in his regards for the tenderness of her sex, struck her a very unmerciful blow with his brawny fist, nearly tantamount to the kick of a coach horse, upon her side. Then in some other exertions of his violence, he pulled down a shelf in the bar upon which was sustained a five gallon cask of Hodges high flavoured cordial gin, which being precipitated upon the exterior of the prosecutrix's head, laid her as prostrate and senseless upon the floor, as if the violence of the material had acted *Ab Interiori*. The prisoner, seeing the mischief he had done, cut and ran to avoid the consequences, but was afterwards brought before a magistrate and consigned for trial. Mr Mainwaring in summing up the evidence for the jury, reprobated such acts of outrage, as wholly incompatible with the necessary duty of the Impress Service. The prisoner was fined forty shillings.'

The Times, 4 December 1805

HINTS

Mrs Harvey, the 'prosecutrix' (the injured party) is the landlady of a pub. The 'prisoner' is the press gang officer, James Fair. From the tone of the piece, what do you think is the reporter's attitude to those involved, and to the whole incident? Consider the effect of:
- **tussle**
- **rather alarmed . . . so materially involved**

- **not very punctilious in his regards for the tenderness of her sex**
- **unmerciful**
- **brawny fist**
- **Hodges high flavoured cordial gin**
- **as if the violence of the material had acted *Ab Interiori* [from the inside].**

The three extracts on pages 28 and 29 are, like the one above, about recruiting for the forces – this time from prisons. The first is from a broadsheet – *The Times*; the second from a tabloid – the *Sun*. The third is an editorial 'leader', offering an opinion on the news item.

TRY THIS

Read the extracts, noticing the differences in style.

1 Compare the presentation of facts in *The Times* and *The Sun* pieces. In particular, look at the nouns used for the offenders, the use of quotes, the headlines, pictures and captions, and how the grammar and lexis are tailored towards the very different audiences.

2 Make a Mind Map of facts, opinions and arguments presented in the *Daily Mail* piece. Comment on the language, and how it differs from that used in the previous two items.

Army turns to crime to find new recruits

By Michael Evans Defence Editor

ARMY recruiting chiefs are turning to young offender institutions, the Commonwealth and to the Internet in an effort to improve enlistment and cut the short-fall of 5,000 soldiers, particularly among infantry regiments.

A Prison Service spokesman said last night that 29 young offenders had applied to join the Army in the past 12 months — and the Army had accepted 14 of them.

Recruiting officers are having to adopt increasingly imaginative schemes to attract the numbers of young men and women that they need.

Two young offenders' institutions, at Dover, in Kent, and Wetherby, in West Yorkshire, have been selected for a pilot scheme early next year in which inmates serving no more than two years will be given the chance to take part in a special 12-week Army training course to see if they are suitable for a soldiering career. The pilot scheme will cost about £100,000.

Although the Army has recruited in prisons in the past on an individual basis, this will be the first time that young offenders have been targeted on a big scale.

At the same time, the Army is planning to set up a recruiting scheme on the Internet so that potential soldiers, both men and women aged between 16 and 25, can log on for information and be invited to enlist through the website — cutting out all the form-filling and Army red tape. Inquiries about an Army career already can be handled on the Internet, and this was becoming increasingly popular with potential recruits.

The Commonwealth connection was another route to recruiting. Army sources said. When the Fijian Army band took part in the last Edinburgh Military Tattoo, several members asked about joining the British Army. And it was a Fijian from the 1st Battalion, the Scots Guards, who sang the Fijian national anthem at Twickenham for the World Cup rugby match between England and Fiji.

Recruiting elsewhere in the Commonwealth, such as Kenya, South Africa, Zimbabwe, New Zealand and Australia, is expected to be stepped up in the Army's drive to defeat its manpower crisis. But the most controversial scheme is the decision, confirmed by the MoD

yesterday, to hunt for new recruits among Britain's young offenders' institutions.

If the pilot scheme at Dover and Wetherby is successful, the Army will spread its recruiting campaign to all 20 institutions. Last year the MoD faced criticism for targeting homeless youngsters in Leeds. Last night Iain Duncan Smith, the Shadow Defence Secretary, said: "We are deeply concerned about such proposals. They leave serious questions unanswered. Who will they recruit? What types of crimes have [they] committed? We do not want a situation where hardened young criminals use the Armed Forces to escape paying their debts to society."

However, a spokesman for the Prison Service, which has been in discussions with the MoD for more than a year, said that the scheme would help to rehabilitate offenders and give them the opportunity of "meaningful employment" once they were released.

The 12-week training course would involve education, self-discipline, personal hygiene and map reading.

The MoD also said that certain young offenders would be barred from taking the course, such as inmates serving sentences for violent crimes and offences involving race, sex or serious drugs charges.

Recruitment is now said to be improving, with more young people joining the Army than leaving the service.

The Times, 9 November 1999

ARMY TARGETS LAGS IN RECRUITING DRIVE

By PAUL GILFEATHER

ARMY top brass are to sign up teenage criminals in a desperate bid to boost falling numbers.

Recruiting officers will be sent to jails to enlist cons due for release – just like in the hit film The Dirty Dozen.

Ministry of Defence chiefs insisted yesterday: "If the best soldiers are in jail, then so be it."

Serve

The tearaways are needed to plug massive gaps in the ranks.

And talks have already been held between the MoD and several young offenders' institutions.

A Defence spokesman added: "The Army is looking for the best new recruits.

"Some excellent young men may have made mistakes but have paid for it and deserve a chance to serve their country."

Cons will only be able to sign up if they were sentenced to two years or less.

And inmates caged for race, sex and drugs offences will be barred.

All inmates will have to prove themselves before being enlisted by undergoing a 12-week military training course, involving physical fitness, drill, military history and map reading.

A pilot scheme, involving youngsters at jails in Dover, Kent, and Wetherby, West Yorkshire, is planned for the New Year.

Convicted criminals were banned from joining the forces until three-and-a-half years ago.

Then the rules were relaxed to allow certain categories of young offenders to join up.

Paul Cavadino, of the National Association for the Care and Resettlement of Offenders, said: "This is an enlightened and imaginative move which we hope other employers will follow.

"Many young offenders have the potential to make first-rate soldiers. This will steer them

away from crime and help them to make something of their lives."

But Tory Shadow Defence Secretary Iain Duncan Smith said: "We are deeply concerned about such proposals. Who will they recruit?"

Desperate

"Defence strategy is in tatters. Our military services are so over-stretched and so desperate for soldiers that they are entertaining the idea of going into prisons to recruit.

"The Government has cut £600 million a year out of the defence budget, with our armed forces more committed across the world.

"They have driven the Ministry of Defence to desperate measures."

● In the 1967 film The Dirty Dozen, Lee Marvin plays an officer who recruits 12 lags for a suicidal commando mission during World War Two.

The Sun, 8 November 1999

COMMENT

The Army is right to recruit where it can

ALL Britain's combat-ready soldiers could be fitted into the new Wembley Stadium. This sobering fact should be borne in mind by those who have criticised the Army's proposal to enlist young offenders to help solve its manpower shortage.

The Army's strength is about 109,000 (of which just over 90,000 are ready for action at any time). Compare this with the figure of 180,000 for France, whose population is barely higher than ours.

Meanwhile, nearly half of all our soldiers are on operational duty from Ulster to East Timor. And if the Prime Minister means what he said earlier this year about the Western democracies intervening militarily to 'solve' humanitarian crises around the globe, then the armed services are destined to be even more severely stretched.

In the circumstances, it is difficult to blame the Army chiefs for casting their recruitment net wider. Besides, not only the Army stands to benefit. If young criminals who would almost certainly offend again are kept off the streets and given a sense of purpose, society as a whole will gain. A minimum four year term in uniform — teaching vital self-discipline — is far more likely to turn them into useful, law-abiding citizens than most other alternatives normally available to them after jail.

And perhaps it is not too fanciful to hope that their example may encourage others to turn away from the prospect of a life of crime in favour of a worthwhile career in the armed forces.

Provided that the selection process weeds out those whose wrongdoing, character or temperament clearly marks them as undesirable recruits, there is no sensible reason why offenders should be stopped from helping to defend this country and its interests. Indeed, the sovereign's uniform has always been worn by some who have fallen foul of the law — and many more who would have fallen foul of it had it not been for their service experience. Over 160 years ago, the Duke of Wellington said that the British army was 'composed of the scum of the earth — the mere scum of the earth'. Doubtless it was. But it also ended Napoleon's dream of European domination.

Of course, this is far from being the state of the army today. But in a still dangerous world, its role is as important now as ever. And if it needs the help of recruits from prison to do the job, so be it. There would be no objection from the Iron Duke.

Daily Mail, 8 November 1999

Language issues

You may be asked to comment on language issues in your exam, or in coursework. There are too many issues to deal with here. Moreover, these change constantly as society changes and language changes with it. Some possible issues to consider are:

- Is English in decline?
- How are the media affecting English use?
- How is the Internet affecting English use?
- How does social class influence English speech patterns?
- Is non-standard English dying out, and is it worth preserving?
- What is the role of slang in English?
- How useful is jargon?
- 'Good English is plain English.' Why use two words when one will do?

CHECKLIST

✓ *Facts* and *opinions* – Be sure you understand the difference.

✓ *Bias* can be unconscious or deliberate. Biased is weighted towards one side of an argument.

✓ *Emotive language* manipulates our emotions.

✓ *Media* style is determined by audience, and by commercial motives.

Summary

This chapter has told you about:

- **reasons for studying English language**
- **the history of English – Old English, Old Norse, Norman French, Latin**
- **forms and structures – grammar**
- **choice of words – lexis and how all words have connotations**
- **how speech and written language differ, especially in register**
- **standard and non-standard English; dialect and accent**
- **the media and advertising**
- **issues in language**

The question of language development is addressed in the news feature on 'Ebonics' on page 30. Read it, then Mind Map the issues that it raises. What are your views?

Black English 'a language' says US school board

Black English, or 'ebonics' – celebrated by rap artists and black activists – has been declared a second language by a California school board, opening the door to extra cash for bilingual teaching and provoking an immediate political row.

Arguing that phrases such as 'he be walkin'' and 'she done did it' are expressions from a language carved out by West African slaves, the Oakland district has ordered schools to teach black children in their own tongue.

But with California embroiled in a legal civil war over the recently approved Proposition 209 – which would end positive discrimination in favour of ethnic minorities – the move is likely to heighten racial tension and fuel conservative opposition to the $130 million (£78,000) already spent on bilingual education in the state.

The US justice department yesterday said it was poised to weigh into the affirmative action case in California, with President Clinton backing the department's view that Proposition 209 was in breach of the US constitution.

Oakland education officials insisted, however, that the decision on ebonics was merely intended to underline the legitimacy of black culture, as well as to help African-American children learn standard English. Teachers are to receive special training to help them bridge the language gulf.

'When children come to school with whatever language – whether they are Filipinos or Chinese or Hispanic – funds are available to support them,' said the board president, Lucella Harrison. 'The African-American community says: "Why aren't our students given that money and support, if they are limited in English?"'

But there were fears that the board's radical stance could backfire and erode support for other, clearer-cut programmes. 'In one sense, this is all we need,' said Jim Lyons, director of the National Association for Bilingual Education. 'Whenever bilingual education is raised in this way, there is a backlash.'

Although Mr Lyons claimed the decision stemmed from legitimate anger from members of the black community at the failure of the school system to recognise their culture, he said the linguistic basis of the new ruling was unsound.

'Ebonics is not a separate language, in the way Spanish is, although the rap movement has done a lot to accentuate the diversity in dialects,' he said.

The two key differences between black English and standard English, according to linguists, are the use of 'be' for a current activity – for example 'she be eatin' lunch' – and the use of double negatives for emphasis, as in 'I ain't got no food.'

Oakland's black mayor, Elihu Harris, disowned the decision, describing ebonics – a combination of 'ebony' and 'phonics' – as little more than slang. Mr Harris said he had been deluged with telephone calls from business leaders afraid that the board decision would discourage investment.

Norm Gold, who oversees California's distribution of federal money for bilingual teaching, said requests for money for ebonics were unlikely to succeed, and that the scheme would have to be funded from existing budgets.

The Guardian, 21 December 1996

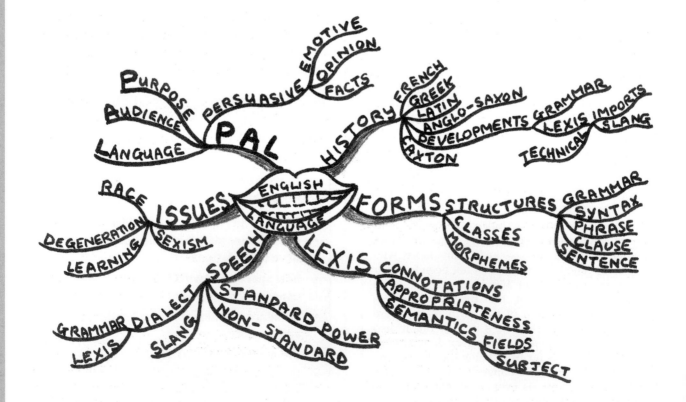

How to write

There is no single tried-and-tested formula for success in writing. However, in this chapter we will suggest some approaches. Try them out and see how you get on. Find what works for you.

Your best PAL

If you've read and absorbed Chapter 2, on how the fine detail of the English language works, then you should already be well equipped as a writer. It will also help enormously if you read as much good writing by other people as you can, both fiction and non-fiction. Refer back to Chapter 2 to see how each piece of writing achieves its effects. Look closely at the writer's choice of words, as well as at the bigger picture created by plot, character, themes and arguments.

In fact, even reading mediocre writing will help you to develop your own style if you get into the habit of thinking critically about what you read. Newspapers and magazines, album notes, even cereal packet blurbs – they can all teach you something.

Keep reminding yourself of the **PAL** formula (see page 8), and apply it to your own writing. Whatever you write, there will always be an **audience**, even if only the one determined by an exam rubric such as 'Write an introduction to Britain for foreign students…' Show your work to friends and relatives, not just your teacher. This will help to develop your sense of audience.

Try to imagine what this audience will make of what you're writing. This applies especially if you're writing about something with which your reader will be unfamiliar. If you're trying to convey the joys of rugby, ice climbing or skiing in the Alps, it doesn't help much to say that it's 'amazing', 'breathtaking' or 'staggering': you need to make your readers feel that they're there, head down in the scrum, dangling from a crampon, or careering across a blurring snowscape.

Equally, every piece of writing you tackle will have a **purpose**, for example to argue persuasively, to entertain, or to inform. Keep your purpose – or purposes – in mind as you write. Anything that does not serve this purpose is irrelevant, and should be pruned.

Know it all

Many people flounder around trying to start a piece of writing, or get lost halfway through it in the tangles of their own thought processes. They think their problem is not knowing what to write, but often the real problem is that they don't really know what they want to say.

Have you ever had the experience of getting very angry with someone and coming out with exactly what you think of them? Sometimes anger makes people inarticulate – words fail them. But just occasionally it has the opposite effect and they discover a facility with words that they didn't know they had. The probable reason is that at this moment they *know*, with startling clarity, what they want to say, and feel uninhibited about saying it.

If you know what you want to say in a piece of writing, and you plan how to say it, actually writing it down will probably be the easiest part. So, how do you get to this point?

Talking about your ideas could be a good start. Just airing ideas with someone else can have an almost magical effect on your thinking. You may get some new ideas or angles from the other person, but above all you'll have a clearer grasp of your own. If your friend is able to ask you questions, all the better. Of course in some cases – for example in writing a poem – you may prefer to ask yourself the questions.

A plan of action

One excellent way of exploring your ideas is Mind Mapping. Refer to the Introduction to this guide if you haven't tried it yet. This technique has the advantage that the product of your exploration can quickly be turned into a plan of action, just by numbering the branches of your Mind Map in a suitable sequence.

Once you have your plan, it is a good idea to go for a walk, or do something else that's not too intellectually taxing (unless you're in an exam!). However, don't let this drift into procrastination – delaying tactics! Even professional authors are capable of becoming terribly absorbed in tidying their room when confronted by the blank page or computer screen.

If you've planned properly, you'll probably feel keen to begin writing. However, if you do have trouble getting started, try:

- dashing off an opening paragraph without worrying too much about precise wording – you can always edit it later

- starting in the middle

- rereading something you've already written – it helps to be reminded that you *can* write! Once you've begun a piece of writing, you can always get yourself back into it by reviewing and editing what you've written already.

Style

Avoid using long or obscure words just to impress. On the other hand, don't be lazy and use the easy option every time just to avoid having to use a dictionary. It is appropriate to write 'Emma feels ambivalent about Knightley,' but in an exam it would be better to say 'Emma has mixed feelings . . .' than to make the mistake of using the word 'ambiguous' instead. Outside of the exam room, make a note to check a word later it you don't want to halt your flow.

As to sentences, vary their length and construction, and don't assume that long sentences are always more impressive than short ones. Moreover, it is better to write two short but correct sentences than to attempt a long, complex one in which your grammar breaks down halfway through.

Write in an appropriate register (see page 21). There is no need to be extremely formal, or to use phrases such as 'it might be argued that' in place of 'I think'. Do not use slang or overly colloquial phrasing. Write in standard English unless there is a good reason for not doing so – for example in dialogue.

Discursive essays

The word **discursive**, strangely, can have two almost opposite meanings. Here it refers to essays in which you present a logical argument, step by step.

Planning, as ever, is essential. In fact it is in this kind of essay that your sequencing – based on your planning – has to be at its most lucid. You must build up your case, making sure that your reader follows at each step how you progress from one idea to the next. You will find that subordinating conjunctions (see page 17) and lead-in adverbs such as *however* and *moreover* are very useful here. They help connect your ideas and signal each new development – as if you were driving a car to your house and your readers were following along behind.

Avoid getting stuck at the introduction. Many students spend far too long giving dictionary definitions of key words in the essay title, exploring the background, or just skirting the issue. Make a brief introduction referring to the title and making it clear what you understand by it – and then just get on with it.

It is, of course, extremely important to 'stick to the question'. Every year teachers tell students this, and every year examiners comment on the numbers of entrants who fail to do this. Even in coursework essays, be sure that you understand the question, or subject, and stick to it.

When you make your points, demonstrate a development of ideas. Too many students write essays that read like shopping lists of only loosely related ideas.

When you get to the end, do not just repeat yourself, or lamely sum up everything you've said so far. Try to pull the strands of your thoughts together, but leave the reader with some new angle or question to think about.

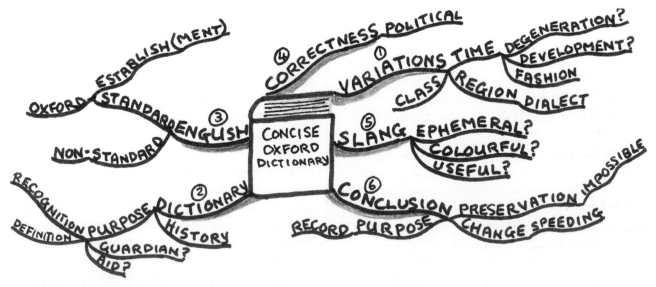

Do dictionary-makers have a duty to preserve only established English usage?

Purists take new dictionary to task for 'dreadful' words

The new *Concise Oxford English Dictionary* is published next month amid claims that it has become a record of slang, junk culture and political correctness.

The ninth edition, which introduces 7,000 new words, including a sweep of Americanisms and popular slang, was condemned yesterday for its 'dreadful and unnecessary' choices. Critics are incensed by American inventions such as *antsy*, meaning agitated and impatient, deriving from 'to have ants in your pants'. *Arvo*, Australian for afternoon, is also causing dismay. Clergywoman, acquaintance rape and glass ceiling are seen as a capitulation to political correctness, defined as 'the avoidance of forms of expression that exclude, marginalise or insult racial or cultural minorities'. *Swipecard* also offends.

Michael Plumbe, vice-chairman of the Queen's English society, said the dictionary should have a separate loose-leaf section for most new terms. 'I deplore the inclusion of some of these new words, many of which I feel have been put there on a whim. I understand that lexicographers must note the changes that affect our language but faddish terms could be recorded in a separate form. Many are used by young people and simply won't stand the test of time.'

An Oxford University Press spokesman said the dictionary was not prescriptive. 'The purpose is to record language as it is and not how people would wish it to be. The Concise Oxford Dictionary is a document of current English and no word is included without evidence of established current usage.' Editors did not make value judgements about words.

Inclusion is based on a search of publications. If a word is used in three separate publications then it is thought worthy of an entry.

The Times, 5 June 1995

Above is a news article about a new edition of the *Concise Oxford Dictionary*. Read it and then see how the Mind Map opposite presents a plan for an essay based on the article, answering the following question:

'Do dictionary-makers have a duty to preserve only established English usage?'

Critical essays

All the points made about discursive essays apply to critical essays on literary texts. Additional points are:

- Use short, carefully selected quotations to back up your arguments.

- Use evidence in the form of plot details or character observations.

- Demonstrate relevant knowledge of social, historical and literary context.

- Do not feel you have to come down firmly on one side of an argument or the other; if you feel that a character is, for example, only partly to blame for an event in a novel, say so.

- Spell the names of authors, characters and places correctly.

Creative writing

If seems only fair to remind you that we, the authors, are not Booker Prize-winning novelists, or poets laureate. In a sense the best source of instruction on creative writing lies in the great works of English literature. You will also learn a lot that you can apply to your own writing by reading what this guide has to say about literature. However, we can offer some practical hints on how you can go about your own writing.

Prose fiction

You will probably not be attempting a novel. A short story is more manageable, but don't try to cram in too much. Some of the best stories feature just one or two characters, with nothing happening that could be called a major event – though of course there is significance in what little does happen. Read a range of short stories to get some ideas about the many different possible approaches.

A basic question is whether you start with characters or plot. There is no hard and fast rule, but on balance you may write a more interesting story if you start with characters. Think of your characters, imagine them in a setting and situation, and ask yourself how each character would behave, and what the outcome might be. If you know what outcome you want, you will have to build traits into the characters that will lead to this outcome. A simple example might be:

- **Characters** – three applicants for a job as a store detective in a department store. One is cocky, jokey, refers a lot to previous successes; one is cynical, doesn't really want the job but needs the money; the third is quiet, nervous and easily offended.

- **Situation** – they are stuck in a lift on the way to the top floor for the interview.

- **Development** – the strain begins to tell; other sides of their characters emerge; conflict sets in; one of them wonders if there is a hidden camera in the lift.

- **Outcome** – the lift arrives, but what next...?

You will have to consider who is telling the story:

- You as omniscient narrator aware of everything going on within each character?

- One of the characters?

- A character who is only marginally involved in the action?

- More than one character?

What tense will you use? If using a character to tell the story, from what point in time is the story told? How will you take the reader into your setting, and how will the setting develop atmosphere?

As always, Mind Mapping can help you brainstorm the options of plot, character and style. You may also find it helpful to use a storyboard to divide the story up into key episodes. Another way in is to write some of the dialogue first.

If you want to write a story but cannot find a good plot, try reading newspaper articles. The French novelist Balzac made good use of them. Truman Capote wrote a chilling piece of 'faction', *In Cold Blood*, based on a real-life murder incident. You could even try the game of choosing three objects at random and working them into a plot – at least as a way of getting your imagination working.

You could also try starting from a theme, or an image, as you may be asked to do in an exam question. For example, you could take 'Unequal competitors' as your theme. A recent exam paper invited entrants to write on 'The Last Train'. One option here would be to take the central image as a metaphor for what happens in the story.

Lastly, a story is as long as it needs to be – and this should not be determined by your determination to write three, four or five pages. Supposedly there was an amateur writer who phoned a publisher and asked, 'How long is the average novel?' 'About 75,000 words,' was the reply. 'Thank God, I've finished!' cried the grateful author.

Plays

When you write dialogue for a story, you may find yourself wanting to write a play instead. In a play, everything is conveyed by action and dialogue: there is no author description. Chapter 7 of this guide describes the basic structure of Shakespeare's plays,

which can be applied to drama generally. The model can be remembered as **STAR**:

- **S**ituation

- **T**ension

- **A**narchy

- **R**esolution

It is not always necessary to enter the Anarchy phase, but it is certainly true that all drama must present some form of tension or conflict, which must somehow be resolved by the end of the play. Therefore, your first task will be to brainstorm the nature of this conflict.

Working with a partner may help. Once you have an idea for a character and a situation, you could try 'hot-seating', in which you take on the persona of the character and answer your partner's questions about your feelings and motivation in the play.

Another technique is to take existing characters, from real life, television, novels or plays, and throw them together in a situation. Try, for example, Lady Macbeth, Robin Hood, Tony Blair and Geri Haliwell on Judgement Day. Or you could just take one and write a dramatic monologue. (See Alan Bennett's *Talking Heads*.)

Remember that every character must have a dramatic role. What function do they perform in the play? Also remember that their language, even if intended to be realistic, must fit the play as a whole. Moreover, even naturalistic drama stylises real speech rather than copying it.

Poetry

This is perhaps the most personal form of creative writing. If you work through Chapter 8 of this guide, you will learn a lot about poetic techniques, and you should be able to apply some of them to your own writing. Poets all have their different ways of writing poetry. Here are a few ways of getting started.

Writing about a single subject

This means writing poetry that is inspired by a single object, animal, tree, bird or person – even though the actual themes of the poem may go far beyond this starting point. Ted Hughes' poems about animals focus very closely on the character of the animal, whereas Romantic poems inspired by nature tend to expand outwards from ideas suggested by their starting point: Shelley's 'Ode to a Skylark' (see page 117) and Keats' 'Ode to a Nightingale' demonstrate this.

Whether you are trying to evoke the very essence of your subject, or using it as a starting point for your ideas, Mind Mapping is a very helpful technique. Draw your image for the subject at the centre, and use the radiating branches to suggest all your personal associations for this subject. Then select and see how those associations selected could be sequenced in a poem.

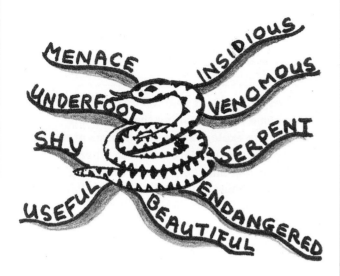

A variant on this technique is to come up with as many metaphors or similes for the subject as you can. You may then decide to focus on one or two of these, or like Sylvia Plath in her poems 'Metaphors' and 'You're', devise a poem composed entirely of these images.

Persona poems

These are discussed on page 110. The technique is to imagine that you are a particular person or thing and write from this persona. You could imagine that you are your cat, or a river in which someone has drowned, or one of your parents talking about you – or a whole range of people talking about you, one in each stanza!

This technique can be wonderfully freeing, particularly if you feel awkward writing about your own feelings or perceptions in the first person.

A variant on this, used by U.A. Fanthorpe in 'Not My Best Side' (and quoted in our *Revise GCSE English*), is to write in the persona of a figure in a painting that you like. You could also use a character, or characters, from a novel or play. W.H. Auden wrote a superb poem, 'The Sea and the Mirror', in the voices of characters from *The Tempest*.

Imitations

One of the best ways to learn is to copy, whatever you have been told at school about copying being the same as cheating! After all, this is how young children learn. You can learn about poetic style by copying the style of published poets. Gradually you will develop your own, using some of the features that you have learned.

When a poet's style is copied for a humorous effect, this is a **parody**. The parody writer does not necessarily scorn the original author's style. Some of the most original poets can be parodied. Here is a parody of T.S. Eliot by Wendy Cope (read Eliot's poems 'Ash Wednesday' and 'Rhapsody on a Windy Night' for the full effect):

> 'A Nursery Rhyme'
> *as it might have been written by T.S. Eliot*
>
> Because time will not run backwards
> Because time
> Because time will not run
> > *Hickory dickory*
>
> In the last minute of the first hour
> I saw the mouse ascend the ancient timepiece,
> Claws whispering like wind in dry hyacinths.
>
> One o'clock,
> The street lamp said,
> 'Remark the mouse that races towards the carpet.'
>
> And the unstilled wheel still turning
> > *Hickory dickory*
> > *Hickory dickory*
>
> *dock*

Writing a summary

Some syllabuses will require you to write a summary of a piece of non-fiction writing. Typically this will be a piece of about 600–750 words, and you will have to reduce it to 200 words. You may also be given a particular purpose and audience.

The first step is to make sure you understand the original fully. What is its central subject matter? Does it present an argument, and if so, what are the stages of its development?

You could sum up the main points in the margin. Another effective technique is to Mind Map them. You may find that each paragraph deals with a separate subject, in which case you should relate each paragraph to one main branch on the Mind Map.

Avoid using whole sentences from the original. Where possible, use your own words, but don't worry about the occasional short phrase here or there, providing it doesn't seem incongruous stylistically in the context of the rest of your summary.

It should be possible for you to write a summary that flows smoothly. If it reads like a 'hatchet job', you need to make some stylistic adjustments, probably in the form of conjunctions to link ideas and signal their introduction.

Lastly, be sure to write in an appropriate register and style for the given audience and purpose. If none are given, then write as far as possible in the style of the original.

Writing for a purpose and text transformation

If you have read all of this guide up to this point, you should by now have got the idea that *all* writing is for a purpose. In an exam, or for coursework, you will have to write strictly for this purpose. This discipline will also be very important if your syllabus requires you to do a 'desk study', which will also require you to select material for a purpose, and possibly to rewrite it for a purpose – applying the skills of an editor, in fact.

Think back to *The Times* news report on page 27, which describes a press gang officer getting carried away and landing his 'brawny fist' on the landlady of a pub – and her being knocked senseless by a barrel of gin. This could be rewritten in a number of ways.

- monologue from one of the characters involved – the press gang officer, the landlady, or one of the reluctant seamen, describing the incident
- letter to the court, or to an MP, from the landlady complaining about the officer getting off with a fine
- poem – perhaps in the persona of the barrel of gin
- official memo to all press gang officers warning against using undue violence
- news article in the style of the *Sun*
- feminist magazine feature
- letter from a reader to the editor of *Press Gang Gazette*, complaining about difficult landladies
- diary entry
- film script
- advertising script for headache tablets

You might like to try your hand at one of these text transformations. Otherwise, the range of possibilities is endless. You may find, for example if you are working on coursework for the popular AQA syllabus, that you are required to transform a literary work into another 'genre'. Your teacher will help you decide

what to do, probably basing your work on a text that you are already studying. This will have the advantage of deepening your insight into that text.

If transforming text into a news feature, bear in mind the 'Journalist's triangle':

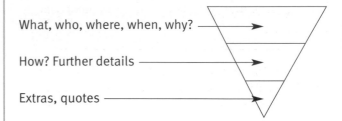

What, who, where, when, why?

How? Further details

Extras, quotes

TRY THIS

The best way to test yourself on this chapter is to do some writing! Failing that, use Mind Mapping to explore some of the forms of writing that you might try. Here are three other exercises that may help you to 'limber up'. You do not even need to lift pen to paper in order to try them!

- As you go through your day, try – for perhaps ten minutes at a time – standing outside yourself mentally and conducting a running commentary on what you are doing and experiencing. This could be in the past or present tense.
- Play 'What's it like?' Practise looking at things around you and brainstorming images for them.
- When you meet people for the first time, quickly think of three physical features that stand out, and think of how you would make these come alive to a reader. Do the same with any special features of their speech and movement.

Summary

This chapter has told you about:

- how to approach writing – getting started, style
- discursive essays – step-by-step ordering of ideas
- critical essays – using evidence and quotes
- creative writing – fiction, plays, poetry
- summary skills – including purpose and audience
- writing for a purpose – including text transformation

PREVIEW

This chapter will tell you about:

- **the nature of non-fiction prose texts**
- **the changing language of prose**
- **the literary and linguistic features of a range of texts**

The Mind Map below shows some of the aspects you should consider when you are studying a non-fiction prose text. You could copy it and add to it as you work through the chapter.

What is prose non-fiction?

Non-fiction prose texts are forms of writing in prose (as opposed to poetry) that are not novels, stories or plays. This category covers a range of writing, including:

- essays
- sermons
- biography
- autobiography
- speeches
- travel writing
- journalism
- letters

Start building your non-fiction knowledge base by answering the following questions.

Questions

Match each of these quotations to one of the categories of writing listed left.

a) Remember me affectionately to Mr de Quincey and tell him that we hope to hear that he intends coming into the North this summer.

b) The bell doth toll for him that think it doth; and though it intermit again, yet from that minute, that that occasion wrought upon him, he is united to God.

c) As I'd watched Momma put ruffles on the hem and cute little tucks around the waist, I knew that once I put it on I'd look like a movie star.

d) At dawn the jungle was half obscured in a heavy morning mist; and through the cloudy layers of rising moisture came the whooping call, the owl-like clear ringing hoot, of the female Borneo Gibbon.

e) No word in English carries a more consistently positive reference than 'creative', and obviously we should be glad of this when we think of the values it seeks to express and the activities it offers to describe.

f) For The Rolling Stones, in October 1962, the most pressing question was whether they could survive another week.

(Answers on page 145)

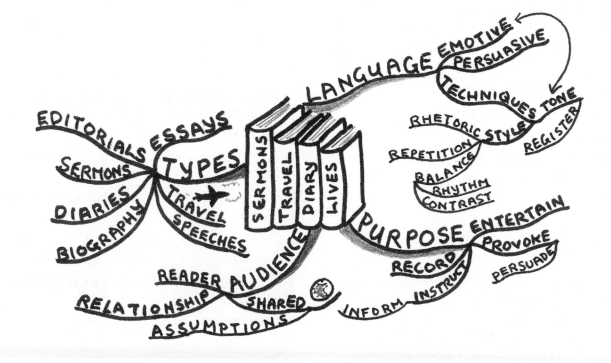

Essays

The essay was a very popular form of writing from the seventeenth to nineteenth centuries. An essay is a composition in which the writer expresses personal views. The views expressed may be about personal, political or social topics. Essays can be philosophical, provocative, argumentative, persuasive, informative, humorous, satirical – in fact, anything the writer wants. The essence of an essay is its personal nature: it is entirely subjective. In recent years other forms of mass communication have become the preferred means of expressing personal points of view, and the published essay in its original form has declined in popularity. However, some magazine and newspaper articles in which the writers give their thoughts and opinions on subjects of their choice could really be called the essays of our time.

? If you were to write an essay on a topic about which you have strong views, what would it be about? What kind of style and approach would you choose? Where would you want to publish it – in a specialist publication, in a national paper or magazine, on the Internet?

Mind your manners

You might think that this expression is rather old-fashioned, or perhaps you have never heard it before. (Do some linguistic research – find out the social context of this and similar phrases to do with 'manners'!) Read the following two essays on manners and behaviour. They are separated by 240 years.

? What differences and similarities do you expect to find?

A Treatise on Good Manners and Good Breeding

Good manners is the art of making those people easy with whom we converse.

Whoever makes the fewest persons uneasy is the best bred in the company.

As the best law is founded upon reason, so are the best manners. And as some lawyers have introduced unreasonable things into common law, so likewise many teachers have introduced absurd things into common good manners.

One principal point of this art is to suit our behaviour to the three several degrees of men; our superiors, our equals, and those below us.

For instance, to press either of the two former to eat or drink is a breach of manners; but a farmer or a tradesman must be thus treated, or else it will be difficult to persuade them that they are welcome.

Pride, ill nature, and want of sense, are the three great sources of ill manners; without some one of these defects, no man will behave himself ill for want of experience; or of what, in the language of fools, is called knowing the world.

Therefore I insist that good sense is the principal foundation of good manners; but because the former is a gift which very few among mankind are possessed of, therefore all the civilised nations of the world have agreed upon fixing some rules for common behaviour, best suited to their general customs, or fancies, as a kind of artificial good sense, to supply the defects of reason.

Jonathan Swift (1754)

Questions

1 According to Swift, the art of good manners is to do what? Pick out the words from the passage that tell you.

2 What does Swift say is the basis of good manners? (He uses the same word three times in the passage, and also uses another expression that conveys the same idea.)

3 What qualities does Swift say are the cause of bad manners?

4 What is Swift's opinion of human beings?

5 What have 'civilised nations' had to agree on?

(Answers on page 145)

HINT

Apply PAL, your friendly way to remember some important aspects of non-fiction prose. Purpose, Audience, Language

Purpose

Audience

Language

TRY THIS

1 What is the purpose of Swift's essay? Is it intended to provoke thought or debate? Is it to explore aspects of human experience? What are the essay's main themes and ideas?

2 For what kind of audience is the essay written? What might be their social position and their level of education? Are any assumptions made about the readers' familiarity with areas of experience?

3 Look at the words Swift uses to present his argument. Are any words unfamiliar to a modern reader? Look at how the sentences are constructed. Are any sentence constructions unfamiliar to a modern reader? What do you notice about the tone of the passage?

4 Make a Mind Map of your ideas. You could compare your map with the one below.

Curse of the Rudest Women in London

It's difficult to write about the rudeness of well-heeled young women without feeling – and almost certainly appearing – a tremendous old fart. But I risk mockery because I've seen some compelling rudeness over the last few weeks and wonder whether this is a trend in what used to be a resolutely genteel class.

Scene one: outside a private school in Notting Hill where parents wait in the afternoon for their unlovely nippers. One woman, a pretty blonde in her late twenties, had double-parked and was yak-yaking on her mobile, oblivious or careless of the traffic building up behind her.

When a driver pulled out from behind her and briefly sounded his horn, she responded by holding her mobile away and leaning from the window to give him a vigorous jerk of the middle finger.

Scene two: Holborn Tube station. Another good-looking woman, this time brunette and younger and dressed for the gym. She was in a hurry to get down to the platform, but there were several queues and she had to wait behind a well-dressed continental gent who was being dense about the ticket machine. First she yelled at him: 'No, the other way! The other way!' he still didn't get it right so she snatched the ticket from him and thrust it into the machine. He went through the barrier but then, of course, forgot to collect his ticket, at which she completely lost her head and shouted, 'Are you senile?' She departed, tapping her temple with a beautifully made hand. The man looked amazed.

Scene three: me dithering in front of the organic-produce counter, looking down at the remaining half dozen wholesomely battered pears that I had decided to buy. Before I could place them in a brown paper bag, there was a flash of pale blue pashmina* in my peripheral vision and two hands darted past me to grab the pears.

'Excuse me, those pears are – were – mine,' I said.

'Paid for them, have you?' returned the woman, a slim executive type in her mid-thirties showing evidence of Hohenzollern† lineage. I stammered that perhaps we might share them. A look of disdain wrinkled her nose, then she revolved like a matador and without a word swept towards the checkout.

Perhaps I haven't proved my case enough to claim a serious trend, but there do seem to be a lot of good-looking, advantaged women, cursing and pushing their way round the capital with less charm than the average puff adder.

* a type of fashionable shawl
† the Prussian imperial family

Henry Porter (1999)

TRY THIS

Apply PAL when answering these questions:

1 Write a sentence summarising the passage's theme. What might be the purpose of the passage? Tick the statement/s with which you agree.

   a) to offer a sociological analysis of contemporary behaviour

   b) to make some observations about contemporary behaviour

   c) to provide a talking point

   d) to entertain

   e) to annoy

   f) to start a campaign against mobile phones

2 What assumptions are made about the audience? What does the reader need to know in order to understanding the passage?

3 Underline any words and references which would be unfamiliar to a reader earlier than the late twentieth century.

4 What kind of language does the writer use? Consider lexis (see Chapter 2 for more about this concept), diction, tone and figurative language.

5 What similarities and differences do you find in the two passages? (Look for tone and attitude or bias as well as theme and subject matter.)

CHECKLIST

When you study a text that seems challenging or difficult:

✓ read the passage at least twice

✓ look up the meaning of unfamiliar words

✓ check that familiar words have not changed their meaning or use

✓ look up unfamiliar references, such as classical or contemporary allusions

✓ read long sentences out loud

✓ pay particular attention to the function of words that link sentences and ideas

✓ write a sentence summarising each section

✓ explain in your own words what the passage is about

Speeches

Formal speeches are intended to be spoken to an audience. The most successful and memorable speeches are those that fulfil their purpose and gain the intended audience reaction. As in all prose writing, the choice of words, the types of sentences, and the use of devices, such as rhythm and repetition, stress and intonation, will all contribute to the overall effect.

One example of repetition is Martin Luther King's famous use of the phrase 'I have a dream…'. This technique of repetition is often used in threes, as in: 'We demand jobs. We demand freedom of speech. We demand equal rights for all'.

TRY THIS

Make a Mind Map of the main factors to consider in studying speeches. You could copy and add to the one below.

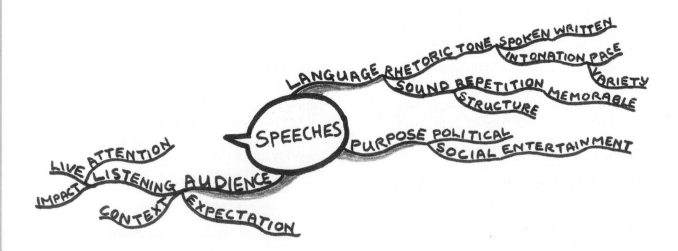

A world crisis

The two extracts below are from speeches delivered in very different contexts, both in reference to Adolf Hitler and the events of the 1930s and 1940s.

Winston Churchill to the House of Commons (1940)

Churchill had just formed a coalition government to fight what seemed to be Hitler's imminent victory.

In this crisis I hope I may be pardoned if I do not address the House at any length today. I hope that any of my friends and colleagues, or former colleagues, who are affected by the political reconstruction, will make allowance, all allowance, for any lack of ceremony with which it has been necessary to act. I would say to the House, as I have said to those who have joined the Government: 'I have nothing to offer but blood, toil, tears and sweat.'

We have before us an ordeal of the most grievous kind. We have before us many, many long months of struggle and suffering. You ask, what is our policy? I will say: it is to wage war, by sea, land and air, with all our might and with all the strength that God can give us; to wage war against a monstrous tyranny, never surpassed in the dark, lamentable catalogue of human crime. That is our policy. You ask, what is our aim? I can answer in one word: It is victory, victory at all costs, victory in spite of all terror, victory, however long and hard the road may be; for without victory there is no survival. Let that be realised; no survival for the British Empire, no survival for all that the British Empire has stood for, no survival for the urge and impulse of the ages, that mankind will move forward towards its goal. But I take up my task with buoyancy and hope. I feel sure that our cause will not be suffered to fail among men. At this time I feel entitled to claim the aid of all, and I say, 'Come, then, let us go forward together with our united strength.'

Winston Churchill (1940)

TRY THIS

Find examples in the speech of the following: *repetition* of words and phrases; *rhetorical* questions; *groups of words* with *cumulative* effect; *emotive* words and phrases; sentences of *different lengths*; *rhythm*; use of *balance* and *contrast*.

You could make a Mind Map of your ideas.

Gideon Hausner at the prosecution of Adolf Eichmann for crimes against the Jewish people (1961)

When I stand before you, O Judges of Israel, to lead the prosecution of Adolf Eichmann, I do not stand alone. With me here are six million accusers. But they cannot rise to their feet and point their finger at the man in the dock with the cry 'J'accuse' on their lips. For they are now only ashes – ashes piled high on the hills of Auschwitz and the fields of Treblinka and strewn in the forests of Poland. Their graves are scattered throughout Europe. Their blood cries out, but their voice is stilled. Therefore I will be their spokesman. In their name will I unfold this terrible indictment.

Gideon Hausner (1961)

TRY THIS

1 How does Hausner make us aware of the huge solemnity of his task?

2 What is the effect of the place names used?

3 What literary and linguistic features help to create the effect of the speech?

FACTFILE

Gideon Hausner's speech at the trial of Adolf Eichmann lasted ten hours.

Anger and admiration

In the following two speeches we hear the speakers' admiration for particular groups of people.

Neil Kinnock speaking at an election meeting in Llandudno (1987)

Why am I the first Kinnock in a thousand generations to be able to get to university? Why is Glenys the first woman in her family in a thousand generations to be able to get to university?

Was it because *all* our predecessors were 'thick'? Did they lack talent – those people who could sing, and play, and recite and write poetry; those people who could make wonderful, beautiful things with their hands; those people who could dream dreams, see visions; those people who had such a sense of perception as to know in times so brutal, so oppressive, that they could win their way out of that by coming together?

Were these people not university material? Couldn't they have knocked off all their A levels in an afternoon?

But why didn't they get it?

Was it because they were weak? – those people who could work eight hours underground and then come up and play football?

Weak? Those women who could survive eleven childbearings, were they weak? Those people who could stand with their backs and their legs straight and face the people who had control over their lives, the ones who owned their workplaces and tried to own them, and tell them, 'No. I won't take your orders.' Were they weak?

Does anybody really think that they didn't get what we had because they didn't have the talent, or the strength, or the endurance, or the commitment?

Of course not. It was because there was no platform upon which they could stand; no arrangement for their neighbours to subscribe to their welfare; no method by which the communities could translate their desires for those individuals into provision for those individuals.

Neil Kinnock (1987)

Alice Walker at a talk convention (1972)

The last time I spoke here I was already involved in a study of black women writers that has tremendously enriched the last couple of years. It began, this study, shortly after my husband and I moved to Mississippi to live. By the time we had overcome our anxiety that we might be beaten up, mobbed or bombed, I had worked up a strong interest in how to teach history to mature women; in this case, fifty and sixty year olds who had an average five years of grammar school. The approach I finally devised was to have them write their own autobiographies. Reading them, we were often able to piece their years together with political and social movements that they were then better able to understand.

Nor were all these women simply waiting around for me to show up and ask them to write about themselves. Mrs Winson Hudson, whose house was bombed more than once by the KKK, was already writing her autobiography when I was introduced to her. A remarkable woman, living in Harmony, Mississippi, a half-day's drive from anywhere of note, she is acutely aware of history, of change, and of her function as a revolutionary leader . . . her defence against the Klan was a big German shepherd dog who barked loudly when he heard the bombers coming, and two shotguns which she and her husband never hesitated to use. She wanted other people to know what it meant to fight alone against intimidation and murder, so she began to write it all down.

From Mrs Hudson I learned a new respect for women and began to search out the work of others.

Alice Walker (1972)

TRY THIS

1 Write a sentence or two summarising the content of each extract.

2 What different emotions do you hear in Neil Kinnock's speech?

3 Find examples of how the use of the personal and the informal shape the speech.

4 In Kinnock's speech, what examples are there of devices used in Churchill's speech earlier in this section?

5 In what ways is Alice Walker's speech similar to Neil Kinnock's? In what ways is it different?

When you study a speech, look for:

✓ **the purpose**
✓ **the audience**
✓ **the context**
✓ **tone and attitude**
✓ **the nature of the appeal – e.g. emotional, intellectual**
✓ **rhythm**
✓ **repetition**
✓ **contrast**
✓ **balance**

Biography and autobiography

Biography and autobiography are usually clearly distinguished – **biography** referring to accounts of people's lives written by someone else, and **autobiography** referring to life stories written by the subjects themselves. However, you may also come across texts that are fictionalised accounts of real lives, or fictional accounts that seem to be factually true. For example, Daniel Defoe's *A Journal of the Plague Year* seems to be written by a contemporary observer giving details of this dramatic period of his life, but in fact the role of the observer is created by Defoe, who would have been about four years old at the time of the plague!

Biography – the eye of the beholder

It might sound obvious, but it is helpful to remember that a biography is written by a biographer. In other words, people who write biographies have their own attitude and bias towards the people about whom they are writing. The amount and nature of the information available to them will vary according to when and in what circumstances they are writing the life story. Also, a biographer may be researching and writing from a particular critical or cultural point of view. It is quite likely, therefore, that you may read different accounts and interpretations of the same person's life.

The extracts below and on pages 44–5 are from books about the life of Diana, Princess of Wales.

Fractured fairytales

From all we know of royalty in history, however, the Prince and Princess were not acting in any way that was new. They were not more immoral, or more promiscuous. What, perhaps, has changed is the attention their lives received. For the first time the public were being let in on something that has always been going on – and not just in royal circles but in every section of society, in every age. The storybook Prince and Princess were actually experiencing, in full view of the world, what has touched every family – brokenness. Diana's life, we realised, contained elements from both the fairytale world and the real world we know so well.

We are creatures of the Oprah Winfrey age, in which stars and ordinary people queue up to speak about their sadness, their trauma, to tell their 'I have suffered too' stories. This is what brings credibility. What stronger images for us, then, than a woman who personified our aspirations, yet had gone through the only thing many of us know and can identify with – suffering and pain?

Languishing in a loveless marriage, burdened with rigid protocol and constant public scrutiny, Diana fell ill. The Princess suffered from bulimia nervosa.

Modern eating disorders are not so modern, their symptoms having been recorded in the early eighteenth century by Georgio Baglivi, Chair of Medical Theory at the Collegio Della Sapienza in Rome, and by name in 1874 by William W. Gull and Charles E. Lasegue. However, eating disorders such as anorexia and bulimia nervosa have become women's diseases of the late twentieth century. They are psychological illnesses, symptoms of something deepseated, for they are caused not just by wanting to be fashionably thin but by a kind of self-loathing and terror of the flesh and sexuality. In 1988, Diana began a course of treatment with a psychiatrist at Guy's Hospital in London. It must have been heartening for her to know that thousands of women went for help as a result of the publicity following the admission of her illness.

Having suffered much, Diana was able to empathise with those who suffered far more. If she was no longer Cinderella, she had become for her admirers something equally potent – the female victim of a brutal world she had thought she could redeem through love. We had constructed her in the context of a fairytale, and now could deconstruct her in the context of a modern parable about power and powerlessness. There was almost nothing she could do to dispel the image of Diana the saint.

J. John

TRY THIS

1 Which words in 'Fractured Fairytales' describe the writer's attitude to the subject of her biography?
   sympathetic, unbiased, analytical, critical, supportive, informed, admiring, objective

2 Which do you agree with?

   a) The information about eating disorders gives the passage authority.

   b) The writer thinks that Diana was a saint.

   c) The writer knows what Diana was thinking and feeling.

HINT

Look for vocabulary and meanings, tone, grammar, inclusion of the reader. Consider the use of metaphor and imagery and of rhetorical questions

3 How does the writer use language to convey ideas and information to the reader?

4 Make a Mind Map of your responses. You could compare your map with the one here.

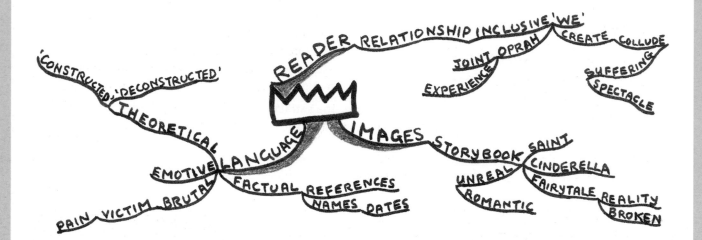

In her own words

I knew the bulimia started the week after we got engaged. My husband put his hand on my waistline and said: 'Oh, a bit chubby here, aren't we?' and that triggered off something in me.

I remember the first time I made myself sick. I was so thrilled because I thought this was the release of tension. The first time I was measured for my wedding dress I was 29 inches around the waist. The day I got married I was 23 and a half inches. I had shrunk into nothing from February to July. I had shrunk into nothing.

I gave everybody a fright. I couldn't sleep, I just never slept. I went for three nights without any sleep at all. I had no fuel to sleep on. I thought my bulimia was secret but quite a few of the people in the house recognised it was going on, but nobody mentioned it. They all thought it was quite amusing that I ate so much but never put any weight on.

I always kept my breakfast down. I don't know what the hell it was. I didn't keep vitamin pills. I just got help from somewhere – I don't know where it came from. I swam every day, I never went out at night, I didn't burn candles at both ends. I got up very early in the morning, on my own, to be on my own and at night-time went to bed early, so it wasn't as though I was being a masochist to my system but not to my energy level. I always had terrific energy, I've always had.

Andrew Morton (1997)

TRY THIS

How can you tell that this passage represents spoken language rather than written language?

HINT

Look for vocabulary and meanings, grammar and punctuation.

Revise AS and A2 Level English

Don't You Want Me

She had wanted to be a dancer, she has shown great ability at working with children, but at the age of twenty vomiting was her new vocation, and her vacation was arranged around it four times a day, just like cleaning your teeth. Bulimia nervosa is a condition affecting thousands of sufferers in this country, nearly all of them female. It might well be called the 'caring disease' on two counts; that it disproportionately affects women in the 'caring' professions, who seeing self-sacrifice as the norm, come to translate their own basic needs and desires – for food, even – as greed and self-indulgence in desperate need of correcting through the penance of purgative medicine. And unlike its haughty older sister, anorexia, which screams its pain in people's faces and stares blank-eyed as the loved ones around it weep to see their little girl turning into an Oxfam poster right in front of their eyes, bulimia tries to protect others, to pretend there's no problem. When men are angry and upset, they rebel by hurting others; when women are angry and upset, they rebel by hurting themselves.

Deprived of any ordinary human comfort, Diana did what confused and powerless young women often do: she became bulimic. And because it was now her job, as surely as any supermodel, to have her photograph taken, and because during their engagement her fiancé had put his arm around her waist and commented on her chubbiness, she was making herself sick four times a day as the Love Boat cruised by Algeria, Tunisia, Sicily, the Greek islands, through the Suez Canal and the Red Sea and into Egypt, and between bouts of sunbathing, swimming, scuba-diving, snorkelling and windsurfing.

She looked beautiful because she was as thin as she would ever be. And she looked thin because she was as sick as she would ever be, her body racked by the constant push and shove of bingeing and purging. When asked about her experience of married life on a photocall, she answered 'I can highly recommend it'. Like many caring, sharing bulimics, she was well on the way to becoming an excellent actress. For the curtain was up, the lights were lit and the show must go on.

Julie Burchill (1998)

TRY THIS

1   **Which words describe the writer's attitude to the subject of her biography?**
    admiring, analytical, biased, critical, balanced, supportive, objective

2   **What use does the writer make of theories about the nature and cause of eating disorders? Compare her approach to this matter with that of the writer of the first passage on page 43.**

3   **What linguistic devices does the writer use to convey ideas and information to the reader?**

4   **Make a Mind Map of your ideas. You could copy and complete the one that has been started here.**

5   **How important is the social and cultural context of the three passages on pages 43, 44 and 45? What insights into contemporary society might you receive from the subject matter and the writers' attitudes?**

HINT

Look at vocabulary and meanings, tone and grammar. Consider aspects such as imagery and the length of sentences.

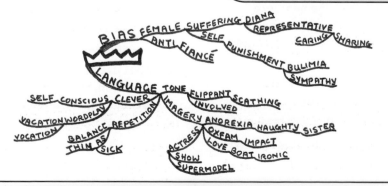

Autograph – I myself

Autobiographical writing can take different forms and fulfil different purposes. Some autobiographies are explorations of the writer's culture and identity, others consist of amusing or entertaining anecdotes. Writers can choose the focus of their autobiographies, and can concentrate on specific areas of their experience, such as childhood and growing up, or their political development.

In the following autobiographical extracts (below and page 47), the writers focus on their fathers.

Sugar Daddy

I would say my father did not prepare me well for patriarchy; himself confronted, on his marriage with my mother, with a mother-in-law who was the living embodiment of peasant matriarchy, he had no choice but to capitulate, and did so. Further, I was the child of his mid-forties, when he was just the age to be knocked sideways by the arrival of a baby daughter. He was putty in my hands throughout my childhood and still claims to be so, although now I am middle-aged myself while he, not though you'd notice, is somewhat older than the present century.

He is a man of immense, nay, imposing physical presence, yet I tend to remember him in undignified circumstances.

One of my first memories is how I bust his nose. (I was, perhaps, three years old. Maybe four.) It was on a set of swings in a public park. He'd climbed up Pooterishly* to adjust the chains from which the swings hung. I thought he was taking too long and set the swing on which I sat in motion. He wasn't badly hurt but there was a lot of blood. I was not punished for my part in this accident. They were a bit put out because I wanted to stay and play when they went home to wash off the blood.

Shortly after this he nearly drowned me, or so my mother claimed. He took me for a walk one afternoon and stopped by the pond on Wandsworth Common and I played a game of throwing leaves into the water until I forgot to let go of one. He was after me in a flash, in spite of the peril to his gents' natty suiting (ever the dandy, my old man) and wheeled me dripping in my pushchair home to the terrible but short-lived recriminations of my mother. Therefore the just apportioning of blame is not one of his specialties, and though my mother tried it on from time to time, he always thought he could buy us off with treats and so he could and that is why my brother and I don't sulk, much.

*Charles Pooter is a character in *Diary of a Nobody* by G. and W. Grossmith. Someone said to be 'Pooterish' is behaving in a dull, unimaginative, fussy way.

Angela Carter (1997)

TRY THIS

1   **Look at the content and vocabulary of the first sentence. What does the sentence suggest about the writer's approach to her subject? Tick the statements you agree with.**

   a) **The writer wants to show that her grandmother was a peasant.**

   b) **The writer is interested in gender issues.**

   c) **The writer assumes that the reader shares her view of the world.**

   d) **The writer is interested in issues of gender and power.**

   e) **The writer is interested in social and personal analysis.**

2   **What use does the writer make of: anecdote, reflection, variations in language and vocabulary, variations in tone?**

And When Did You Last See Your Father?

My father does not like waiting in queues. He is used to patients in queues waiting to see him, but he is not used to waiting in queues himself. A queue, to him, means a man being denied the right to be where he wants to be at a time of his own choosing, which is at the front, now. Ten minutes have passed. What is happening up ahead? What fathead has caused this snarl-up? Why are no cars coming the other way? Has there been an accident? Why are there no police to sort it out? Every two minutes or so my father gets out of the car, crosses to the opposite verge and tries to see if there is movement up ahead. There isn't. He gets back in and steams some more. The roof of our Alvis is down, the sun beating on to the leather upholstery, the chrome, the picnic basket. The hood is folded and pleated into the mysterious crevice between the boot and the narrow back seat where my sister and I are scrunched together as usual. The roof is nearly always down, whatever the weather: my father loves fresh air, and every car he has owned has been a convertible, so that he can have fresh air. But the air today is not fresh. There is a pall of high-rev exhaust, dust, petrol, boiling-over engines.

In the cars ahead and behind, people are laughing, eating sandwiches, drinking from beer bottles, enjoying the weather, settling into the familiar indignity of waiting-to-get-to-the-front. But my father is not like them. There are only two things on his mind: the invisible head of the queue and, not unrelated, the other half of the country lane, tantalisingly empty.

'Just relax, Arthur,' my mother says. 'You're in and out of the car like a blue-tailed fly.'

But being told to relax only incenses him. 'What can it be?' he demands. 'Maybe there's been an accident. Maybe they're waiting for an ambulance.' We all know where this last speculation is leading, even before he says it. 'Maybe they need a doctor.'

Blake Morrison (1993)

TRY THIS

1 **This passage describes the writer's family caught in a traffic jam. How does the writer use this incident to reveal aspects of his father's character and their family life?**

HINT

Look at the use of: vocabulary, direct speech, indirect speech, descriptive detail, tense and sentence structure.

2 **What similarities and differences do you find in the two passages?**

CHECKLIST

Consider the following points when you study writing about the self:
- ✓ objectivity
- ✓ subjectivity
- ✓ selection of material
- ✓ purpose
- ✓ point of view
- ✓ tone
- ✓ vocabulary
- ✓ authority

Summary

This chapter has told you about:
- categories of non-fiction
- applying PAL – Purpose + Audience → Language
- vocabulary
- tone
- bias
- attitude
- structure
- context
- how to approach a difficult text

What is prose fiction?

'Prose' is any kind of writing that isn't verse; 'prose fiction' is the term that describes novels and short stories.

Types of novels

Novels can be categorised in different ways. We often place or describe novels in terms of their subject matter – **a war novel** or a **social problem novel**, for example. Sometimes we describe novels according to their tone or intention – we use adjectives like **humorous** or **satirical**. There are novels that may be

described as **allegorical**, because the characters and events have a symbolic function, representing other characters, events or qualities. Another category you may come across is **picaresque**, which refers to novels that feature, in a series of episodes, the adventures of a 'wandering rogue' kind of character.

Many people today enjoy novels and films with a **Gothic** flavour; the Gothic novel, popular in the late eighteenth and early nineteenth centuries, featured mysterious happenings in castles, and thrilling, violent events. Some nineteenth-century novels are called **industrial** because they focus on issues raised by the effects of the industrial revolution, particularly in the north of England. You may come across novels that consist of letters exchanged between the characters: these are called **epistolary** novels. **Faction** describes works that are a mixture of fact and fiction, presenting true events in fictional form. Another category is **magical realism**, a term referring in the first place to South American writers like Gabriel Garcia Marquez, whose work combines mythical elements, bizarre events and a strong sense of local cultural tradition.

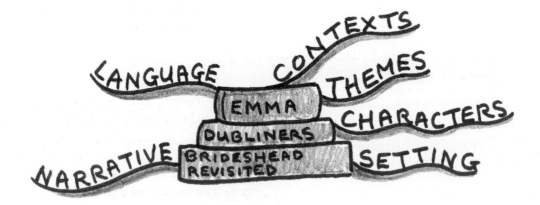

FACTFILE

Dictionary definitions of a novel:

- An extended fictional work of prose dealing with character, action, thought etc., especially in the form of a story.

- A fictitious prose narrative presenting a picture of real life, especially of the emotional crises in the lives of the men and women portrayed.

Questions

1 Sharpen your research skills and match these novels with an appropriate category description. You can use more than one category for individual titles.

   i) *Animal Farm* by George Orwell
   ii) *North and South* by Elizabeth Gaskell
   iii) *Tom Jones* by Henry Fielding
   iv) *The History Man* by Malcolm Bradbury
   v) *In Cold Blood* by Truman Capote

   a) humorous b) allegorical c) faction
   d) picaresque e) satirical f) industrial

2 a) Who published novels under the names of Ellis, Currer and Acton Bell?
   b) Mary Ann Evans is better known as which author?
   (Answers on page 145)

Short stories display many of the same features as novels, and should be studied with the same kind of care and consideration with which you approach longer works of fiction. Don't think of the short story as an easy option! It is likely that you will be studying a collection of short stories by the same author, and questions will focus on specific aspects of the text, in the same way as questions on novels.

TRY THIS

1 Make a Mind Map of the novel you are studying, showing how it reflects the definitions in the Fact File above.

2 Think of a short story you know, a fairy tale for example. How is it similar to and different from a novel?

3 Draw a timeline of the plot of the novel you are studying. You could illustrate it with colours and symbols. If you prefer, you could make a Mind Map, or a storyboard.

4 If the novel you are studying is very long or has a complicated structure, you could work with a friend or group of friends and write each main event on a separate slip of paper, put all the slips of paper in a pile, then take it in turns to select one of the slips and put it in the correct sequence.

Plot

The plot describes the story, the events that take place, and how the novel is arranged. Focus on **how** the novel is structured and **how** the events unfold. Is the story told chronologically, or does it move backwards and forwards in time? It is important to know the plot of your novel, not just in terms of what happens, but in terms of how the plot provides a framework for the themes and ideas. Imagine a garden plot, in which plants and flowers are arranged in a certain order and formation based on colour, contrast, overall effect. A novel's plot has the same sense of organic design.

Theme

Theme is the word that describes a novel's central or leading idea. Some novels have several themes. Usually the themes, or main concerns, emerge through the details of plot and character, through images and symbols and through the narrative tone and stance. Ask yourself what issues are being addressed in the text and what ideas form the focus of the author's interest.

HINT

Themes are often expressed through conflict. This may be conflict between characters, conflict between characters and the society in which they live, and internal conflict, when characters are in opposition to themselves.

The passage below from *Hard Times* by Charles Dickens describes Mr Gradgrind's reaction to finding his children visiting a circus. Think about what theme or themes the extract presents.

Dumb with amazement, Mr Gradgrind crossed to the spot where his family was thus disgraced, laid his hand upon each erring child, and said, 'Louisa!! Thomas!!'

Both rose, red and disconcerted. But Louisa looked at her father with more boldness than Thomas did. Indeed, Thomas did not look at him, but gave himself up to be taken home like a machine.

'In the name of wonder, idleness and folly!' said Mr Gradgrind, leading each away by a hand. 'What do you do here?'

'Wanted to see what it was like,' returned Louisa, shortly.

'What it was like?'

'Yes, father.'

There was an air of jaded sullenness in them both, and particularly in the girl: yet struggling through the dissatisfaction of her face, there was a light with nothing to rest upon, a fire with nothing to burn, a starved imagination keeping life in itself somehow, which brightened its expression.

'Thomas, though I have the fact before me, I find it difficult to believe that you, with your education and resources, should have brought your sister to a scene like this.'

'I brought him, father,' said Louisa quickly. 'I asked him to come.'

TRY THIS

1. What does the fact that Mr Gradgrind is 'dumb with amazement' at the behaviour of his 'erring' children suggest? What about his opinion that the circus represents 'idleness and folly'?

2. What is the effect of the imagery in the passage?

3. What do you gather about the relationship between Mr Gradgrind and his children? What do you gather about the characters of Louisa and Thomas?

4. Make a Mind Map showing the main themes or ideas that emerge. You could compare it with the one shown here.

HINT

Look at the simile 'like a machine', and at the imagery of light and fire. Does the circus itself have a metaphorical function?

5. Make a Mind Map of the themes in one of the novels you are studying. You could work with a partner and draw a map together, or make individual maps and discuss them.

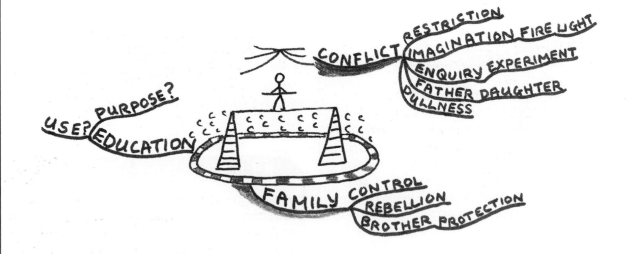

Characterisation

When you think about the characters in a prose text you should consider their appearance, personality and behaviour; how the author presents them; how they fit into the development of the text's plot, themes and ideas. Although it is important that you should engage with the characters and develop your response to them, try not to think of them as real people with an independent life of their own. The characters in a novel are literary constructions created by the author, and are there to contribute to the text's ideas and purpose.

There are various methods of characterisation.

Character through appearance

A character's appearance can reflect important aspects of personality and attitude. In this passage from *Look at Me* by Anita Brookner, what do you gather about the character and her life from the details of her appearance?

I had never thought myself interesting to look at, but now I could not help noticing that my eyes were wider, my expression lively with anticipation. I began to study my appearance in the glass. I looked through my clothes and put the dull sensible things to one side. I got rid of the heavy walking shoes, and gave my navy coat to Nancy. I bought a couple of pullovers, and a wool shirt, in light fresh colours, sky blue and white. I resurrected a pale grey dress with a white puritan collar and a black bow at the neck that I had not worn for a couple of years and had folded up and put aside because I thought it looked too elaborate for the sort of life I led. Now, as I examined myself with a franker sort of appreciation, I thought it made me look interesting, almost unusually so. I began to look forward to dressing up for the day that lay before me.

TRY THIS

1 **Think about these questions.**

   • **What does the passage suggest about the character's former appearance?**

   • **What kind of present appearance does she describe?**

   • **What development in character do these changes suggest?**

   • **What details suggest that the character's life has changed?**

2 **Make a Mind Map showing what aspects of the character in the passage are revealed through details of her appearance. You could develop the map that is shown below.**

3 **What is significant about the appearance of the characters in the text you are studying? Make a chart or Mind Map of your ideas. You could draw the characters and label relevant aspects of their appearance.**

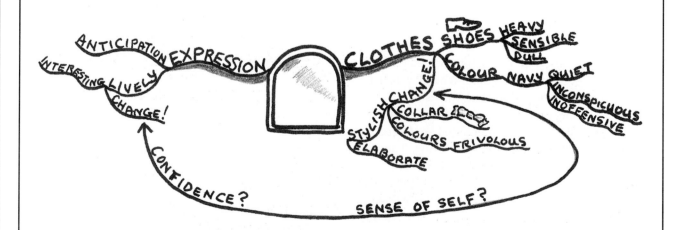

In this passage from *Middlemarch* by George Eliot (published 1871) Mrs Bulstrode has discovered that her husband is facing public disgrace and ruin. She is preparing to go downstairs to let him know that she knows.

> When she had resolved to go down, she prepared herself by some little acts which might seem mere folly to a hard onlooker; they were her way of expressing to all spectators visible or invisible that she had begun a new life in which she embraced humiliation. She took off all her ornaments and put on a plain black gown, and instead of wearing her much-adorned cap and large bows of hair, she brushed her hair down and put on a plain bonnet-cap.

? What message does Mrs Bulstrode's changed appearance give to her husband? What similarities and differences do you see between Mrs Bulstrode and the character in the previous extract?

Character through speech

Characters are also revealed through their speech, both what they say and how they say it. In the extract below from *Jane Eyre* by Charlotte Brontë, Jane and Helen are pupils at Lowood School. Jane goes to the sickroom to see Helen, who is very ill. What do you gather about each character?

Jane Eyre

'Why are you come here, Jane? It is past eleven o'clock: I heard it strike some minutes since.'

'I came to see you, Helen: I heard you were very ill, and I could not sleep till I had spoken to you.'

'You came to bid me goodbye, then: you are just in time probably.'

'Are you going somewhere, Helen? Are you going home?'

'Yes, to my long home – my last home.'

'No, no, Helen!' I stopped, distressed. While I tried to devour my tears, a fit of coughing seized Helen; it did not, however, wake the nurse. When it was over, she lay some minutes exhausted; then she whispered, 'Jane, your little feet are bare; lie down and cover yourself with my quilt.' I did so. After a long silence she resumed, still whispering, 'I am very happy, Jane; and when you hear that I am dead, you must be sure and not grieve: there is nothing to grieve about. We all must die one day, and the illness which is removing me is not painful; it is gentle and gradual; my mind is at rest. I leave no one to regret me much: I have only a father, and he is lately married, and will not miss me. By dying young, I shall escape great sufferings. I had not qualities or talents to make my way very well in the world: I should have been continually at fault.'

'But where are you going to, Helen? Can you see? Do you know?'

'I believe; I have faith; I am going to God.'

'Where is God? What is God?'

'My Maker and yours, who will never destroy what He created. I rely implicitly on his Power, and confide wholly in His goodness. I count the hours till that eventful one arrives which shall restore me to Him, reveal Him to me.'

'You are sure, then, Helen, that there is such a place as heaven, and that our souls can get to it when we die?'

'You will come to the same region of happiness, be received by the same mighty universal Parent, no doubt, dear Jane.'

Again I questioned, but this time only in thought. 'Where is that region? Does it exist?'

Charlotte Brontë

TRY THIS

1 Which of the following qualities do you see in Helen, and which do you see in Jane? Some words might describe both characters.
questioning, sceptical, accepting, self-aware, passionate, seeking, conventional, determined, other-worldly, affectionate, trusting, tender, confident

2 Does the conversation also reveal anything about the novel's themes?

3 Choose three passages of dialogue from the novel you are studying. What does the subject matter and language reveal about the characters? Present your ideas in notes or a Mind Map.

Hint: Look for conflict. In what ways do Jane and Helen disagree?

You might conclude that one of the novel's themes could be religion and the authority of religious belief. You could also consider the extent of the influence that Helen has on Jane, and how this will affect Jane as she goes through life.

CHECKLIST

Speech and dialogue in a novel can:
- ✓ reveal characters' thoughts and feelings
- ✓ indicate how characters react to each other
- ✓ further the plot
- ✓ create a range of effects such as humour, tension, realism

Character through action

? The actions and reactions of characters in different situations shape our view of them. What do you learn from the behaviour of the characters in the extract below?

Birdsong

Two officers in the First World War explore an underground tunnel beneath their trench to locate a German explosive mine. The canary is used to detect gas.

'Can you make it?' said Stephen.

'I've broken my arm. Maybe a rib too. I'll have to crawl on one hand. You take the bird.'

Stephen reached back to the cage. Its flimsy wooden frame had been crushed in the fall of earth; it was empty.

'The bird's gone,' he said. 'Let's go.'

'Damnation,' said Weir. 'We can't leave it. We'll have to find it and take it back. Otherwise if the Boche find it they'll know we –'

'For Christ's sake, they know there's a tunnel anyway.

That's why they blew it.' Weir spat through his pain. 'You cannot under any circumstances leave a bird free. Ever. It's in the handbook. I'd be court martialled. Find the bird.'

Birdsong – *cont*

Stephen crawled back over Weir's prostrate body. He felt himself close to tears as he searched the murk of the clay with the feeble light of his helmet. A little to the left of the hole made by the fall he saw gleam of yellow. Gently, he reached out his hand towards it.

He could feel his heart pummeling the floor of the tunnel; his clothes were sodden with sweat. It ran down into his eyes. He held his hand steady, the fingers opening in the gloom as he moved towards the bird. Please god, he muttered, please, please . . . When his hand was no more than six inches from the canary he made a lunge for it. The bird took off and its wings brushed the back of his hand as it flew past him. Stephen screamed. His body convulsed and his legs kicked back into Weir's thighs.

'For Christ's sake! What's the matter? You're going to bring the tunnel down.'

Stephen lay face down, panting, with his eyes closed.

'Keep still,' said Weir. 'For God's sake keep still. It's up near me now.'

Stephen lay quietly, saying nothing. Weir made no movement. Stephen heard him make little whistling noises. He was trying to soothe the startled bird, or trick it into his hand. Stephen was still facing the wrong way. Weir's body was blocking his exit back to the light.

He felt Weir make a sudden movement. 'I've got it,' he said. 'It's in my hand.'

'All right. Let's go. You start off and I'll follow.'

'I've only got one hand. I can't take the bird.'

'Well, kill it. It's only a canary. Come on. I want to turn round. I'm getting cramp. I want to get out of here.'

There was a silence. Weir made no movement. Eventually he said, 'I can't kill it. I can't do it.'

Stephen felt a strange weight in his stomach. 'You must kill it,' he said. His voice came softly through his dry mouth.

There was another silence. Then Weir said, 'I can't do it, Wraysford. I can't do it. It's just a tiny bird. It's done nothing wrong.'

Stephen, trying to keep control of himself, said, 'For God's sake kill it. Just squeeze it in your hand. Bite its head. Anything.'

'You do it.'

'No! It's too risky passing it back to me. It might escape again.'

Weir rolled over on to his back and held his left fist towards Stephen. The bird's head appeared between the forefinger and the thumb. 'There it is,' Weir said. 'I'll hold it still while you take your knife and cut its throat.'

Stephen felt Weir's eyes boring into him. He reached into his pocket and found his knife. He opened the blade and reached up over Weir's knees. Weir, straining up on his back was able to meet his gaze as Stephen's head appeared between his shins. The two men looked at each other over the tiny yellow head between them. Stephen thought of the lines of men he had seen walking into the guns; he thought of the world screaming into the twilight at Thiepval. Weir looked steadily at him. Stephen put the knife away in his pocket. He fought back the rising tears. Weir might let the bird go. It might touch him.

'I'll take it,' he said.

Sebastian Faulks (1993)

Revise AS and A2 Level English

FACTFILE

Some novels with war settings that you could read include:

- *The Regeneration Trilogy* by Pat Barker (*The Eye in the Door, The Ghost Road, Regeneration*)
- *An Ice Cream War* by William Boyd
- *Birdsong* by Sebastian Faulks
- *Catch-22* by Joseph Heller
- *A Farewell to Arms* by Ernest Hemingway
- *Officers and Gentlemen* by Evelyn Waugh

TRY THIS

1 How does each character behave in this extract? You could go through the passage and, with a different colour for each of them, underline important aspects of their behaviour.

2 What does the behaviour reveal about the characters? Add your ideas to the Mind Map below. You could include words and references from the passage if you like.

3 What themes do you find in the passage? Jot down some ideas.
You might have identified ideas like: the experience of war, the nature of courage, shared humanity, compassion, responsibility.

4 How does the dialogue in the passage affect your knowledge of and response to the characters?

HINT

Think about how the length of the sentences reflects the characters' state of mind. Look for how the characters express themselves, and for variations in tone and what this indicates.

Look at how the characters behave in this passage from *Vanity Fair* by William Thackeray, published 1886.

Vanity Fair

Rawdon Crawley returns home unexpectedly and finds his wife Rebecca in a compromising situation with Lord Steyne.

Rawdon opened the door and went in. A little table with a dinner was laid out – and wine and plate. Steyne was hanging over the sofa on which Becky sat. The wretched woman was in a brilliant full toilette, her arms and all her fingers sparkling with bracelets and rings; and the brilliants on her breast which Steyne had given her. He had her hand in his, and was bowing over to kiss it, when Becky started up with a faint scream as she caught sight of Rawdon's white face. At the next instant she tried a smile, a horrid smile, as if to welcome her husband; and Steyne rose up, grinding his teeth, pale, and with fury in his looks.

He, too, attempted a laugh – and came forward holding out his hand. 'What, come back! How d'ye do, Crawley?' he said, the nerves of his mouth twitching as he tried to grin at the intruder.

There was that in Rawdon's face which caused Becky to fling herself before him.

She clung hold of his coat, of his hands: her own were all covered with serpents, and rings, and baubles. 'I am innocent! Say I am innocent!' she said to Lord Steyne.

He thought a trap had been laid for him, and as furious with the wife as with the husband. 'You innocent! Damn you,' he screamed out. 'Why, every trinket you have on your body is paid for by me. I have given you thousands of pounds which this fellow has spent, and for which he has sold you. Innocent, by –! Make way, sir, and let me pass,' and Lord Steyne seized up his hat, and, with flame in his eyes, and looking his enemy fiercely in the face, marched upon him, never for a moment doubting that the other would give way.

But Rawdon Crawley springing out, seized him by the neck-cloth, until Steyne, almost strangled, writhed, and bent under his arm. 'You lie, you dog!' said Rawdon. 'You lie, you coward and villain!' And he struck the Peer twice over the face with his open hand, and flung him bleeding to the ground. It was all done before Rebecca could interpose. She stood there trembling before him. She admired her husband, strong, brave and victorious.

'Come here,' he said. She came up at once.

'Take off those things.' She began, trembling, pulling the jewels from her arms, and the rings from her shaking fingers, and held them all in a heap, quivering and looking up at him. 'Throw them down,' he said, and she dropped them. He tore the diamond ornament out of her breast, and flung it at Lord Steyne. It cut him on his bald forehead. Steyne wore the scar to his dying day.

William Thackeray

TRY THIS

1 **Take a different colour for each of the three characters and underline or circle their significant actions. You could make a Mind Map of the actions of each.**

2 **What is the effect of the words used to describe their behaviour?**

HINT

Look at phrases like: grinding teeth, attempting to laugh, screaming, seizing, looking fiercely, marching upon (Steyne); springing, seizing, striking, tearing, flinging (Rawdon).

3 **What do you think of Becky's behaviour here? Is she innocent, as she claims?**

Character through imagery

Sometimes characters are described through images and symbols which are associated with them throughout the novel. For example, in *The Go-Between* by L.P. Hartley (published 1953) Marian is associated with the plant belladonna or deadly nightshade. Here the narrator, Leo, describes his response to the plant.

It looked the picture of evil and also the picture of health, it was so glossy and strong and juicy-looking: I could almost see the sap rising to nourish it.

I stood on the threshold, not daring to go in, staring at the button-bright berries and the dull, purplish, hairy, bellshaped flowers reaching out towards me. I felt that the plant could poison me, even if I didn't touch it, and that if I didn't eat it, it would eat me.

Aspects of Marian's character and role are suggested by her association with the plant – notice the mixture of attraction and danger created by the description. The plant attracts and repulses the narrator with its triumphant display of strength. The plant, like Marian, is strong and intimidating, and draws the helpless narrator towards it. The image of the plant is sustained throughout the novel. The belladonna grows and flourishes in the heat of summer, suggesting a parallel with the dangerous sexual heat of Marian's affair with her lover, Ted. Leo's ritual destruction of the plant is a desperate attempt to control the threat of sexual passion.

Darcy in *Pride and Prejudice* is a thoroughbred horse, handsome and proud.

I see Cordelia in *King Lear* as a white rose with a thorny stem.

Narrative viewpoint

All the prose fiction you read is written from a particular point of view. Someone tells the story – maybe more than one person. Don't assume that the author is the narrator. Writers choose how to present their stories, and they can create narrators whose characters and voices shape and influence our responses.

The omniscient narrator

Omniscient means 'knowing everything'. An omniscient narrator is a storyteller who has a complete overview of the characters and action, and who has total knowledge of their thoughts and behaviour. These narrators can move backwards and forwards in time, can move from one setting to another, can reveal what characters are thinking and feeling, can put in or leave out whatever they wish.

An omniscient narrator will have a distinctive tone and voice, and an attitude to the characters and events described. Sometimes the narrator's opinion will be made clear in a direct address to the reader; sometimes it will emerge through the tone of the narrative.

Read these descriptions of characters from novels by Jane Austen and then answer the questions on page 58.

a) Mrs Allen was one of that numerous class of females whose society can raise no other emotion than surprise at there being any men in the world who could like them well enough to marry them. She had neither beauty, genius, accomplishment, nor manner. The air of a gentlewoman, a great deal of quiet, inactive good temper, and a trifling turn of mind, were all that could account for her being the choice of a sensible, intelligent man like Mr Allen.

Northanger Abbey, 1818

b) Vanity was the beginning and end of Sir Walter Elliot's character; vanity of person and of situation. He had been remarkably handsome in his youth; and at fifty-four, was still a very fine man. Few women could think more of their personal appearance than he did; nor could the valet of any new made lord be more delighted with the place he held in society. He considered the blessing of beauty as inferior only to the blessing of a baronetcy; and the Sir Walter Elliot, who united these gifts, was the constant object of his warmest respect and devotion.

Persuasion, 1818

Mark each of these statements True or False.

1 The narrator does not judge the characters.

2 The narrator thinks that Mrs Allen makes an impact on the people she meets.

3 The narrator thinks that Mrs Allen is intelligent.

4 The narrator thinks that Mr and Mrs Allen are suited to each other.

5 The narrator admires Sir Walter.

6 Sir Walter thinks that beauty doesn't count.

7 Sir Walter admires his valet.

8 Mrs Allen is an undistinguished character who was fortunate to be Mr Allen's wife.

9 Sir Walter is a vain, self-centred man who is obsessed with rank and personal appearance.

(Answers on page 145)

FACTFILE

- Jane Austen's characteristic technique is to reveal her judgements and her opinions through an ironic tone.

- Her observations are detached and pointed.

Direct communication with the reader

Some narrators directly address the reader, or offer their own thoughts and reflections on what is happening. George Eliot, for example, presents analysis and comment in a grave and measured tone which helps to create a sense of the narrator as an observer who may be troubled, dismayed or even amused by the behaviour of her characters, and draws the reader into her thoughts and judgements. Expressions such as 'I think…' and 'Do not imagine that…' underline the thrust of the narrative and direct the reader's response. Some of the comments are generalisations about human behaviour. In *Middlemarch*, for example, the narrator says, 'We are all of us born in moral stupidity' (Chapter 22), and in Chapter 23, describing a character who needs someone to sign a guarantee for money he owes, she observes: 'With a favour to ask we review our list of friends, do justice to their more amiable qualities, forgive their little offences, and concerning each in turn, try to arrive at the conclusion that he will be eager to oblige us'. In this way the actions and motives of the characters are linked to our shared human experience, and the direct inclusion of the reader intensifies the realism of the situation.

Sometimes a third-person narrative shifts into adopting the point of view of one of the characters. Unless you read carefully, you may assume that it is still the narrator's voice. For example, this description from *Emma* may seem to be the narrator's third-person description, but attentive reading reveals that the description of the future Mrs Elton is filtered through the perception of Mr Elton and his society:

> The charming Augusta Hawkins, in addition to all the usual advantages of perfect beauty and merit, was in possession of an independent fortune, of so many thousands as would always be called ten.

TRY THIS

- **Does the narrator think that Augusta is charming?**

- **Does the narrator think that Augusta has perfect beauty and merit?**

- **Is there an implied connection between Augusta's charms and her independent fortune?**

FACTFILE

The technique in which the narrator's voice merges with the voice of a character or characters is sometimes called *free indirect speech*.

The first-person narrator

A first-person narrative is one where the story is told by the person to whom the events happen. In this kind of narrative, everything is presented through the narrator's eyes. This means that the only access we have to other characters is through the narrator's perception of them. It also means that you should be aware that the narrators' own characters will affect their judgement. The use of a first-person narrator whose point of view is limited by lack of self-knowledge, by poor judgement or by youth can create a range of effects, including tension, irony and humour. The gap between the narrator's awareness and the reader's awareness is a major factor in many novels.

The first-person narrator Lockwood begins the story of *Wuthering Heights* by Emily Brontë (published 1847)

Chapter 1

I have just returned from a visit to my landlord – the only neighbour that I shall be troubled with. This is certainly, beautiful country! In all England, I do not believe that I could have fixed on a situation so completely removed from the stir of society. A perfect misanthropist's Heaven – and Mr Heathcliff and I are such a suitable pair to divide the desolation between us. A capital fellow! he little imagined how my heart warmed towards him when I withheld his black eyes withdraw so suspiciously under their brows, as I rode up, and when his fingers sheltered themselves, with a jealous resolution, still further in his waistcoat, as I announced my name.

Chapter 2

Yesterday afternoon set in misty and cold. I had half a mind to spend it by my study fire, instead of wading through heath and mud to Wuthering Heights . . . and, after a four miles' walk, arrived at Heathcliff's garden gate just in time to escape the first feathery flakes of a snow shower.

? Who is the narrator? What impression have you gained of Lockwood's character?

You might conclude that Lockwood's narration may not be entirely reliable, since it is soon obvious that he is not a good judge of his own character.

Multiple narrators

Sometimes a story is told by more than one narrator. When you read a novel told in this way, look for how different narrators' views of people and events differ from each other, and consider the effects that are created by the reader being drawn into separate yet complementary worlds. In *Wuthering Heights*, for example, a series of narrators take over the story at different points, contributing to the novel's dense, multi-layered effect. *Bleak House* by Charles Dickens has two distinct narrative voices, the character Esther Summerson, and a third-person narrator who presents the parts of the narrative in which Esther does not feature.

What kind of narrators can you identify in the novels you are studying? How does the choice of narrator affect the text and your response? Make a Mind Map of your ideas.

HINT

Look for signs of contradiction in what Lockwood says, thinks about himself and how he behaves. Make a Mini Mind Map of your ideas. You could compare your map with the one shown below.

CHECKLIST

✓ **With every text, make sure you know who is the narrator.**

✓ **Remember that a narrator is a constructed character.**

✓ **The narrator may give an unreliable or untrustworthy account.**

Setting and environment

In many novels the environment plays an important part. The actual place or places in which events take place can be significant for several reasons.

Physical environment

The physical environment can reflect the moods and behaviour of the characters in the novel, and establish the mood of the narrative. Read the beginning of *The Return of the Native* by Thomas Hardy (published 1878).

The Return of the Native

A Saturday afternoon in November was approaching the time of twilight, and the vast tract of unenclosed wild known as Egdon Heath embrowned itself moment by moment. Overhead the hollow stretch of whitish cloud shutting out the sky was as a tent which had the whole heath for its floor.

The heaven being spread with this pallid screen and the earth with the darkest vegetation, their meeting-line at the horizon was clearly marked. In such contrast the heath wore the appearance of an instalment of night which had taken up its place before its astronomical hour was come: darkness had to a great extent arrived hereon, while day stood distinct in the sky. Looking upwards, a furze-cutter would have been inclined to continue work; looking down, he would have decided to finish his faggot and go home. The distant rims of the world and of the firmament seemed to be a division in time no less than a division in matter. The face of the heath by its mere complexion added half an hour to evening; it could in like manner retard the dawn, sadden noon, anticipate the frowning of storms scarcely generated, and intensify the opacity of a moonless midnight to a cause of shaking and dread.

In fact, precisely at this transitional point of its nightly roll into darkness the great and particular glory of the Egdon waste began, and nobody could be said to understand the heath who had not been there at such a time.

Thomas Hardy

TRY THIS

1 **What impression of Egdon Heath do you receive from this passage? Go through the passage and underline words and phrases that create a particular effect.**

2 **How would you describe the mood and atmosphere that the description creates? Choose some of the following list of words to help you with your description:**
   sombre, light-hearted, impressive, pretty, inviting, intense, forbidding, eternal, living, stern, powerful, mysterious, reassuring, fateful, portentous, hopeful, dominating, bleak, warm-hearted, insignificant, timeless, unchanging, desolate.

3 **What kind of narrative does the physical environment suggest? You could choose one of these:**
   romance, comedy, satire, epic, family, saga, tragedy.

4 **Make a Mind Map of your responses. You could copy and complete the one that has been started here.**

5 **What is the importance of the physical environment in the text you are studying? Make a Mind Map of your ideas.**

Revise AS and A2 Level English

Place as symbol

Sometimes the place or setting of a text assumes a symbolic role. In *Mansfield Park* by Jane Austen (published 1814) the house in the title is not only the setting of significant events, but also represents certain values. The description of the house unfolds gradually, and its status as a representative of order and stability is questioned. The house, the park and the garden are presented in a variety of contexts through a range of viewpoints. Fanny Price is intimidated by the grandeur of the house: 'The grandeur of the house astonished, but could not console her. The rooms were too large for her to move in with ease' (Chapter 2). Mary Crawford assesses Mansfield Park in terms of what it will mean to her if she marries the heir to the estate: 'She looked about her with due consideration, and found almost everything in his favour, a park, a real park five miles round, a spacious modern-built house, so well placed and well screened as to deserve to be in any collection of engravings of gentlemen's seats in the kingdom' (Chapter 5). Other places have symbolic significance. London, for example, is seen as the embodiment of corrupt sophistication in contrast to the morality represented by Mansfield Park.

TRY THIS

1   **In the novels you are studying, are there examples of symbolic use of place? Make a Mind Map showing how place is presented and what it represents.**

2   **What ideas could each of these settings represent or symbolise?**

The novel's world

The setting can also refer to the world of the novel, that is, the society the novel describes. This can include geographical setting, but also encompasses social and historical factors that help to identify the nature of the novel's world. The world of the novel may be as small as a family; it could be a whole country. To understand the environment the author has created you will find it helpful to ask yourself questions like:

* What is the structure of this world?

* What are its values?

* How are people expected to behave?

* What happens to people who don't accept aspects of the society?

* What is the author's attitude to the world of the novel?

* How do I know what the author's attitude is?

Read this extract from *The Dickies*, a short story by Jane Gardam published in 1981.

The Dickies

Pam lives in a pretty house – The Rookery, though she has successfully discouraged birds – all beams and black metal window-frames and prints and pelmets and dogs. She's a widow. I don't know anything about her husband except that he died all of thirty years ago. It is generally assumed that she didn't think much of him, though as she has never done a day's paid work in her life he must have been well-heeled and that usually rates pretty high with Pam.

She is my mother's friend rather than mine. She has little in common with my mother except that they are constantly on the telephone to one another about things like does she remember Mabel Crawford and if so or even if not would she be able to put her up for a few nights as she's coming to Sloane Street to have her dog done over.

Pam and I have nothing in common at all. She boils down – she has boiled down and been removed from the heat: she is a reduction, a glaze – to everything I most dislike. She hates children, blacks and Jews. She despises education and the working man ('Of course I can tile a bathroom. ➡

The Dickies – *cont*

If *they* can tile a bathroom then I can. If they could do anything better they wouldn't have that sort of job, would they?) and I don't think she has ever read a book. When anyone breathes the faintest whisper of the arts or the sciences in her presence she cries out, 'Oh, I say! Brainy.'

Her time is arranged pleasantly and well in advance and according to the Surrey social almanac: Chelsea Flower Show, Henley, Wimbledon, Motor Show, Ideal Home Exhibition and Harrods at Christmas where because she lives just within the limit she makes their vans deliver free all her little Christmas boxes of handkerchiefs separately gift-wrapped. She gets a kick out of watching the pence and cares like a new mother about her possessions,

a new woman about her rights. She goes to church on Easter Day because it is the thing to do.

That she thinks it is the thing to do gives Pam away as being pretty old. I don't know how old: perhaps seventy – but she is trim, well-dressed and spare, with a good perm and plenty of hair in the right places. Driving her car full of meals-on-wheels she might well be fifty. Jane Austen said that you are pretty clear of being desired by the time you're fifty-five but she might well have thought again had she met Pam. A classy driver in her Ford Capri. I have seen men look at Pam with respect and interest as they've caught up with her at traffic lights too blatantly at red for even Pam to disregard.

Jane Gardam

TRY THIS

1 First, think about the narrative viewpoint. Who is the character telling the story? What is this character's attitude to the people and world being described?

HINT

Skim the text and underline references to the narrator. You might notice that she (the gender isn't clear from this extract) is of a different generation from Pam, the character she is describing. The narrator also has different attitudes and values from Pam, who is described in a critical tone.

2 Go on to identify the world Pam lives in. What social class would you place her in? Where does she shop? How does she spend her time?

3 Make a Mind Map of your responses. You could finish the one that has been started here.

4 Choose one of the novels or short stories you are studying, and make a Mind Map of the world it portrays.

5 Imagine a different setting for the novel. How is the novel's total effect changed?

Revise AS and A2 Level English

The author builds up a picture of the characters and their social environment through her use of the narrative voice and through the range of references which help to place the story in a particular social setting.

> ### CHECKLIST
>
> ✓ **Setting can create a particular mood.**
> ✓ **Place can be used to create a moral and social environment.**
> ✓ **Setting can have symbolic value.**
> ✓ **The world of a novel can be the focal point of conflict.**

Language and style

A writer's style is the combination of factors that are discussed in this chapter, and you will have been considering matters of language and style as you worked through the previous sections. Style refers to how authors write, and to the choices they make about what language they use and how they use it. When you consider style in prose, look for the same features that you analyse in poetry: author's voice, tone, vocabulary, imagery, rhythm and length of sentences, associations of words, and the use of assonance and alliteration.

Read the opening paragraphs of (1) *David Copperfield* by Charles Dickens (published 1849–50) and (2) *The Catcher in the Rye* by J.D. Salinger (published 1951):

(1) Whether I shall turn out to be the hero of my own life, or whether that station will be held by anybody else, these pages must show. To begin my life with the beginning of my life, I record that I was born (as I have been informed and believe) on a Friday, at twelve o'clock at night. It was remarked that the clock began to strike, and I began to cry, simultaneously.

In consideration of the day and hour of my birth, it was declared by the nurse, and by some sage women in the neighbourhood who had taken a lively interest

in me several months before there was any possibility of our becoming personally acquainted, first, that I was destined to be unlucky in life; and secondly, that I was privileged to see ghosts and spirits: both these gifts inevitably attaching, as they believed, to all unlucky infants of either gender born towards the small hours on a Friday night.

(2) If you really want to hear about it, the first thing you'll probably want to know is where I was born, and what my lousy childhood was like, and how my parents were occupied and all before they had me, and all that David Copperfield kind of crap, but I don't feel like going into it. In the first place, that stuff bores me, and in the second place, my parents would have about two haemorrhages apiece if I told anything pretty personal about them. They're quite touchy about anything like that, especially my father. They're *nice* and all – I'm not saying that – but they're also touchy as hell. Besides, I'm not going to tell you my whole goddam autobiography or anything.

? What differences in style do you find in the two passages? Jot down your ideas in notes or a Mind Map.

> ### HINT
>
> **Look for differences in narrative voice, vocabulary and sentence construction.**

Get planting

In the section on Plot (see page 49), you may remember a reference to a garden plot. Let's pick up the horticultural theme again – think of the works of prose fiction you read as living, organic. **PLANTS**, made up of:

People or characters
Language and style
Action or plot
Narrative voice
Themes
Setting.

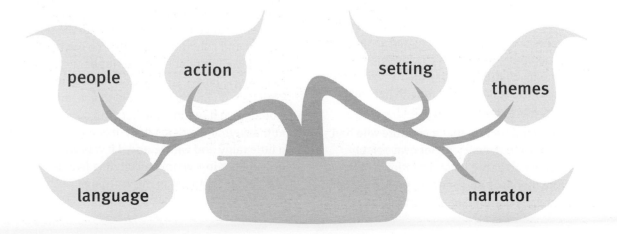

people   action   setting   themes

language   narrator

Social, historical and cultural context

The social, historical and cultural contexts in which works of literature are written and discussed are like the soil that nourishes and feeds the plants. Some knowledge of the background that shaped writers' lives and ideas will help you towards a deeper understanding and appreciation of their work.

The novel in the eighteenth century

The following chart shows some important events of the eighteenth century. Add to it if you wish.

1714	George I comes to the throne
1719	*Robinson Crusoe* by Daniel Defoe published
1726	*Gulliver's Travels* by Jonathan Swift published
1727	George II comes to the throne
1749	*Tom Jones* by Henry Fielding published
1760	George III comes to the throne
1765	Steam engine invented by James Watt
1769	Spinning Jenny invented by Richard Arkwright
1775–83	War of American Independence
1794	*The Mysteries of Udolpho* by Ann Radcliff published
1795	*Vindication of the Rights of Women* by Mary Wollstonecraft published
1793–1802	War with France
1807	Trading in slaves by British ships abolished

Read this extract from *Tom Jones* by Henry Fielding (published in 1749). The passage describes Squire Allworthy discovering the infant Tom Jones, who has been abandoned by his mother and placed in the Squire's bed. As you read, apply the PLANTS technique, and make a Mind Map of your ideas.

Tom Jones

He came to his house very late in the evening, and after a short supper with his sister, retired much fatigued to his chamber. Here, having spent some minutes on his knees, a custom which he never broke through on any account, he was preparing to step into bed, when, upon opening the clothes, to his great surprise he beheld an infant, wrapt up in some coarse linen, in a sweet and profound sleep, between his sheets. He stood some time lost in astonishment at this sight; but as good nature had always the ascendant in his mind, he soon began to be touched with sentiments of compassion for the little wretch before him. He then rang his bell, and ordered an elderly woman servant to rise immediately and come to him, and in the meantime he was so eager in contemplating the beauty of innocence that his thoughts were too much engaged to reflect that he was in his shirt, when the matron came in. She had indeed given her master sufficient time to dress himself; for out of respect for him, and regard to decency, she had spent many minutes in adjusting her hair at the looking-glass, notwithstanding all the hurry in which she had been summoned by the servant, and though her master, for ought she knew, lay expiring in a fit.

It will not be wondered at, that a creature who had so strict a regard to decency in her own person should be shocked at the least deviation in it from another. She therefore no sooner opened the door, and saw her master standing by the bedside in his shirt, with a candle in his hand, than she started back in a most terrible fright, and might perhaps have swooned away, had he not now recollected his being undressed, and put an end to her terrors by desiring her to stay without the door until he had thrown some clothes over his back and was become incapable of shocking the pure eyes of Mrs Deborah Wilkins, who, though in the fifty-second year of her age, vowed she had never beheld a man without his coat.

When Mrs Deborah returned into the room and was acquainted by her master with finding the little infant, her consternation was rather greater than his had been; nor could she refrain from crying out, with great horror of accent as well as look, 'My good sir! What's to be done?' Mr Allworthy answered she must take care of the child that evening, and in the morning he would give orders to provide it with a nurse. 'Yes, sir,' says she, 'and I hope your worship will send out your warrant to take up the hussy its mother and I should be glad to see her committed to Bridewell (a prison) and whipped at the cart's tail. Faugh, how it stinks! It doth not smell like a Christian. If I might be so bold to give my advice, I would have it put in a basket, and sent out and laid at the church-warden's door. It is a good night, only a little rainy and windy; and if it was well wrapped up, and put in a warm basket, it is two to one but it lives until it is found in the morning.'

Henry Fielding

You will be pleased to learn that Tom is not left outside to die, and lives to experience many adventures and changes in fortune. Your PLANTS response might have included some of the following ideas.

People: Squire Allworthy (as name suggests) identified as essentially good natured and moral – says prayers, feels instinctive compassion, acts in child's interests. Mrs Deborah Wilkins is hypocritical – claims to be 'decent' but actions show the opposite – identifies herself with Christian values but is unforgiving, harsh and judgemental.

Language and style: formal language – long, balanced sentences – elaborate sentence construction – archaic references – effective use of direct speech – focus on key word 'decent'.

Action or plot: situation used to show contrast between the squire and the servant – enables themes to be dramatically conveyed.

Narrative voice: omniscient narrator – aware of reader – includes reader – ironic tone – humorous – shows criticism of Mrs Deborah by merging her voice with his and allowing her to condemn herself – pretends to share her point of view.

Themes: good and bad in human nature – hypocrisy – class – moral duty.

Setting: sense of important household – social status established.

The novel in the nineteenth century

The following chart shows some important events of the nineteenth century. Add more entries of your own.

1802–15	Napoleonic Wars
1813	*Pride and Prejudice* by Jane Austen published
1815	Battle of Waterloo
1818	*Persuasion* by Jane Austen published
1818	*Frankenstein* by Mary Shelley published
1820	George IV comes to the throne
1830	William IV comes to the throne
1832	Great Reform Bill
1834	New Poor Law
1837	Queen Victoria comes to the throne
1842	Industrial strikes in the north of England
1847	*Jane Eyre* by Charlotte Brontë published; *Wuthering Heights* by Emily Brontë published
1847	Factory Act – women and children to work maximum ten hours per day
1859	Charles Darwin's *On the Origin of Species* published
1861	*Great Expectations* by Charles Dickens published
1861–65	American Civil War
1870	Education Act
1871	*Middlemarch* by George Eliot published
1874	First Impressionist exhibition
1886	*The Mayor of Casterbridge* by Thomas Hardy published
1901	Queen Victoria dies

Read the extract from *North and South* on page 66 by Elizabeth Gaskell (published in 1855). Margaret Hale and her parents have moved from the south of England to the northern town of Milton. They have met the local mill owner, Mr Thornton, and his mother. As you read, apply the PLANTS technique and make a Mind Map of your ideas like the one below.

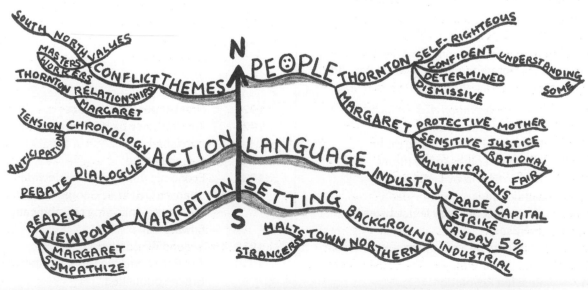

Prose fiction

North and South

Mr Thornton came that evening to Mr Hale's. He was shown up into the drawing room, where Mr Hale was reading aloud to his wife and daughter.

'I am come partly to give you a note from my mother, and partly to apologise for not keeping to my time yesterday. The note contains the address you asked for; Dr Donaldson.'

'Thank you!' said Margaret hastily, holding out her hand to take the note, for she did not wish her mother to hear that they had been making any enquiry about a doctor. She was pleased that Mr Thornton seemed immediately to understand her feeling; he gave her the note without another word of explanation.

Mr Hale began to talk about the strike. Mr Thornton's face assumed a likeness to his mother's worst expression, which immediately repelled the watching Margaret.

'Yes; the fools will have a strike. Let them. It suits us well enough. But we gave them a chance. They think trade is flourishing as it was last year. We see the storm on the horizon, and draw in our sails. But because we don't explain our reasons, they won't believe we're acting reasonably. We must give them line and letter for the way we choose to spend or save our money. Henderson tried a dodge with his men, out at Ashley, and failed. He rather wanted a strike; it would have suited his book well enough.

So when the men came to ask for the five per cent they were claiming, he told 'em he'd think about it, and give them his answer on the pay day; knowing all the while what his answer would be, of course, but thinking he'd strengthen their conceit of their own way. However, they were too deep for him, and heard something about the bad prospects of trade. So in they came on the Friday, and drew back their claim, and now he's obliged to go on working. But we Milton masters have today sent in our decision. We won't advance a penny. We tell them we may have to lower wages; but can't afford to raise. So here we stand, waiting for their next attack.'

'And what will that be?' asked Mr Hale.

'I conjecture, a simultaneous strike. You will see Milton without smoke in a few days, I imagine, Miss Hale.'

'But why,' asked she, 'could you not explain what good reason you had for expecting a bad trade? I don't know whether I use the right words, but you will understand what I mean.'

'Do you give your servants reasons for your expenditure, or your economy in the use of your own money? We, the owners of capital, have the right to choose what we will do with it.'

'A human right,' said Margaret, very low.

Elizabeth Gaskell

? Compare your Mind Map with the one on page 65. Did you have similar ideas?

The novel in the early twentieth century

The chart below shows some significant events of the twentieth century before the Second World War. Add any events that you think should be included.

1900	*The Interpretation of Dreams* by Sigmund Freud published
1901	Edward VII comes to the throne
1910	George V comes to the throne
1910	*Howard's End* by E.M. Forster published
1913	*Sons and Lovers* by D.H. Lawrence published
1914	*Dubliners* by James Joyce published
1914–18	First World War
1917	Russian Revolution
1924	First Labour Government
1925	*Mrs Dalloway* by Virginia Woolf published
1926	General Strike
1930	Economic depression worldwide
1936	Spanish Civil War; George VI comes to the throne, following the abdication of Edward VIII
1939–45	Second World War
1940	*The Power and the Glory* by Graham Greene published

Revise AS and A2 Level English

Mrs Dalloway

Mrs Dalloway said she would buy the flowers herself.

For Lucy had her work cut out for her. The doors would be taken off their hinges; Rumpelmayer's men were coming. And then, thought Clarissa Dalloway, what a morning – fresh as if issued to children on a beach.

What a lark! What a plunge! For so it had always seemed to her when, with a little squeak of the hinges, which she could hear now, she had burst open the French windows and plunged at Bourton into the open air. How fresh, how calm, stiller than this of course, the air was in the early morning; like the flap of a wave; the kiss of a wave; chill and sharp and yet (for a girl of eighteen as she then was) solemn, feeling as she did, standing there at the open window, that something awful was about to happen; looking at the flowers, at the trees with the smoke winding off them and the rooks rising, falling; standing and looking until Peter Walsh said, 'Musing among the vegetables?' – was that it? – 'I prefer men to cauliflowers' – was that it? He must have said it at breakfast one morning, when she had gone out on to the terrace – Peter Walsh. He would be back from India one of these days, June or July, she forgot which, for his letters were awfully dull; it was his sayings one remembered; his eyes, his pocket knife, his smile, his grumpiness and, when millions of things had utterly vanished – how strange it was! – a few sayings like this about cabbages.

Virginia Woolf

? The above extract is the beginning of *Mrs Dalloway* by Virginia Woolf. As you read it, apply the PLANTS technique and make a Mind Map of your ideas. You could note any ways in which this passage differs from the previous two extracts.

You may have noticed the writer's distinctive style, in which thoughts are expressed almost at random, in a 'stream', with no definite structure or formal order. This technique is known as the 'stream of consciousness', and is particularly associated with writers such as Virginia Woolf and James Joyce. Novelists used this technique to express the thought processes and unconscious minds of their characters, and to explore individual experience in a world which questioned the old certainties of religion and the social order.

Questions

Can you find two writers (non-fiction) in the timecharts of the nineteenth and twentieth centuries who have changed the way we think about human life and the workings of the human mind?

(Answers on page 145)

The novel after the Second World War

The following chart shows some significant events of the second half of the twentieth century. Which other events do you think should be included?

1945	Hiroshima destroyed by an atomic bomb
1946	National Health Service founded
1947	India becomes independent
1949	*1984* by George Orwell published
1952	Queen Elizabeth II comes to the throne
1963	President Kennedy assassinated
1962	The Beatles' first record
1965–73	Vietnam War
1968	Martin Luther King assassinated
1969	First moon landing; British troops sent in to Northern Ireland
1970	*The Female Eunuch* by Germaine Greer published
1979	Margaret Thatcher becomes Prime Minister
1982	Falklands War

? Read the following extract from *The Robber Bride* by Margaret Atwood, published 1994. Use the PLANTS technique to help you to identify significant elements in the passage's content and style.

The Robber Bride

Larry is asleep in his bed, his single bed, one arm thrown over his eyes. His hair is feathery on the pillow, hair lighter than the twins', straighter, more like Mitch's hair. He's growing it longer, with a thin rat-tail braid at the back. It looks like heck, in her opinion, but not a word has she said.

Roz stands stock-still, listening for his breathing. She's always done that, ever since he was a baby; listened to see if he was still alive. He had weak lungs, as a child; he had asthma. With the twins she didn't listen because it didn't seem called for. They were so robust.

He draws in a breath, a long sigh, and her heart turns over. Her love for him is different in quality from her love for the twins. They're tough and wiry, they have resilience; it's not that they won't get any wounds, they have wounds already, but they can lick their wounds and bounce back. Also they have

each other. But Larry has an exiled look to him, the look of a lost traveller, as if he's stuck in some no man's land, between borders and without a passport. Trying to figure out the road signs. Wanting to do the right thing.

Under the young moustache his mouth is tidy, and also gentle. It's the mouth that worries her the most. It's the mouth of a man who can be wrecked by women, by a whole bunch of women in succession. Or else by one woman: if she was mean enough, it would only take one. One really slick mean-minded woman, and poor Larry will fall in love, he'll fall in love earnestly, he'll trot round after her with his tongue hanging out, like a sweet, loyal, house-trained puppy, he'll set his heart on her, and then one flick of her bony gold-encircled wrist and he'll be just a sucked-out shell.

Margaret Atwood

You might have commented on some of these points.

- the narrative is told from the point of view of the mother
- the focus on the female experience and perspective
- the focus on family group and emotional life
- the narrative expresses thoughts as they occur
- punctuation and sentence structure show the flowing nature of thoughts and reflections
- the imagery of travelling
- the variety of sentence structures used
- the use of the present tense
- colloquial idiom

? Choose one of the prose fiction works you are studying. Identify which century it belongs to and mark it on the relevant timechart. Use the PLANTS approach to make a Mind Map of your text.

Writing about prose

Writing about prose is no different from writing about poetry or drama. You will get a good grade if your essay addresses the question, makes clear points supported by appropriate quotation, follows a line of argument and is written in a pleasing style. You will get an excellent grade if you also show informed personal response.

CHECKLIST

Make sure you know:
- ✓ when your text was written
- ✓ the main events of the time
- ✓ the influence of contemporary thought and experience on the text
- ✓ TAT – the relationship between *Text*, *Author*, *Time* (or period).
- ✓ how the novel is structured
- ✓ the novel's main themes
- ✓ the identity and type of narrator
- ✓ the role of the setting and environment

CHECKLIST

Some Dos and Don'ts for writing about prose:
- ✓ Do write in the present tense
- ✓ Don't quote long passages
- ✓ Do learn how to use 'quote' as a verb i.e. Don't say 'in *The Go-Between* Leo quotes...'
- ✓ Don't tell the story or repeat irrelevant details of the plot
- ✓ Don't write prepared character studies
- ✓ Don't write about characters as if they are real people
- ✓ Do address the key words in the question

Tackling the unseen

Working your way through this chapter will have given you practice in dealing with unseen prose, as well as helping you with your set texts. Apply the same principles and techniques, and focus on how the writer uses language and the particular effects that are created. The PLANTS approach will help you to prepare your response.

TRY THIS

Below is the opening of *Enduring Love* by Ian McEwan, published 1997. Write about its effectiveness as the beginning of a novel, and show what you find interesting about the passage. Before you read the suggested answer on page 70, prepare your own response. You could write a full essay, or make a Mind Map of your ideas.

Enduring Love

The beginning is simple to mark. We were in sunlight under a turkey oak, partly protected from a strong, gusty wind. I was kneeling on the grass with a corkscrew in my hand, and Clarissa was passing me the bottle – a 1987 Daumas Gassac. This was the moment, this was the pinprick on the time map: I was stretching out my hand, and as the cool neck and the black foil touched my palm, we heard a man's shout. We turned to look across the field and saw the danger. Next thing, I was running towards it. The transformation was absolute: I don't recall dropping the corkscrew, or getting to my feet, or making a decision, or hearing the caution Clarissa called after me. What idiocy, to be racing into this story and its labyrinths, sprinting away from our happiness among the fresh spring grasses by the oak. There was the shout again, and a child's cry, enfeebled by the wind that roared in the tall trees along the hedgerows. I ran faster. And there, suddenly, from different points around the field, four other men were converging on the scene, running like me.

I see us from three hundred feet up, through the eyes of the buzzard we had watched earlier, soaring, circling and dipping in the tumult of currents: Five men running silently towards the centre of a hundred-acre field. I approached from the south-east, with the wind at my back. About two hundred yards to my left two men ran side by side. They were farm labourers who had been repairing the fence along the field's southern edge where it skirts the road. The same distance beyond them was the motorist, John Logan, whose car was banked on the grass verge with its door, or doors, wide open. Knowing what I know now, it's odd to evoke the figure of Jed Parry directly ahead of me, emerging from a line of beeches on the far side of the field a quarter of a mile away, running into the wind. To the buzzard Parry and I were tiny forms, our white shirts brilliant against the green, rushing towards each other like lovers, innocent of the grief this entanglement would bring. The encounter that would unhinge us was minutes away, its enormity disguised from us not only by the barrier of time but by the colossus in the centre of the field that drew us in with the power of a terrible ratio that set fabulous magnitude against the puny human distress at its base.

What was Clarissa doing? She said she walked quickly towards the centre of the field. I don't know how she resisted the urge to run. By the time it happened – the event I am about to describe, the fall – she had almost caught us up and was well placed as an observer, unencumbered by participation, by the ropes and the shouting, and by our fatal lack of co-operation. What I describe is shaped by what Clarissa saw too, by what we told each other on the time of obsessive re-examination that followed: the aftermath, an appropriate term for what happened in a field waiting for its early summer mowing. The aftermath, the second crop, the growth promoted by that first cut in May.

I'm holding back, delaying the information. I'm lingering in the prior moment because it was a time when other outcomes were still possible; the convergence of six figures in a flat green space has a comforting geometry from the buzzard's perspective, the knowable, limited plane of the snooker table. The initial conditions, the force and the direction of the force, define all the consequent pathways, all the angles of collision and return, and the glow of the overhead light bathes the field, the baize and all its moving bodies, in reassuring clarity. I think that while we were still converging, before we made contact, we were in a state of mathematical grace. I linger on our dispositions, the relative distances and the compass point – because as far as these occurrences were concerned, this was the last time I understood anything clearly at all.

What were we running towards? I don't think any of us would ever know fully. But superficially the answer was, a balloon. Not the nominal space that encloses a cartoon character's speech or thought, or, by analogy, the kind that's driven by mere hot air. It was an enormous balloon filled with helium, that elemental gas forged from hydrogen in the nuclear furnace of the stars, first step along the way in the generation of multiplicity and variety of matter in the universe, including our selves and all out thoughts.

We were running towards a catastrophe, which itself was a kind of furnace in whose heat identities and fates would buckle into new shapes. At the base of the balloon was a basket in which there was a boy, and by the basket, clinging to a rope, was a man in need of help.

Ian McEwan

Suggested answer

The first sentence is an effective beginning, the short direct statement arousing interest and suggesting that a story of some significance will follow. The passage describes a balloon accident, which seems to have been the starting point for some momentous development, as the narrator refers to the 'encounter that would unhinge us'. The narrator is recreating what happened on a sunny day some time ago. He gives information which can only have been gathered later, and the sense of the past and the present combining gives the passage an eerie and almost prophetic atmosphere.

The narrator seems to be an educated man, reflective, with a scientific background. The imagery with which he evokes the incident includes mathematical allusions like 'angles of collision', and he refers to the 'comforting geometry' of the pattern the six figures make as they converge on the balloon. I find the phrase 'we were in a state of mathematical grace' particularly effective, as it conveys both the idea that the moment before they converged on the balloon was the last time they would be in a state of grace, untouched by the evil that is to come, and also reinforces the image of pattern and order that will shortly be disrupted. References to gas, matter and the universe add to the impression of the narrator's knowledge of and perhaps involvement in science.

The reader is very aware of the narrator organising and manipulating the narrative. His presence is obvious and quite compelling. Phrases such as 'I'm holding back, delaying the information' make us aware that he is shaping the narrative, making choices about the information he gives. They also make the narrator seem vulnerable, heightening our sense of the 'enormity' of what is to happen.

At the beginning of the passage, the narrator and Clarissa are having a picnic. The moment is captured almost in slow motion as the man's shout coincides with the sensation of the cool foil and the glass of the bottle. With almost obsessive accuracy, the narrator identifies the wine they were about to drink. There seems to be the assumption that the reader will recognise the wine, which I find quite flattering and rather off-putting at the same time. The narrator and Clarissa belong to a clever, cultured world in which people discuss ideas and drink good wine. However, the tone is far from smug, because the sense of impending disaster – a disaster which is not just the balloon accident – pervades the whole passage.

Suspense is effectively created by phrases such as 'sprinting away from our happiness' and 'knowing what I know now'. Each of the men who arrives at the scene is named, but Jed Parry appears to be the most significant. The narrator and Parry are described as 'rushing towards each other like lovers, innocent of the grief this entanglement would bring'. This could refer to a later, disastrous relationship between the two. The catastrophe towards which they are running is both the balloon and whatever events are to come, which will forge new identities and fates for the participants. The image of the furnace is powerful, suggesting fiery heat which will change them irrevocably. The events of the passage build up to the final picture of the 'man in need of help' clinging to the rope; we already know he is going to fall, and that the lack of cooperation among the men grabbing the ropes is to be 'fatal'. We want to know the details of what happened next, and how this incident affected the lives of those involved.

The relationship between the narrator and Clarissa is presented as happy; there is a sense of closeness in their 'obsessive re-examination' of what happened. The warmth of feeling is in contrast to the images of science and rational thought. The passage suggests ideas about the insignificance of human beings and the randomness of chance and time. The combination of a tense narrative and abstract ideas is intriguing, and provides a stimulating beginning to the novel.

Remember that this is one person's interpretation of the passage. Your own ideas may be different. The important thing is to read carefully and refer closely to the text to support and illustrate your observations.

Questions

Answer the following questions on the novel genre:

1 In which century did the novel emerge?

2 In which period was the Gothic novel popular?

3 An **epistolary** novel is told through…

4 A novel's **plot** is its…

5 The… are the central ideas of a novel.

6 The **narrator** is the author of a novel. True or false?

7 The technique in which characters' thoughts are presented through a pattern of association rather than through logical, grammatical structure is known as the… of…

(Answers on page 145) ➡

Questions – *cont*

8 From which novel, author or period does each of the extracts below come? What stylistic clues can you find?

   a) Even if they were to leave Europe, and inhabit the deserts of the new world, yet one of the first results of those sympathies for which the demon thirsted would be children, and a race of devils would be propagated on the earth who might make the very existence of the species of man a condition precarious and full of terrors. Had I right, for my own benefit, to inflict this curse upon everlasting generations?

   b) Wednesday was fine, and soon after breakfast the barouche arrived, Mr Crawford driving his sisters; and as everybody was ready, there was nothing to be done but for Mrs Grant to alight and the others to take their places. The place of all places, the envied seat, the post of honour, was unappropriated. To whose happy lot was it to fall? While each of the Miss Bertrams were mediating how best, and with the most appearance of obliging the others, to secure it, the matter was settled by Mrs Grant's saying, as she stepped from the carriage, 'As there are five of you, it will be better that one should sit with Henry, and as you were saying lately, that you wished you could drive, Julia, I think this will be a good opportunity for you to take a lesson.' Happy Julia! Unhappy Maria!

   c) We talked, for the rest of the journey, about this and that. We ascertained that I was getting off at the station before he was, though neither of us disclosed the cause of our journeys into unexpected Kent. He let me have the other Gauloise, and smoked the tipped cigarettes himself. He said he did not like them: I asked him why he carried them around with him, and he said that he had got them for the woman he had taken out for the evening. As my station drew nearer and nearer, and he still did not know my name or who I was or anything about me, I began to feel sick: waves of terror kept pouring through me.

   d) [A group of people travelling in a coach have come across a man who has been robbed and stripped.] The two gentlemen complained they were cold, and could not spare a rag; the man of wit saying with a laugh, that charity began at home; and the coachman, who had two great-coats under him, refused to lend either, lest they should be made bloody; the lady's footman desired to be excused for the same reason, which the lady herself, notwithstanding her abhorrence of a naked man, approved; and it is more than probable that Joseph must have perished, unless the postilion (a lad who has since been transported for robbing a hen-roost) had voluntarily stripped off a great-coat, his only garment; at the same time swearing a great oath, for which he was rebuked by the passengers, that he would rather ride in his shirt all his life, than suffer a fellow-creature to lie in so miserable a condition.

   e) Two hours later, Dorothea was seated in an inner room or boudoir of a handsome apartment in the Via Sistina. I am sorry to add that she was sobbing bitterly, with such abandonment to this relief of an oppressed heart as a woman habitually controlled by pride on her own account and thoughtfulness for others will sometimes allow herself when she feels securely alone. And Mr Casaubon was certain to remain away for some time at the Vatican.

Summary

This chapter has told you about:

- **different types of novels**
- **what is meant by 'plot'**
- **how novels' themes are presented**
- **ways of presenting character**
- **different types of narrator**

- **the importance of setting and environment**
- **features of language and style**
- **the social, historical and cultural background to novels of the eighteenth, nineteenth and twentieth centuries**

Curtain up

Not every play begins with a curtain going up – how many different ways to begin a performance can you identify? What the audience sees and hears when the play begins, the set, the scenery, the lighting effects – all these are aspects of the play in performance. The difference between a play and a novel, for example, is the public nature of drama. Plays are written to be performed for an audience, not to be read individually and privately. A play is a shared experience, to be seen and heard. Its effect is gained by a combination of the text, the director's interpretation of the text, the actors' performances, the staging and the audience's reaction. This complex combination of factors means that drama is essentially a living and changing medium. You might have been to different performances of the same production, and found each one an entirely different experience.

HINT

As you read your drama text, try to visualise it. See the actions and hear the words. Imagine you are the director and think about the effect you want to create. Imagine that you are a member of an audience and react as if you were in the theatre.

FACTFILE

A dictionary definition of drama: a story showing life and action, intended for representation by actors.

Scenery and setting

In general, modern playwrights give more directions than dramatists from earlier periods about setting and other aspects of a play's performance. The stage set can be used to establish the period of the play, to give information about the characters' way of life, or to create a mood. Read this description of what we see at the opening of *A Doll's House* (1879) by Henrik Ibsen, the influential Norwegian playwright.

> SCENE – *A room furnished comfortably and tastefully but not extravagantly. At the back a door to the right leads to the entrance hall; another to the left leads to* HELMER'S *study. Between the doors stands a piano. In the middle of the left-hand wall is a door and beyond a window. Near the window are a round table, armchairs and a small sofa. In the right-hand wall, at the farther end, another door; and on the same side, nearer the footlights, a stove, two easy chairs and a rocking chair; between the stove and the door a small table. Engravings on the wall. The floors are carpeted, and walls; a cabinet with china and other small objects; a small bookcase with well-bound books. A fire burns in the stove. It is winter.*

Exit, pursued by a bear

The line above is a **stage direction** from William Shakespeare's *A Winter's Tale*. What difficulties does this direction present to a director? Some playwrights give detailed instructions about how the actors should move and speak; others are less prescriptive and allow the director freedom to choose. Where stage directions are included, they are part of the play's purpose and often convey important aspects of character, plot or theme.

The description for the stage **setting** at the beginning of *A Doll's House* is followed by some instructions for the **action**. Read them carefully and think about how they add to our understanding of the situation.

> *Enter* NORA, *humming a tune and in high spirits. She is in outdoor dress and carries a number of parcels; these she lays on the table to the right. She leaves the outer door open after her, and through it is seen a* PORTER *who is carrying a Christmas tree and a basket, which he gives to the* MAID *who has opened the door.*

> [Nora asks the maid to hide the Christmas tree, and gives the porter a big tip.]

> *The* PORTER *thanks her and goes out.* NORA *shuts the door. She is laughing to herself as she takes off her hat and coat. She takes a packet of macaroons from her pocket and eats one or two, then goes cautiously to her husband's door and listens.*

1 What information does the setting of *A Doll's House* reveal? Make a Mind Map of your ideas. You could copy and complete the one that has been started here.

2 Choose a drama series that you watch regularly. Make notes of some of the settings that are used. What do they establish about the characters and the action?

3 In the drama text you are studying, does the dramatist include descriptions of the scenery and setting? If so, make a Mind Map of what aspects of the play are established through the details. If not, draw or write your own suggestions for the major settings.

CARPET SEASON
WINTER
FIRE
ENJOYMENT
PICTURES
FURNITURE COMFORTABLE
PLEASANT
INEXPENSIVE FAMILY £££
CAREFUL

Questions

Read these statements about the effect of the stage directions and what we learn from them, and tick the ones with which you agree.

1 Nora is excited about Christmas.

2 Nora is careful with money.

3 The atmosphere is grim and foreboding.

4 The atmosphere is light and optimistic.

5 Nora wants to give her husband a macaroon.

6 Nora is wary of her husband.

(Answers on page 145)

Choose a scene from the text you are studying and decide how the characters should speak and act. If you are working with a friend or a group you could compare ideas and explain your choices.

Costumes

The **costumes** that characters wear can convey ideas about features such as personality, social status, occupation. They can also have a symbolic function. For example, in *A Doll's House* Nora's costume for the tarantella she is to dance includes a 'long, variegated shawl'. When she does perform the dance, she wears a 'large, black shawl'. What might the change in colour indicate about the mood and atmosphere and Nora's state of mind?

Lights and music

Modern dramatists can make use of lighting and music in a way that was not available to writers in Shakespeare's time, for example. Lighting can create different moods; it can change the appearance of the stage; it can indicate the passing of time. Music can also create a range of effects. For example, it can establish a period in time; it can enhance the action; it can create tension; it can heighten emotion.

1   What kind of physical appearance should the characters in your drama text convey? Use the playwright's instructions, if applicable, and choose the actors you would like to play each part. They could be people you know, or professional actors.

2   Design a costume or costumes for each actor. If you like, you could find and cut out pictures of the actors and the costumes.

3   What piece of music would you choose to be the overture to the drama text you are studying? If you are working with friends, you could arrange to hear and discuss each other's choices.

4   Is there a particular scene in the text you are studying where the effect would be enhanced by music? Choose a piece of music and explain how you would use it.

Plays are meant to be performed. Aspects of a play's performance are:

✓   scenery
✓   stage settings
✓   stage directions
✓   costume
✓   lighting
✓   music

In on the act

Plays are divided into acts and scenes, through which the **plot** and **structure** emerge. 'Plot' refers to the story of the play, but also encompasses the idea of the play's overall design. (The chapter on **Prose fiction** discusses similar issues concerning the function of the plot in novels.) Most plays are structured in a similar pattern.

1   **Opening or exposition.** This is the beginning of the play where the characters are introduced and the situation established. There may be the beginning of dramatic conflict between the characters.

2   **Dramatic trigger or incitement.** Something happens to change the situation and to spark off the action.

3   **Complication.** This is the main part of the play. The characters react to the incitement and to any further developments arising from it.

4   **Crisis.** At this point the climax of the play is reached.

5   **Resolution.** Finally, everything is worked out and a conclusion is reached.

Before you go on, turn to Chapter 7 on Shakespeare to find a 'stellar' way to remember this structure.

Plot and structure in *A Doll's House*

Act 1

Nora and Helmer Torvald have three young children. He is a bank official whose recent promotion will mean an increase in salary. He is patronising and dominant, treating Nora as if she were a doll-like child. Nora is visited by an old friend, Mrs Linde, an impoverished widow who is looking for work. Helmer offers Mrs Linde work at the bank. Nora reveals to Mrs Linde that she borrowed money to pay for a holiday that Helmer needed when he was very ill, and that she has secretly worked and saved to meet the repayments. Another visitor arrives, Nils Krogstad. He is a money-lender, and is the person who lent Nora the money. He knows that Nora forged her father's signature on the loan bond. Krogstad now has a respectable job in the bank, but is in danger of losing it. He blackmails Nora into using her influence with Helmer on his behalf. Helmer, however, is determined to dismiss Krogstad.

Act 2

Mrs Linde wrongly assumes that a family friend, Dr Rank, lent Nora the money. Dr Rank is dying from a disease inherited from his father. Nora flirts with Dr Rank, hoping that he will be able to lend her enough money to pay off the debt, but when Dr Rank reveals his love for her, she is unable to go ahead. Krogstad puts in Helmer's letter box a letter with details of the loan and the forgery. Nora persuades Helmer not to open his post until the next day, and Mrs Linde goes to persuade Krogstad to take back the letter before Helmer reads it. Krogstad has left town for the night.

Act 3

Mrs Linde and Krogstad were once romantically involved, but she married a man with better prospects. They renew their relationship. Krogstad offers to take back his letter, but Mrs Linde thinks it would be better if the truth came out. Helmer reads the letter. He feels that his life and marriage are ruined, but he wants to maintain appearances for the sake of his respectability. Krogstad delivers another letter, enclosing the bond and expressing his regret and repentance. Helmer is delighted that the matter has been settled, and offers Nora his forgiveness. Nora, however, is not willing to be a 'doll wife' any more. Helmer's response to the blackmail threat has disappointed and disillusioned her. Ready to assert her independence, she leaves the house and the marriage.

TRY THIS

1 Take five pencils of different colours, and underline each different stage of the plot development. (If you apply the STAR approach, use four pencils and combine steps 3 and 4.) You might identify this structure:

- **Exposition or situation:** the nature of the marriage and the relationship between Nora and Helmer; the loan

- **Dramatic incitement or trigger:** Krogstad's blackmail attempt

- **Complication:** Nora's response; Mrs Linde's involvement

- **Crisis:** Helmer reads the letter

- **Resolution:** Nora leaves

2 Choose one of the plays that you are studying. Fill in the diagram to show the steps in the development of the play.

Subplot

Many dramatists make use of **subplots**. A subplot is a secondary plot which runs parallel to the main story. It adds interest and variety, and usually deals with similar themes to the main plot. The subplot will illuminate the main plot in some way. Look for contrasts and similarities in the characters and the action of the main plot and the subplot.

In *A Doll's House*, the Nora–Helmer–Krogstad story is the main plot, and the Krogstad–Christine Linde story is the subplot.

TRY THIS

1 Even if you don't know the play, you will be able to complete the chart below by reading the outline carefully. Fill in the gaps, and make any other entries that occur to you.

Main plot	Subplot
Nora leaves her marriage	Christine Linde . . .
Helmer . . .	Krogstad is a villain at the beginning, then redeems himself

2 Identify the subplot in the text you are studying. Add what happens in the subplot to your main plot diagram.

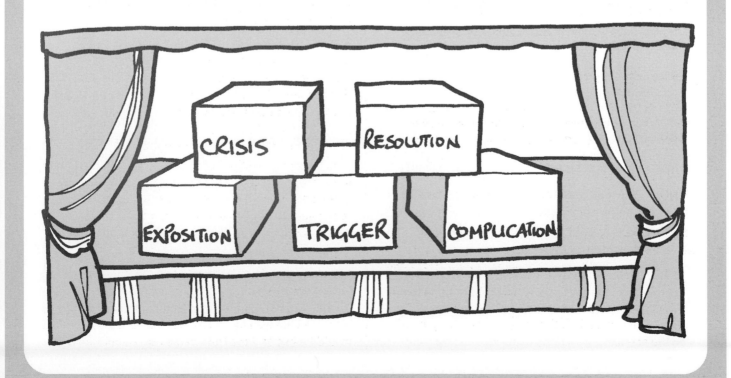

CHECKLIST

✓ **Plot refers to a play's story and the pattern and structure of events.**

✓ **The structure of plays usually follows a particular pattern.**

✓ **Subplots are thematically related to the main plot.**

A cast of characters

Character in drama is presented differently from character in prose fiction. In a novel we can have access to a character's inner thoughts and feelings; on stage, we find out about characters only through what we see and hear. When you study your drama text, look for what characters do, what they say, and what others say about them. You should also think about their purpose in the plot and how they relate to the play's themes and ideas. Try to identify what conflicts or tensions the characters experience, and how they develop through the course of the play. In this extract from Act 1 of *A Doll's House*, Nora has just offered to ask her husband to find work for Mrs Linde.

A Doll's House

MRS L: How kind you are, Nora, to be so anxious to help me! It is doubly kind in you, for you know so little of the burdens and troubles of life.

NORA: I? I know so little of them?

MRS L (*smiling*): My dear! Small household cares and that kind of thing! You are a child, Nora.

NORA (*tosses her head and crosses the stage*): You ought not to be so superior.

MRS L: No?

NORA: You are just like the others. They all think that I am incapable of anything really serious –

MRS L: Come, come

NORA: – that I have gone through nothing in this world of cares.

MRS L: But, my dear Nora, you have just told me all your troubles.

NORA: Pooh! – those were trifles. (*Lowering her voice*) I have not told you the important thing.

MRS L: The important thing? What do you mean?

NORA: You look down on me altogether, Christine – but you ought not to. You are proud, aren't you, of having worked so hard and so long for your mother?

MRS L: Indeed, I don't look down on anyone. But it is true that I am both proud and glad to think that I was privileged to make the end of my mother's life almost free from care.

NORA: And you are proud to think of what you have done for your brothers?

MRS L: I think I have the right to be.

NORA: I think so too. But now listen to this; I too have something to be proud and glad of.

MRS L: I have no doubt you have. But what do you refer to?

NORA: Speak low. Suppose Torvald were to hear! He mustn't on any account – no one in the world must know, Christine, except you.

MRS L: But what is it?

NORA: Come here. (*Pulls her down on the sofa beside her*) Now I will show you that I too have something to be proud and glad of. It was I who saved Torvald's life.

MRS L: 'Saved'? How?

NORA: I told you about our trip to Italy. Torvald would never have recovered if he had not gone there.

MRS L: Yes, but your father gave you the necessary funds.

NORA (*smiling*): Yes, that is what Torvald and the others think, but –

MRS L: But –

NORA: Papa didn't give us a shilling. It was I who procured the money.

TRY THIS

1 What does the dialogue reveal about Nora and about Christine Linde? Make a Mind Map of your ideas. You could compare your map with the one below.

2 Make a pack of cards (use index cards, or cut up squares of paper) for each of the characters in the text you are studying. On each card write something significant that the character does or says, or something that is said about the character, or some reaction to the character. With a friend (or by yourself) deal cards in turn from the individual packs. Make a comment or a note on what you learn about the characters from each pair of cards.

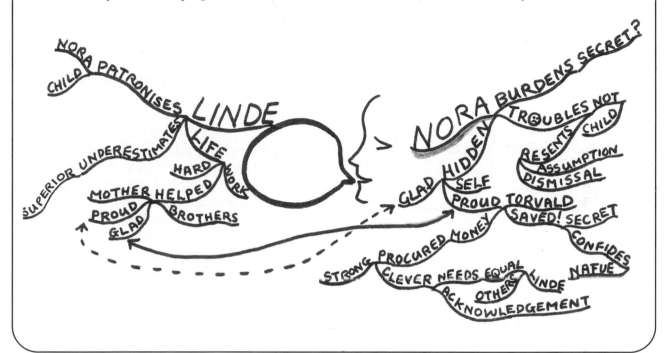

Learning the lines

The words spoken between the characters in a play are known as **dialogue**. The dialogue reveals characters and themes and furthers the plot or action. The type of language a character uses reveals aspects of personality and contributes to the overall mood or atmosphere of the play.

HINT

To appreciate the depth and subtlety of characterisation, look for what lies behind characters' words, and for any differences between what they say and what they do.

Dialogue and development

Nora's language in *A Doll's House* is often excited and emotional: 'This dreadful thing is going to happen! It will happen in spite of me! No, no, no – it can't happen – it shan't happen!' At the end of the play, her new strength and determination may be seen in the simplicity and directness of her speech: 'Now it is all over. I have put the keys here. The maids know all about everything in the house – better than I do. Tomorrow, after I have left her, Christine will come here and pack up my own things that I brought with me from home.'

TRY THIS

Choose five key pieces of dialogue from the text you are studying. Explain why they are significant.

Soliloquies and asides

These are techniques that dramatists use to enable characters to reveal their inner thoughts. A **soliloquy** is a speech in which a character, alone on the stage, reveals thoughts and feelings, sharing them with the audience; an **aside** is a comment a character makes that is not intended to be heard by the other characters on stage. Nora's state of mind as she tried to persuade herself that things will be all right may be seen in her brief soliloquy in Act 1: 'The horrible man! It's all nonsense – there's nothing wrong. The tree shall be splendid!'

CHECKLIST

✓ *Character* in drama refers to a person in the play.

✓ *Characterisation* in drama is achieved through action and dialogue.

✓ *Dialogue* furthers the action and reveals character.

Themes and ideas

When you study your drama text it is important to identify the themes and issues that are explored through the text. It is also important to distinguish between the ideas that are the dramatist's own and the ideas that are those of the characters. The playwright's own thoughts and attitude to what is being presented are seen in the overall message that the play conveys.

TRY THIS

1   From the account of the plot (see page 74) and the discussion throughout this chapter, can you identify any themes that are explored in *A Doll's House*? Make a Mind Map of your ideas, and compare it with the one below.

2   What are the central ideas in the drama text that you are studying? What is the playwright's attitude to these ideas?

HINT

A helpful way to approach this question would be to identify the beliefs and values of each of the characters in the play, then decide if the play as a whole supports or attacks these beliefs. For example, Torvald Helmer values appearance and respectability, and believes that in a marriage the man should be dominant. Does the development and resolution of *A Doll's House* endorse these ideas?

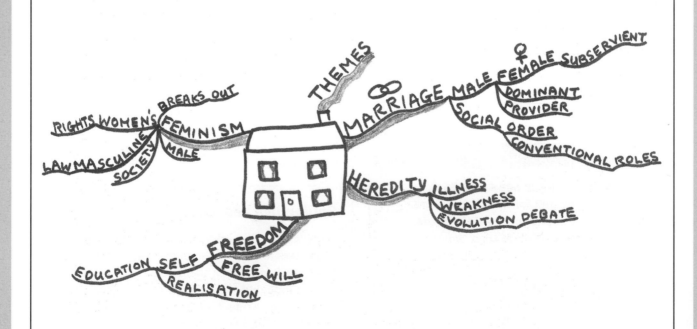

Imagery

The imagery in a play reflects the themes and ideas. The title of *A Doll's House* suggests some of the central ideas of the play.

Questions

Which of the following ideas might be suggested by the image of the doll's house? Tick the ones you agree with.

1 Nora enjoys playing with a doll's house.

2 Nora's children enjoy playing with a doll's house.

3 Nora is treated like a doll.

4 Helmer wants to buy Nora a doll's house for Christmas.

5 A miniature world.

6 A make-believe world.

7 A world in which conventional roles are imitated.

8 A world in which social roles are imitated.

(Answers on page 145)

TRY THIS

How does the imagery in the play you are studying reflect its themes and concerns? Make a Mind Map of your ideas.

Dramatic developments

Mysteries, miracles and moralities

This may sound like an introduction to a weird sect – in fact, it's an introduction to the earliest forms of English drama, performed in the Middle Ages. There weren't any theatres then (the first theatre was built in 1576) so plays were performed in the open air, on carts that moved from place to place. Mystery plays and miracle plays were dramatised versions of Bible stories, involving huge numbers of episodes and crowds of actors. Don't search for the 'whodunnit' element in a mystery play – trade guilds (a guild was like a union or professional association) referred to their crafts as 'mysteries', and the guilds took over the responsibility for mounting the plays. Morality plays developed slightly later in the period. These plays were **allegorical**, that is to say the characters represented specific virtues and vices. The most famous of these plays is *Everyman* (about 1500), which presents some of the difficulties and temptations we all experience during life's journey. Some knowledge of *Everyman* and the tradition of morality plays may be helpful to you if you study Chaucer's use of allegory, in *The Pardoner's Tale*, for example (see Chapter 9).

Elizabethan and Jacobean drama

These terms are used to categorise the drama that was written during the reigns of Elizabeth I (1558–1603) and James I (1603–25). The section on **Shakespeare's times** in Chapter 7 gives you information about the social, historical and literary events of this period. If you are studying a play from this era, write it in on the time chart (see page 93).

The Mind Map below shows some examples of Elizabethan and Jacobean drama. You could copy it and add to it as you work through this section.

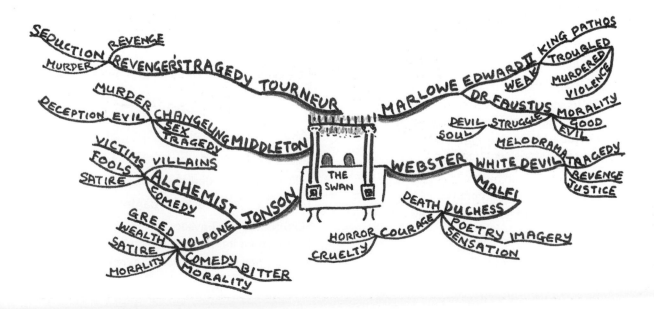

Drama of this period has some of the following characteristics:

✓ lots of blood and gore

✓ a focus on death and evil

✓ violent language and action

✓ horrific events

✓ a sense of corruption

✓ satirical wit

✓ a feeling of melancholy

✓ serious, philosophical issues

✓ humour and sensation

✓ elaborate and powerful poetry

The Duchess of Malfi by John Webster (1612)

A secret marriage

The Duchess is a widow, who declares that she has no intention of remarrying. However, she secretly marries her steward, Antonio, disregarding the wishes of her brothers, Ferdinand and the Cardinal, who are opposed to her marrying. The brothers, suspecting that she may be up to something, get Bosola to spy on her and report back to them. Bosola finds out and reveals to the brothers that the Duchess and Antonio are married. The couple flee and separate.

Torture and torment

The Duchess is captured. Ferdinand and Bosola subject her to a series of horrific experiences, such as showing her what they tell her is her husband's corpse and having her attended by madmen. Finally she is strangled. Two of her children and Cariola, her waiting woman, are also strangled.

Retribution

Ferdinand develops lycanthropy, which is a kind of madness in which the person has fantasies of being a wolf. Bosola repents, and kills the Cardinal. Ferdinand kills Bosola. What happened to Antonio? He is already dead, killed by Bosola who mistook him for the Cardinal.

The Duchess of Malfi

FERDINAND: How doth our sister Duchess bear herself
In her imprisonment?

BOSOLA: Nobly. I'll describe her:
She's sad, as one long used to't, and she seems
Rather to welcome the end of misery
Than shun it; a behaviour so noble
As gives a majesty to adversity.
You may discern the shape of loveliness
More perfect in her tears than in her smiles;
She will muse four hours together, and her silence,
Methinks, expresseth more than if she spake.

FERDINAND: Her melancholy seems to be fortified
With a strange disdain.

BOSOLA: 'Tis so, and this restraint,
Like English mastiffs, that grow fierce with tying,
Makes her too passionately apprehend
Those pleasures she's kept from.

FERDINAND: Curse upon her!
I will no longer study in the book
Of another's heart. Inform her what I told you.

(*Exit* FERDINAND. *Enter* DUCHESS)

BOSOLA: All comfort to your grace.

DUCHESS: I will; I have none.

Pray thee, why dost thou wrap thy poisoned pills
In gold and sugar?

BOSOLA: Your elder brother, the Lord Ferdinand,
Is come to visit you, and sends you word,
'Cause once he rashly made a solemn vow
Never to see you more, he comes i'th' night;
And prays you, gently, neither torch nor taper
Shine in your chamber. He will kiss your hand,
And reconcile himself; but, for his vow,
He dares not see you.

DUCHESS: At his pleasure.
Take hence the lights;

(BOSOLA *removes the lights and walks apart. Enter* FERDINAND)

he's come.

FERDINAND: Where are you?

DUCHESS: Here, sir.

FERDINAND: This darkness suits you well.

DUCHESS: I would ask you pardon.

FERDINAND: You have it;
For I account it the honourabl'st revenge,
Where I may kill, to pardon. Where are your cubs?
➡

The Duchess of Malfi – *cont*

DUCHESS: Whom?

FERDINAND: Call them your children,
For though our national law distinguish bastards
From true legitimate issue, compassionate nature
Make them all equal.

DUCHESS: Do you visit me for this?
You violate a sacrament o'th' church
Shall make you howl in hell for't.

FERDINAND: It had been well,
Could you have lived thus always; for indeed
You were too much i'th' light. But no more,
I come to seal my peace with you: here's a hand,

(*Gives her a dead man's hand*)

To which you have vowed much love; the ring
upon't

You gave.

DUCHESS: I affectionately kiss it.

FERDINAND: Pray do, and bury the print of it in your
  heart.
I will leave this ring with you for a love-token;
And the hand, as sure as the ring; and do not doubt
But you shall have the heart too. When you need a
  friend
Send it to him that owed it; you shall see
Whether he can aid you.

DUCHESS: You are very cold.
I fear you are not well after your travel.
Ha! Lights!

(*BOSOLA brings up lights*)

O horrible!

TRY THIS

1 **Read the extract. What impression does this
   scene create of:**
   a) the Duchess
   b) Bosola?
   **Make a Mind Map of your ideas. You could
   compare your map with the one below.**

2 **If you were directing this scene, how would
   you want the audience to react?**

3 **Look at the checklist opposite showing the
   characteristics of drama in this period. Which
   of the characteristics do you find in this
   scene?**

Restoration comedy

Following the rule of Oliver Cromwell and the Commonwealth, Charles II came to the throne. The theatres in England had been closed for eighteen years, by order of the Puritans. They now reopened, and a form of drama emerged that was very different from the Jacobean style.

FACTFILE

- 'Restoration' is the word used to describe the reinstatement of a monarch or the monarchy.
- In Restoration drama, women played the female roles.
- The diarist Samuel Pepys (diary begun in 1660) enjoyed watching plays.

1625	Charles I comes to the throne
1629	Parliament dissolved
1642	Civil War – theatres closed
1649	Trial and execution of Charles I
1653	Oliver Cromwell becomes Lord Protector
1660	Charles II restored to throne – theatres reopen
1665	Great Plague of London
1675	*The Country Wife* by William Wycherley
1666	Great Fire of London
1685	James II comes to the throne
1700	*The Way of the World* by William Congreve

CHECKLIST

You would expect to find some of the following in Restoration comedy.

✓ wit
✓ slick, sophisticated dialogue
✓ bawdy comedy
✓ sexual intrigue
✓ satire
✓ young rakes, amoral and fashionable
✓ foolish men, obsessed with appearance and status
✓ country bumpkins
✓ town/country contrasts
✓ pure young women
✓ lusty, frustrated older women
✓ lots to do with money, inheritances, legal entanglements, marriage dowries

The Way of the World by William Congreve (1700)

A legacy

The central couple in the play are the heroine Millament and the hero Mirabell. The plot hinges on conflict over a legacy. Mirabell wants to marry Millament, but Millament's aunt and guardian, Lady Wishfort, has to give her consent. Lady Wishfort has control over Millament's fortune and also over the fortune of her own daughter, Mrs Fainall, a widow who has recently married. Lady Wishfort hates Mirabell because he pretended to be in love with her in order to conceal his courtship of Millament. Who tells Lady Wishfort about this? Mrs Marwood, mistress of Mirabell's pretended friend Fainall.

What does Mirabell do?

Naturally, he gets his servant Waitwell to pretend to be his uncle Sir Rowland, and to pretend to want to marry Lady Wishfort. Mirabell hopes that this will make Lady Wishfort agree to his marrying Millament. But before the scheme begins, Waitwell really does marry Lady Wishfort's maid, Foible.

Does it work?

It might have worked – but Mrs Marwood puts her oar in again. She finds out the plot and conspires with her lover Fainall to tell Lady Wishfort. Furthermore, they plan to reveal that Mirabell used to be involved with Mrs Fainall, Lady Wishfort's daughter. Fainall will use these facts to pressurise Lady Wishfort into giving him full control of Mrs Fainall's and Millament's property, threatening to divorce Mrs Fainall unless he gets the money.

The baddies are foiled

Mirabell produces a legal document which shows that he is in fact trustee of Mrs Fainall's property, an arrangement Mrs Fainall made before she married. Lady Wishfort is so grateful to be saved from Fainall's threats that she forgives Mirabell and agrees that he and Millament can marry.

FACTFILE

Restoration comedy is an example of *comedy of manners*. This is satirical comedy dealing with the manners or fashions of a social class.

TRY THIS

1 The mini Mind Map shows some themes that you may identify from the brief outline opposite. Can you find the places in the outline that suggest these themes?

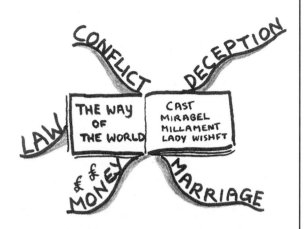

2 Choose some of the following words to describe Millament.

shy, straightforward, teasing, confident, self-centred, taunting, competitive

3 Choose some of the following words to describe Mirabell.

indifferent, tolerant, jealous, lying, sincere, clever, tongue-tied

4 Choose some of the following words to describe the dialogue.

sharp, halting, witty, gritty, terse, polished, clever

5 Imagine that you are directing this scene. What directions would you give the two actors about how they should speak and move? You could write your instructions on the script.

Questions

Read this dialogue between Mirabell and Millament, and answer the questions.

MIRA: I would beg a little private audience too. You had the tyranny to deny me last night, though you knew I came to impart a secret to you that concerned my love.

MILLA: You saw I was engaged.

MIRA: Unkind. You had the leisure to entertain a herd of fools, things who visit you from their excessive idleness, bestowing on your easiness that time which is the encumbrance of their lives. How can you find delight in such society? It is impossible they should admire you, they are not capable: or if they were, it should be to you as a mortification; for sure to please a fool is some degree of folly.

MILLA: I please myself. Besides, sometimes to converse with fools is for my health.

MIRA: Your health! Is there a worse disease than the conversation of fools?

MILLA: Mirabell, if you persist in this offensive freedom, you'll displease me. I think I must resolve after all not to have you. We shan't agree. I shan't endure to be reprimanded, nor instructed; 'tis so dull to act always by advice, and so tedious to be told of one's faults. I can't bear it. Well, I won't have you, Mirabell – I'm resolved – I think – you may go. Ha, ha, ha. What would you give, that you could help loving me?

MIRA: I would give something that you did not know I could not help it.

MILLA: Come, don't look grave then. Well, what do you say to me?

MIRA: I say that a man may as soon make a friend by his wit, or a fortune by his honesty, as win a woman with plain-dealing and sincerity.

1 At the beginning of the passage, why is Mirabell annoyed?

2 What does Mirabell think of the people with whom Millament spent the evening?

3 What does Millament say that she dislikes about Mirabell's behaviour?

(Answers on page 145)

Post-Restoration comedy

Towards the end of the eighteenth century, too late to be accurately termed Restoration, two dramatists were writing plays that were very similar to the earlier comedies of manners. The best-known of these plays are *She Stoops to Conquer* by Oliver Goldsmith and *The Rivals* by Richard Sheridan.

The Rivals by Richard Sheridan (1775)

Complications in love

The action of the play takes place in Bath, in the course of a single day, and as the title suggests, the play features rivals in love. The lady in question is Lydia Languish, who has sentimental ideas about love and marriage and thinks it would be romantic to marry a poor man. This is bad news for Captain Absolute, son and heir to baronet Sir Anthony, who is in love with Lydia. He pretends to be Ensign Beverley, an impoverished soldier, and Lydia responds favourably to him! But there's a further complication – Lydia can marry only with the consent of her aunt Mrs Malaprop, or she will lose her fortune. Mrs Malaprop wants her to marry a rich man, and agrees to Sir Anthony's proposal that his son and Lydia should marry. Captain Absolute is scared to reveal his true identity to Lydia, and furthermore, she has another suitor, his friend Bob Acres.

Crisis of identities

Sir Lucius O'Trigger goads Acres into asking Captain Absolute to deliver a challenge to Ensign Beverley. Lucius himself believes that Lydia has sent him love letters, and wants to fight his perceived rival Captain Absolute. When the real identity of Beverley is revealed, Acres gives up all claim to Lydia. It emerges that Mrs Malaprop, not Lydia, wrote the letters to Lucius. Lydia forgives her lover for his deception.

Subplot

The subplot concerns another pair of lovers, Julia and Faulkland, whose love is jeopardised by Faulkland's romantic notions of how the ideal woman should behave. In the end they are reconciled.

FACTFILE

The word 'malapropism', meaning a word that is pronounced correctly but used wrongly, comes from the character Mrs Malaprop.

TRY THIS

What words is Mrs Malaprop misusing here? What words do you think are the correct ones to use?

He is the very pineapple of politeness.

She's as headstrong as an allegory on the banks of the Nile.

Revise AS and A2 Level English

The passage below is from the beginning of *The Rivals*. Lydia's friend Julia arrives unexpectedly.

The Rivals

LYDIA: My dearest Julia, how delighted am I! (*Embrace*) How unexpected was this happiness!

JULIA: True, Lydia, and our pleasure is the greater. But what has been the matter? You were denied me at first!

LYDIA: Ah! Julia, I have a thousand things to tell you! But first inform me, what has conjured you to Bath? – Is Sir Anthony here?

JULIA: He is – we are arrived within this hour – and I suppose he will be here to wait on Mrs Malaprop as soon as he is dressed.

LYDIA: Then before we are interrupted, let me impart to you some of my distress! I know your gentle nature will sympathise with me, though your prudence may condemn me! My letters have informed you of my whole connexion with Beverley – but I have lost him, Julia! – my aunt has discovered our intercourse by a note she intercepted, and has confined me ever since! Yet, would you believe it? She has fallen absolutely in love with a tall Irish baronet she met one night since we have been here, at Lady Macshuffle's rout.

JULIA: You jest, Lydia!

LYDIA: No, upon my word. She really carries on a kind of correspondence with him, under a feigned name though, till she chooses to be known to him; – but it is a *Delia* or a *Celia,* I assure you.

JULIA: Then, surely, she is now more indulgent to her niece.

LYDIA: Quite the contrary. Since she has discovered her own frailty, she is become more suspicious of mine. Then I must inform you of another plague! – That odious Acres is to be in Bath today; so that I protest I shall be teased out of all spirits!

JULIA: Come, come, Lydia, hope the best. Sir Anthony shall use his interest with Mrs Malaprop.

LYDIA: But you have not heard the worst. Unfortunately I had quarrelled with my poor Beverley, just before my aunt made the discovery, and I have not seen him since, to make it up.

JULIA: What was his offence?

LYDIA: Nothing at all! – But, I don't know how it was, as often as we had been together, we never had a quarrel! And somehow I was afraid he would never give me an opportunity. So, last Thursday, I wrote a letter to myself, to inform myself that Beverley was at that time paying his addresses to another woman. I signed it *your Friend unknown*, showed it to Beverley, charged him with his falsehood, put myself in a violent passion, and vowed I'd never see him more

Richard Sheridan

Questions

1 What plot points are introduced in this passage? Use the outline to help you. Look for ideas and information that will lead to developments in plot and character.

2 What aspects of Lydia's character are established here?

3 Julia shows good feeling and common sense. How should she speak and move during this scene? Use the ideas in the illustration to help you.

(Answers on page 145)

Drama in the nineteenth century

Ibsen, Shaw and Wilde

Three important dramatists of this period are Henrik Ibsen, Oscar Wilde and George Bernard Shaw. Wilde and Shaw are really turn-of-the-century writers, with Shaw in fact carrying on writing well into the twentieth century. You will have discovered something about Ibsen if you worked through the discussions of *A Doll's House* earlier in this chapter. Shaw was influenced by Ibsen. His work deals with intellectual ideas and social issues which he treated realistically and uncompromisingly. Although his themes are strong (prostitution, slum landlordism, arms manufacture), Shaw's work has great life and comic spirit. His drama could be called 'literary'; it is characterised by thought and language, and contains long prefaces, stage directions and descriptions of characters. Oscar Wilde's drama, on the other hand, is characterised by its witty, elaborate wordplay and its concentration on style and effect rather than on realism.

The Importance of Being Earnest by Oscar Wilde (1899)

The background

John Worthing (Jack) and Algernon Moncrieff are two fashionable young men on the London social scene. Jack is pursuing Algy's cousin, Gwendolen Fairfax, and Algy is pursuing Jack's ward, Cecily Cardew.

Double deceptions

Jack goes by the name Ernest when he is in London, and tells his ward Cecily, who lives in the country, that he has a wicked brother called Ernest. Algy has invented an invalid friend, Bunbury, to give him an excuse to get out of social engagements.

The truth emerges

After much confusion, it is revealed that Jack and Algy are brothers. Jack was parted from his family as a baby when Cecily's governess, Miss Prism, left him in a handbag at Victoria Station. Jack's real name is Ernest, which is just as well because Gwendolen is obsessed with marrying someone of that name. All ends happily with both sets of marriages arranged.

In the extract below, Algernon is asking his servant Lane about the quality of wine that is served at dinner parties.

The Importance of Being Earnest

LANE: I have often observed that in married households the champagne is rarely of a first-rate brand.

ALGERNON: Good heavens! Is marriage so demoralising as that?

LANE: I believe it *is* a very pleasant state, sir. I have had very little experience of it myself up to the present. I have only been married once. That was in consequence of a misunderstanding between myself and a young person.

ALGERNON (*languidly*): I don't know that I am much interested in your family life, Lane.

LANE: No, sir; it is not a very interesting subject. I never think of it myself.

ALGERNON: Very natural, I am sure. That will do, Lane, thank you.

LANE: Thank you, sir.

(LANE *goes out*)

ALGERNON: Lane's views on marriage seem somewhat lax. Really, if the lower orders don't set us a good example, what on earth is the use of them? They seem, as a class, to have absolutely no sense of moral responsibility.

(*Enter* LANE)

LANE: Mr Ernest Worthing.

(*Enter* JACK. LANE *goes out*)

ALGERNON: How are you, my dear Ernest? What brings you up to town?

JACK: Oh, pleasure, pleasure! What else should bring one anywhere? Eating as usual, I see, Algy!

ALGERNON (*stiffly*): I believe it is customary in good society to take some slight refreshment at five o'clock. Where have you been since last Thursday?

JACK (*sitting down on the sofa*): In the country.

ALGERNON: What on earth do you do there?

➡

The Importance of Being Earnest – *cont*

JACK (*pulling off his gloves*): When one is in town one amuses oneself. When one is in the country one amuses other people. It is excessively boring.

ALGERNON: And who are the people you amuse?

JACK (*airily*): Oh, neighbours, neighbours.

ALGERNON: Got nice neighbours in your part of Shropshire?

JACK: Perfectly horrid! Never speak to one of them.

ALGERNON: How immensely you must amuse them! (*Goes over and takes sandwich*) By the way, Shropshire is your county, is it not?

JACK: Eh? Shropshire? Yes, of course. Hallo! Why all these cups? Why cucumber sandwiches? Why such reckless extravagance in one so young? Who is coming to tea?

ALGERNON: Oh! merely Aunt Augusta and Gwendolen.

JACK: How perfectly delightful!

ALGERNON: Yes, that is all very well; but I am afraid Aunt Augusta won't quite approve of your being here.

JACK: May I ask why?

ALGERNON: My dear fellow, the way you flirt with Gwendolen is perfectly disgraceful. It is almost as bad as the way Gwendolen flirts with you.

JACK: I am in love with Gwendolen. I have come up to town expressly to propose to her.

ALGERNON: I thought you had come up for pleasure? . . . I call that business.

JACK: How utterly unromantic you are!

ALGERNON: I really don't see anything romantic in proposing. It is very romantic to be in love. But there is nothing romantic about a definite proposal. Why, one may be accepted. One usually is, I believe. Then the excitement is all over. The very essence of romance is uncertainty. If ever I get married, I'll certainly try to forget the fact.

JACK: I have no doubt about that, dear Algy. The Divorce Court was specially invented for people whose memories are so curiously constituted.

ALGERNON: Oh! there is no use speculating on that subject. Divorces are made in Heaven – (JACK *puts out his hand to take a sandwich.* ALGERNON *at once interferes.*) Please don't touch the cucumber sandwiches. They are ordered specially for Aunt Augusta. (*Takes one and eats it*)

Oscar Wilde

Questions

1 Which would you say is more important in the extract, character or dialogue?

2 Which words from this list would you use to describe the describe the dialogue?

   (a) hard-hitting (b) clever (c) coarse (d) sparkling (e) colloquial (f) self-conscious (g) stylised (h) mundane (i) witty

(Answers on page 145)

FACTFILE

Oscar Wilde makes very effective use of *paradox* and *epigram*. A *paradox* is a statement that appears to be contradictory but which often contains some truth. An *epigram* is a short, witty statement.

TRY THIS

1 **Wilde called *The Importance of Being Ernest* 'a trivial comedy for serious people'. Is the comedy entirely trivial? See if you can find examples of serious themes and issues in the passage, or examples of satire.**

HINT

Look for topics such as class, marriage, social behaviour and conventions.

2 **Find in the passage some examples of the use of paradox and epigram.**

Drama in the twentieth century

Bertolt Brecht

A dramatist who had a great influence in the 1930s and 40s was Bertolt Brecht, whose ideas moved drama away from naturalism and towards concentration on plays' themes and political messages. You may see the connection between Brecht's theories, Ibsen's 'theatre of ideas' and Shaw's focus on social and philosophical issues.

> **FACTFILE**
>
> In drama, *naturalism* refers to plays in which the dramatist recreates real life in great detail. *Realism* refers to plays in which the dramatist creates psychological realism and presents fundamental issues about the inner lives of human beings.

Verse drama

In the first half of the century poetic or verse drama became popular. T.S. Eliot's *Murder in the Cathedral* is a good example of this genre, which was influenced by Greek and Elizabethan drama.

Drama after the Second World War

In the mid-1950s there was a resurgence of British drama, which became the dominant literary form for a number of years. The time chart on page 67 will give you information about the social, historical and cultural background to this period. If you are studying a play from this era, write it on the chart. The Mind Map below shows some aspects of drama at this time. You could copy it and add your own ideas.

> **CHECKLIST**
>
> Some characteristics of drama of this period:
> - ✓ breaking of conventions
> - ✓ wider representations of social classes
> - ✓ sense of the absurd
> - ✓ various levels of audience involvement
> - ✓ reflects a range of social and political perspectives
> - ✓ challenges traditional attitudes and conventions
> - ✓ reflects predicaments associated with living in a scientific, post-nuclear age

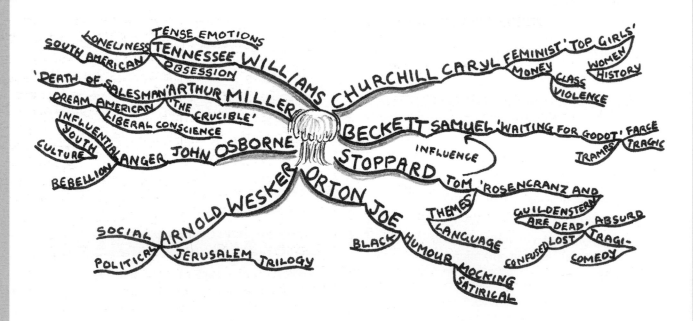

Look Back in Anger by John Osborne (1956)

Jimmy Porter and Alison are a seemingly ill-matched couple: he is a jazz-loving ex-student who works on a market stall, and she is a colonel's daughter. Jimmy rails against everything Alison's background and her parents represent. Alison's friend Helena wants to rescue Alison from this unsuitable marriage. Alison leaves with her father, and Helena takes her place with Jimmy. (She also takes Alison's place in other ways – Act 1 opens with Alison ironing, and Act 3 opens with Helena ironing.) Alison returns. She has lost the baby she was expecting. She and Jimmy are reconciled through their own way of communicating, a mixture of games, fantasy and humiliation.

FACTFILE

- *Look Back in Anger* was produced at the Royal Court Theatre on 8 May 1956.
- The play was a landmark in British drama.
- Characters such as Jimmy and his creator John Osborne were called 'angry young men'.
- They were angry and disillusioned about contemporary life:
  the class system; the establishment; the lack of political idealism; declining standards.
- The play is an example of 'kitchen sink drama', with a true-to-life, realistic, shabby setting.

All the action takes place in the Porters' one-room flat. It is Sunday evening. Alison is ironing. Jimmy and their friend Cliff have been reading the papers. Jimmy is criticising Alison's family.

JIMMY: Have you ever seen her brother? Brother Nigel? The straight-backed, chinless wonder from Sandhurst? I only met him once myself. He asked me to step outside when I told his mother she was evil minded.

CLIFF: And did you?

JIMMY: Certainly not. He's a big chap. Well, you've never heard so many well-bred commonplaces come from beneath the same bowler hat. The Platitude from Outer Space – that's brother Nigel. He'll end up in the Cabinet one day, make no mistake. But somewhere in the back of that mind is the vague knowledge that he and his pals have been plundering and fooling everybody for generations. (*Going upstage and turning*) Now Nigel is just about as vague as you can get without being actually invisible. And invisible politicians aren't much use to anyone – not even to *his* supporters! And nothing is more vague about Nigel

than his knowledge. His knowledge of life and ordinary human beings is so hazy, he really deserves some sort of decoration for it – a medal inscribed 'For Vaguery in the Field'. But it wouldn't do for him to be troubled by any stabs of conscience, however vague. (*Moving down again*) Besides, he's a patriot and an Englishman, and he doesn't like the idea that he may have been selling out his countryman all these years, so what does he do? The only thing he can do – seek sanctuary in his own stupidity. The only way to keep things as much like they have always been as possible, is to make any alternatives too much for your poor, tiny brain to grasp. It takes some doing nowadays. But they knew all about character building at Nigel's school, and he'll make it all right. Don't you worry, he'll make it. And, what's more, he'll do it better than anybody else!

TRY THIS

1 **How should the audience react to Jimmy's speech? Mark on the script places where you would expect a particular response, such as laughter.**
2 **Find examples of: wit; irony; punning.**
3 **What directions would you give the actor about delivering this long speech?**

Questions

Mark each of these statements: True or False.

1 Nigel was born without a chin.
2 Nigel lives in Sandhurst.
3 Nigel was an army officer.
4 Nigel is a politician.
5 Nigel's speech consists of vague, trite remarks.
6 Nigel's speech is common.
7 Nigel does not want political and social change.
8 Nigel's lack of conviction affects people's lives.
9 Nigel went to a stage school.
10 Jimmy admires Nigel.
11 Jimmy thinks that Nigel will have a successful political career.
12 Jimmy feels that Nigel represents a privileged social class.
13 Jimmy despises Nigel.
14 Jimmy thinks that Nigel should receive a medal for his contribution to society.

(Answers on page 145)

Writing about drama

The most important thing to remember when you write about your drama text is that the play is written to be performed. The text is a construct, and your responses to it should be based on a consideration of its dramatic effectiveness.

TRY THIS

In this extract from *A Streetcar Named Desire* by Tennessee Williams (1947), Blanche has just arrived to visit her sister Stella. Stella and her husband Stanley live in an apartment building in a poor area of New Orleans.

How does the playwright establish the characters of Blanche and Stella and the relationship between them? Make a Mind Map of your answer, or write an essay in response.

Then look at the suggested answer on pages 91–92.

CHECKLIST

Some Dos and Don'ts for writing about drama:

✓ **Do write in the present tense (e.g. 'Jimmy despises Nigel').**

✓ **Do consider the visual impact of the drama.**

✓ **Do consider characters' functions in the text.**

✓ **Do relate character to theme.**

✓ **Do relate the language to the dramatic effect.**

✓ **Don't just describe what happens.**

✓ **Do analyse actions and words.**

✓ **Do consider the play in its context.**

✓ **Do develop your own critical response to the text.**

✓ **Don't just repeat material from critical introductions.**

A Streetcar Named Desire

Suddenly (Blanche) notices something in a half-opened closet. She springs up and crosses to it, and removes a whisky bottle. She pours a half tumbler of whisky and tosses it down. She carefully replaces the bottle and washes out the tumbler at the sink. Then she resumes her seat in front of the table.

BLANCHE (*faintly to herself*): I've got to keep hold of myself!

STELLA *comes quickly around the corner of the building and runs to the door of the downstairs flat.*

STELLA (*calling out joyfully*): Blanche!

For a moment they stare at each other. Then BLANCHE *springs up and runs to her with a wild cry.*

BLANCHE: Stella, oh, Stella, Stella! Stella for Star!

She begins to speak with feverish vivacity as if she feared for either of them to stop and think. They catch each other in a spasmodic embrace.

BLANCHE: Now, then, let me look at you. But don't you look at me, Stella, no, no, no, not till later, not till I've bathed and rested! And turn that over-light off! Turn that off! I won't be looked at in this merciless glare! (STELLA *laughs and complies*) Come back here now! Oh, my baby! Stella! Stella for Star! (*She embraces her again*) I thought you would never come back to this horrible place! What am I saying? I didn't mean to say that. I meant to be nice about it and say – Oh, what a convenient location

and such – Ha-a ah! Precious lamb! You haven't said a *word* to me.

STELLA: You haven't given me a chance to, honey! (*She laughs but her glance at Blanche is a little anxious*)

BLANCHE: Well, now you talk. Open your pretty mouth and talk while I look around for some liquor! I know you must have some liquor on the place! Where could it be, I wonder? Oh, I spy, I spy!

She rushes to the closet and removes the bottle; she is shaking all over and panting for breath as she tries to laugh. The bottle nearly slips from her grasp.

STELLA (*noticing*): Blanche, you sit down and let me pour the drinks. I don't know what we've got to mix with. Maybe a coke's in the icebox. Look'n see, honey, while I'm –

BLANCHE: No coke, honey, not with my nerves tonight! Where – where – where is –?

STELLA: Stanley? Bowling! He loves it. They're having a – found some soda! – tournament . . .

BLANCHE: Just water, baby, to chase it! Now don't get worried, your sister hasn't turned into a drunkard, she's just all shaken up and hot and tired and dirty! You sit down, now, and explain this place to me! What are you doing in a place like this?

STELLA: Now, Blanche – ➡

A Streetcar Named Desire – cont

BLANCHE: Oh, I'm sure not going to be a hypocritical, I'm going to be honestly critical about it! Never, never in my worst dreams could I picture – Only Poe! Only Mr Edgar Allan Poe! – could do it justice! . . . Why didn't you tell me, why didn't you write me, honey, why didn't you let me know?

STELLA (*carefully, pouring herself a drink*): Tell you what, Blanche?

BLANCHE: Why, that you had to live in these conditions?

STELLA: Aren't you being a little intense about it? It's not that bad at all! New Orleans isn't like other cities.

BLANCHE: This has got nothing to do with New Orleans. You might as well say – forgive me, blessed baby! (*She suddenly stops short*) The subject is closed!

STELLA (*a little dryly*): Thanks.

(*During the pause,* BLANCHE *stares at her. She smiles at* BLANCHE.)

BLANCHE (*looking down at her glass, which shakes in her hand*). You're all I've got in the world, and you're not glad to se me!

STELLA (*sincerely*): Why, Blanche, you know that's not true.

BLANCHE: No? – I'd forgotten how quiet you were.

STELLA: You never did give me a chance to say much, Blanche. So I just got in the habit of being quiet around you.

BLANCHE (*vaguely*): A good habit to get into . . . (*then abruptly*) You haven't asked me how I happened to get away from the school before the spring term ended.

STELLA: Well, I thought you'd volunteer that information – if you wanted to tell me.

BLANCHE: You thought I'd been fired?

STELLA: No, I – thought you might have – resigned . . .

BLANCHE: I was so exhausted by all I'd been through – my nerves broke (*nervously tamping cigarette*). I was on the verge of – lunacy, almost! So Mr Graves – Mr Graves is the high school superintendent – he suggested I take a leave of absence. I couldn't put all of those details into the wire . . . (*she drinks quickly*). Oh, this buzzes right through me and feels so *good*!

STELLA: Won't you have another?

BLANCHE: No, one's my limit.

Tennessee Williams

Suggested answer

The stage directions at the beginning of the passage help to establish Blanche's character. Her drinking of half a tumbler of whisky suggests that she is tense and nervous and needs the alcohol to steady her. The secretive way that Blanche washes the glass and replaces the bottle indicates that she doesn't want Stella to know that she needs to drink. This aspect of Blanche's character is dramatically reinforced throughout the passage: she pretends she doesn't know where the liquor is kept and that she spots it by chance, but the way she is seen as 'shaking all over' and 'panting for breath' reveals her dependence. Furthermore, Blanche doesn't want her drink to be diluted too much – 'Just water, baby, to chase it! – and admits that alcohol stimulates her as it 'buzzes' through her. Her declaration to Stella that one drink is her limit clearly isn't true. Her reassurance that 'your sister hasn't turned into a drunkard' suggests the opposite. Through the stage directions and the dialogue, Williams shows us Blanche's relationship with alcohol and suggests something of her unstable,

insecure, frail character and the way she deludes herself about the truth.

Blanche's feelings for Stella emerge through her excitable, nervy speech. The phrase 'Stella for Star!' sounds as if it might belong to their shared childhood. The repetition of the phrase and the exclamatory way it is declaimed show that Blanche is emotional and very fond of Stella. The direction that she speaks with 'feverish vivacity' indicates that she prefers the rush of emotion to probing conversation. Blanche repeatedly calls Stella 'baby' and seems to be concerned that her sister lives in 'a place like this'. She shows a protective attitude to Stella, as if she still regards Stella as a child, and it is clear that she is not comfortable about Stella's husband. When Blanche asks where he is, her speech falters and she cannot mention his name.

Blanche's insecurity is shown in her relationship with Stella. She says, 'You're all I've got in the world, and you're not glad to see me.' This line shows her need for affection and makes us aware of her loneliness. Another indication of Blanche's insecurity may be seen in her concern for her looks and her appearance, as she asks Stella to lower the lights and not to look at her until she is bathed and rested. This concern also reinforces the idea that Blanche cherishes illusions and hides from the truth. The background to Blanche leaving her teaching position is hinted at. Blanche's references to her nerves, her exhaustion and being on the verge of 'lunacy' suggest a breakdown of some kind, and Blanche's vague and allusive comments create a sense of shame and secrecy.

The dialogue suggests that Stella is overshadowed by Blanche; in this passage Blanche speaks much more than Stella does, and the lines that Stella does speak sound cautious and a little defensive. She is genuinely pleased to see Blanche, greeting her 'joyfully', and 'sincerely' reassuring Blanche of her pleasure in seeing her. Stella's concern about Blanche's recent past and her reason for visiting is seen in her reluctance to ask Blanche outright about why she has left her job.

Stella seems to have become part of a different life from Blanche. She lives in a poor area and is married to a man who loves bowling. The tone and rhythm of her speech is different from Blanche's – it sounds blunter and less self-conscious. Although there is strong affection between the sisters, we feel that Blanche's presence will cause tension, possibly in Stella's marriage. When Blanche remarks that Stella has hardly said a word, Stella glances at her sister a little anxiously. Williams creates the sense that both sisters are hiding something, and that conflict will be inevitable.

Questions

Answer the following questions on drama:

1 Name three aspects of a play's **staging.**

2 Plays are often divided into... and...

3 The end of a play could be called its r...n.

4 A plot which runs parallel to the main plot is called a...

5 What is dialogue?

6 Name a famous morality play.

7 Why is the Restoration period so called?

8 Two nineteenth-century dramatists are G... B... S... and O... W...

9 Name two influential European dramatists.

10 Name an influential play first performed in 1956 at the Royal Court Theatre.

11 What period or play do you think each of these extracts comes from?

a) ... don't let us be familiar or fond, nor kiss before folks, like my Lady Fadler and Sir Francis: nor to go to Hyde Park together the first Sunday, in a new chariot, to provoke eyes and whispers, and then never be seen there together again; as if we were proud of one another the first week, and ashamed of one another ever after.

b) *The stage represents a comfortless flat in Manchester and the street outside. Jazz music. Enter* HELEN, *a semi-whore, and her daughter* JO. *They are loaded with baggage.*

c) One would suspect it for a shop of witchcraft, to find in it the fat of serpents, spawn of snakes, Jews' spittle, and their young children's ordures, and all these for the face. I would sooner eat a dead pigeon, taken from the soles of the feet of one sick of the plague, than kiss one of you fasting.

(Answers on page 145)

Summary

This chapter has told you about:

- **how scenery and setting contributes to drama**

- **the function of stage directions**

- **how costume, lights and music contribute to performance**

- **how plays are structured**

- **how character is presented**

- **the functions of dialogue**

- **how themes and ideas are presented**

- **characteristics of drama in different periods**

- **how to write about drama**

Background

You will relate more easily to the plays of William Shakespeare if you know a little about the man who wrote them, so this section gives some basics. More importantly, to help develop understanding of the plays, and for exam purposes, the historical, social and literary context in which the plays were written and performed is also covered.

Shakespeare the man

Surprisingly little is known about Shakespeare. Some critics, such as A.L. Rowse, have specialised in literary work to try to establish who the 'dark lady' of Shakespeare's sonnets was, and whether Shakespeare had a homosexual relationship with his wealthy patron the Earl of Southampton. Recent findings have even suggested that Shakespeare was groomed as a Catholic spy in a secret hide-out in the north of England. There has also been speculation that he served as a sailor or a soldier, because of the knowledge of these trades shown by his imagery.

We do know that William Shakespeare was born to John and Mary Shakespeare in 1564 in the market town of Stratford, in Warwickshire. John was a skilled craftsman, a glovemaker, and he became a respected man in the town, holding the post of Chamberlain for four years: one of his duties was to pay visiting players. William was the third child of the marriage, but the first to live beyond infancy. His sister Joan lived to be 77. William died at 52, his three brothers younger than this.

William went to Stratford Grammar School, where he learnt Latin and secured a wide knowledge of Roman writers such as Ovid, whose retellings of myths and legends found their way into so many of the plays. It was also there that he read a translation of *Plutarch's Lives*, from which he adapted the description of Cleopatra on her barge 'like a burnish'd throne' which appears in *Antony and Cleopatra*.

What evidence of Shakespeare's classical education can you find in the play you're studying?

At 18, Shakespeare married a woman six years older than him – unusual at that time. His wife, Anne Hathaway, gave birth to their first child, Susanna, a mere six months later, and to twins, Kate and Hamnet, two years after that. None of these children survived into adulthood: Shakespeare was to become all too familiar with the deaths of children.

Shakespeare moved to London and became first an actor, and then an increasingly respected playwright. He died in Stratford in 1616. Make of it what you will that the only thing he left his widow, Anne, was his 'second-best bed'.

Social context

Shakespeare's times

1564	Shakespeare born. Sculptor and painter Michelangelo dies
1580	Last ever religious 'miracle' play performed in England
1583	English merchants make commercial expeditions to India and Persia
1586	Sir Walter Raleigh introduces tobacco from the New World
1587	Catholic Mary Queen of Scots beheaded for treason
1588	Sir Francis Drake defeats the Spanish Armada in the Channel
1592	Plague kills 15,000 in London – theatres shut
1593	Playwright Christopher Marlowe dies in a tavern brawl in Deptford
1594	Death of the painter Tintoretto
1595	Spanish invade Cornwall; high heels become fashionable for men
1596	Flushing toilets invented
1600	Rome: Giordano Bruno executed for claiming the Earth revolves round the Sun
1601	Earl of Essex executed for revolt against Elizabeth I
1603	Elizabeth I dies. James VI of Scotland becomes James I of England
1605	Catholic Guy Fawkes executed for trying to blow up the Houses of Parliament
1608	Telescope invented
1616	Death of Shakespeare

Arts, commerce and the world view

Shakespeare lived in exciting times. There were advances in science and the arts; America was being explored by the first European settlers. England had become a great sea power, with fast, manoeuvrable ships captained by men such as Francis Drake, who in 1580 sailed right round the world. International commerce was expanding, though still fraught with the kind of perils that sink Antonio's ships in *The Merchant of Venice*.

Although most people in England still went to church and believed in God, thinkers had started to question the meaning of life. We see this trend in Shakespeare's tragedies. Scientists were beginning to challenge the medieval view, which placed the Earth at the centre of the universe. The Church was still powerful, but was beginning to lose its iron grip on daily life and beliefs. A religious-based society was giving way to a secular (non-religious) one. Many of Shakespeare's plays question man's relationship with God (e.g. *Hamlet*), or the gods (e.g. *King Lear*), and whether we have free will or are the slaves of fate.

? What evidence of this debate can you find in the play you're studying?

FACTFILE

- In *King Lear* a despairing Gloucester suggests that we are at the mercy of fate:

    As flies to wanton boys, are we to th'Gods;

    They kill us for their sport (Act 4, scene 1)

- John Webster in *The Duchess of Malfi* (1614?) expresses the same idea in a line that now sounds rather silly:

    We are but the stars' tennis balls.

At the same time, most English people were proud to be Protestants, not Catholics. Hence Kent in *King Lear* quips that he eats no fish (Catholics were not meant to eat meat on Fridays, and often ate fish instead). Catholics were regarded as an evil threat to national stability, a prejudice not helped by Spain launching its Armada against England in an attempt to restore it to Catholicism, or by Guy Fawkes' attempts to rearrange the architecture of the Houses of Parliament.

There were similar prejudices against Jews, as shown in the attitudes of Antonio and others in *The Merchant of Venice*. Jews were banned from most professions. At the same time, moneylending was seen as a sin, and yet the economy depended on merchants being able to borrow. Hence Antonio's hypocrisy in condemning Shylock.

? What evidence of prejudice can you find in the play you're studying?

Women also had a difficult time, their only career options being marriage or a nunnery (Hamlet tells Ophelia, 'Get thee to a nunnery!'). A wife had no legal property rights. Women had to obey first their father, then their husband. Though wealthy women could command male servants – as does Olivia in *Twelfth Night* – all were in an inferior position in relation to men of their own rank. The exception was Queen Elizabeth, and her power depended at least in part on her remaining – supposedly – the 'Virgin Queen'.

Social certainties and personal perils

A key point for you to understand about the social context of Shakespeare's plays is that Elizabethan society was very hierarchical. Kings – and even queens – were seen as having a Divine Right to rule. In other words, rebellion against the monarch was rebellion against God. Society was rigidly structured in class terms. Nobles were seen as superior to commoners, and were not expected to work for a living, though noblemen might enter politics or the armed forces. Shakespeare was not especially conservative, but nor was he a socialist. His plays generally accept that an ordered society is based on hierarchy, with everyone knowing where they stand and fulfilling their social duties.

Perhaps people were more inclined to cling to such certainties when so much else was uncertain. In

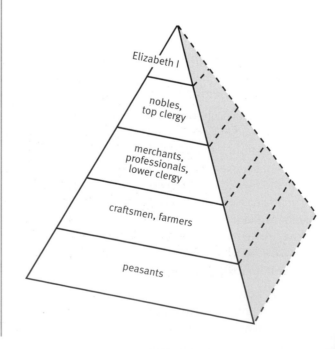

particular, death could strike at any time. A whole host of diseases were widespread and incurable. Venereal disease, often known as 'the pox', was associated with brothels, but men with money to spare were still frequent visitors to them. Plague – Black Death – came in waves. In 1592 it killed 15,000 in London alone. Thus images of disease occur frequently in Shakespeare's plays, and the whole nation is often seen in metaphor as a diseased body.

Magic and mystery

Shakespeare's audiences, especially the 'groundlings', accepted the existence of the supernatural. Thus the Witches in *Macbeth* would have seemed plausible – even frightening, and strange portents, such as an owl flying by day and killing a falcon, would have been accepted as sure signs of something being deeply wrong. James I believed in witchcraft, and wrote a book on the subject.

Nor would audiences have doubted the reality of the Ghost in *Hamlet*, or the possibility of Prospero's magic working in *The Tempest* – especially on a remote island. Elizabeth I kept a magician, John Dee – and across the seas, who knows what might happen? Sailors, after all, were returning from America with tales of men with their eyes and mouths in their chests, and other wonders.

Astrology was also taken more seriously than now, though not universally believed in. Gloucester, in *King Lear*, believes that unnatural events have been caused by eclipses of the sun and moon. Edmund, however, devotes a lengthy speech to ridiculing astrology as a determiner of character.

Literary context

Shakespeare, like other poets and playwrights of the time, was much influenced by Roman writers. The educated nobles who made up the wealthiest and most influential part of his audiences had similarly classical educations. This meant that they would understand when, for example, Orsino in *Twelfth Night* compares himself to Actaeon, a Greek youth torn apart for seeing the goddess Diana naked. They would also be aware of major figures in classical history, such as Caesar.

Shakespeare also used stories from classical and later historical writers as the basis for his plots. *Twelfth Night* is based on 'The Tale of Apolonius and Silla', told by Barnable Riche in *Riche his Farewell to Militaire Profession* (1581). *Hamlet* is probably based on a now lost play by Thomas Kyd, which was more squarely in a popular tradition of the time, the **revenge tragedy**. Plays of this type all end with most of the cast dead on stage. True to type, Shakespeare's *Hamlet* leaves the corpses of Hamlet himself, the wicked Claudius, Gertrude and Laertes to be buried. Ophelia has already drowned herself in the wake of her father Polonius. In Kyd's play she threw herself over a cliff.

Shakespeare was the best of a prolific throng of writers. Like others, he wrote mostly in **blank verse** – otherwise known as unrhymed iambic pentameter. His friend Ben Jonson wrote more bitingly satirical plays. Christopher Marlowe, author of *Doctor Faustus* (1601), occasionally comes close to Shakespeare poetically, but lacks Shakespeare's genius for character and staging.

The Elizabethan theatre

Some key points on Elizabethan theatre:

- There was no stage curtain, very little scenery, and no electric lighting. Setting and atmosphere were conveyed by the text, and perhaps by music.

- A very socially varied audience, from 'groundlings' to nobility – and sometimes the Queen herself – stood, sat, or wandered around eating and drinking. Plays had to appeal to all classes.

- Women's parts were played by boys – creating even greater irony and confusion in the comedies in which women pretend to be men (e.g. *Twelfth Night*).

Above all, remember that Shakespeare's plays are meant to be performed. As you read, consider how each scene could be staged for maximum effect – you could be given an exam question on staging. Try to see at least one good production of the play you're studying. If possible, see a play at the New Globe in London, which imitates the design of Shakespeare's theatre. You can be a 'groundling' very cheaply – but take an umbrella, because this area is open to the sky!

Questions

1 When was Shakespeare born?

2 Elizabethan society was more *secular* than medieval society. What does this mean?

3 Shakespeare explores whether we have *free will*. If not, what controls us?

4 Catholics were (a) in all the top jobs (b) viewed as a threat (c) taking over.

5 Why did Jews become moneylenders?

6 Who was the 'Virgin Queen'?

7 Why was it so bad a sin to kill a king or queen?

8 What is the common name for Black Death?

9 Who succeeded Elizabeth I?

10 Who in *King Lear* ridicules astrology?

11 What would be lying around on stage at the end of a revenge tragedy?

12 Why didn't Elizabethan actors take 'curtain calls'?

(Answers on page 146)

Types of Shakespeare play

Audience expectations

Shakespeare's audiences were used to a number of types of play, or **genres**, as we might call them now. Whereas modern cinema audiences might go to see a disaster or horror movie, a romance, a thriller or a

TRY THIS

1 Consider the plot of the play you're studying. In what ways is it influenced by social and historical context? Make a Mind Map.

HINT

Think about – the social position of the characters, and how this is reflected in their dramatic role; social conventions; the role played by female characters; any philosophical speculation, especially in soliloquies (e.g. *Hamlet*); religion; the kind of imagery used.

2 Draw a pyramid to show the characters, in social ranking, from top to bottom.

HINT

Think about where characters are positioned in relation to each other. King Lear might tower above his subjects at the start of the play and sit or kneel below them when he is later humbled – literally 'brought low'. Hamlet might tend to stand apart from other characters.

3 Choose a lively scene and plan how it could be staged on an Elizabethan stage for maximum effect.

comedy, Shakespeare's audiences would go to see a play expecting it to be one of three types:

- tragedy
- comedy
- history

Modern critics have termed some of the comedies **romances**. This special term is given to Shakespeare's last – and strangest – plays. Of these, *The Tempest* (see page 106) is generally thought to be the best.

Whichever type you are studying, it is worth knowing something about the others in order to place your play in context. So we recommend that you read the whole of this section! Build up a Mind Map as you go, and compare it with the one on page 99.

FACTFILE

Through Polonius in *Hamlet* Act 2, scene 2, Shakespeare pokes fun at the subdivisions of play types:

'The best actors in the world, either for tragedy, comedy, history, pastoral, pastoral–comical, historical–pastoral, tragical–historical, tragical–comical–historical–pastoral, scene individable, or poem unlimited.'

Tragedy

The word **tragedy** is used loosely in modern English. In Elizabethan theatre it refers to something more exact, stemming from ancient Greek and Roman drama, which Shakespeare would have read in translation. Greek tragedy features a hero struck down by the gods, or by fate. This hero was typically a great and noble man, but often one guilty of the sin of **hubris** – the kind of pride that puts him almost in competition with the gods.

The word 'tragedy' comes from the Greek words, *tragos* (goat) and *oide* (song), suggesting a song relating to a goat sacrificed for the community – a 'scapegoat'. This is important, as in Greek tragedy the hero's dramatised death was meant to purge the audience of dangerous emotions, achieving the peace and calm which arises from conflict resolved, known as **catharsis**.

This *catharsis* is still the aim of Shakespeare's tragedies, which is why they end with order restored. However, they are not classic Greek tragedies. Shakespeare was influenced by the Roman writer Seneca, whose tragic heroes develop courage and dignity in the face of death. Shakespeare develops this, so that Hamlet's dying act is to name his successor, thus ensuring order. Similarly, Lear's dying thoughts are for the deaths of his daughter Cordelia, and his Fool, not for his own misfortune.

Another important development is that Shakespeare's tragic heroes die because of a **character flaw** – an imperfection which makes them more like us: Othello's naivety and jealousy; Hamlet's inability to take action; the arrogance and rash misjudgement that make Lear reject a loving daughter. The Shakespearean hero is never completely innocent. In fact, one of the greatest tragic heroes, Macbeth, is actually very wicked, yet it is Shakespeare's dramatic achievement that Macbeth's noble qualities shine through the battle smoke of his crimes to win our sympathy and even our admiration.

The tragedies question the nature of human life – whether we are beasts or fallen angels. Shakespeare seems to say that we have the potential to face life heroically, to accept our fate – and our death – philosophically. As Edgar says in *King Lear*, 'Ripeness is all.'

? If you are studying a tragedy, think about what causes the downfall of the hero.

FACTFILE

You may have studied *Romeo and Juliet* for GCSE, or even earlier. This is not a typical tragedy. It has a hero *and* a heroine, and neither of them is royal, or a fatally flawed great leader. They both have noble qualities, but such greatness as they possess lies in their love and their commitment to each other. Their downfall is not owing to flaws in themselves, but to the world in which they live, and to fate. In a sense the tragic hero of the play is love itself.

Comedy

You may have studied a comedy, such as *Twelfth Night* or *A Midsummer Night's Dream*, for GCSE or even earlier. You may now be studying a more complex comedy, such as *As You Like It*. Even if you are studying a tragedy or history, there will be comic elements in it. On the other hand, some comedies have some very sinister elements in them. *The Merchant of Venice* and *Measure for Measure* are not exactly a barrel of laughs, yet they are officially classified as comedies. Some critics prefer to call them 'problem plays'.

The word **comedy** comes from the Greek *komos*, meaning a village festival to honour Dionysus, god of wine and fertility. His worship was wild and orgiastic. Hence there is a wildness in Shakespearean comedy. People flout social conventions, there are confusions of rank, disguises, women dressed as men, and a lot of trickery. This is all necessary, but temporary. In the end the confusions are resolved, there are marriages (remember the fertility) and happy endings with order restored.

One thing all Shakespeare's comedies have in common is the theme of love. A light-hearted comedy such as *Twelfth Night* acknowledges the disturbing power of love, but it also celebrates the harmless folly that people find themselves caught up in when they fall in love. It undermines stiff social conventions and encourages us to laugh at ourselves. *Much Ado About Nothing*, on the other hand, looks at the harmful consequences of people's nastier follies, that place love under threat.

In Shakespearean comedy there is no permanently unrequited love. Love always leads to marriage. And marriage is a kind of 'social glue' that sticks people together to form the building blocks of the social framework.

? If you are studying a comedy, what confusions does it contain? What aspects of love are shown by the different characters? What threats are there to love or harmony?

History

You may be studying a history such as *Richard II* or *Henry IV* (*Part I* or *II*). These are more straightforward in concept, being based on real historical events and characters, safely distant from Shakespeare's own time. Shakespeare got the basic facts from historical writers such as Raphael Holinshed and fleshed them out for himself.

The central themes of the histories are kingship and leadership, and how they relate to the stability of the social order. They set up an ideal of God in His Heaven, the king on his throne, and happy and obedient subjects who know their place. A flaw in a king throws all this into jeopardy.

The histories have some of the characteristics of tragedy – especially deaths and a sense of order restored. *Richard II* features a king whose weakness as a ruler condemns him to death, but who grows in character as his fortunes decline. *Henry IV Part II* (which centres on the king who killed Richard II) hints at tragedy in the scene of the uneasy king's death, showing how he has lived with guilt, even though he felt obliged to seize power and then take Richard's life to make his own position secure. However, in general the histories focus more on society, and the tragedies more on the development of the individual hero.

The Roman tragedies *Julius Caesar* and *Antony and Cleopatra* are based on ancient history. *Julius Caesar* can be seen both as Roman history play and the tragedy of Brutus, an honourable man who lacks the political astuteness to survive in the cutthroat world of Roman politics.

? If you are studying a history, consider what situation or event throws the state into disorder. How is order restored? Who suffers as a consequence?

FACTFILE

Some common history themes are:

- **kingship and its problems**
- **time: seizing the moment; the passage of time; the quality of 'the times'**
- **appearance and reality**
- **war and conflict**
- **rebellion**
- **honour and duty**

Romance

You may be studying one of Shakespeare's last plays – especially *A Winter's Tale* or *The Tempest*. The other two, less often studied at A level and AS level, are *Pericles* and *Cymbeline*. All four have similar plots, based on the idea of the family as a part of social order, and on an ideal of family harmony within the greater harmony of society. In each case, a noble family is divided through folly or wickedness, separated for years, then reunited and reconciled.

These plays are not 'romances' in the modern sense, but in the literary sense of being based on rather fanciful, magical, mysterious events that we cannot take literally – for example Hermione being restored to life in *A Winter's Tale* or the magical storm of *The Tempest*. The romances have strong moral and spiritual messages, and the key characters seem to suffer in order to become better, wiser people. Yet there is less emphasis on convincing, life-like characterisation than in Shakespeare's other plays. The characters have a mythical quality, although they embody human desires and follies – such as Prospero's craving for power in *The Tempest*.

If studying one of these plays, who develops, and how?

Overlaps

Bear in mind that there are overlaps between the types of play.

- **Comic elements** appear in all Shakespeare plays. For example in *King Lear* the Fool cracks jokes, often at Lear's expense. In *Macbeth* there is **comic relief** featuring the drunken Porter at the gates of Macbeth's castle. Even in *Othello* there is some humour provided by the Clown. *Henry IV Part II*, a history, alternates between affairs of state and the bawdy hilarity provided by Falstaff and his friends.

- **Tragic elements** appear in the history plays. There is also sadness in some comedies. In *Much Ado About Nothing* Hero suffers because of her lover's willingness to believe Don John's lies about her. Even in the light-hearted *Twelfth Night*, Malvolio is tricked and locked up as a madman, and in his final line he swears revenge.

- **History** – loosely adapted by Shakespeare – is the basis for some of the tragedies; for example *Macbeth* is based on a real-life king. However, the comedies exist in more of a make-believe world.

Remember the guiding principle that all Shakespeare plays start with an ideal of social order, descend into chaos brought about by events and human behaviour, and then reach a point where order – and sometimes even harmony – can be restored.

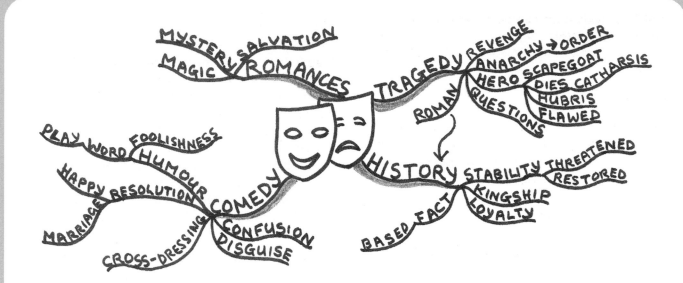

TRY THIS

1 Identify the genre of the play you are studying. Make a table or Mind Map of the genre's characteristics; add how exactly these appear in the play you're studying.

2 What would need to be changed in your play to turn it into a different genre?

HINT

To rewrite *Othello* as a comedy, it would be necessary to save Desdemona's life and have Othello apologise instead of stabbing himself.

3 What evidence can you find in your play of the social order collapsing?

HINT

Look for comments, such as 'The time is out of joint' (*Hamlet*); imagery suggesting chaos – e.g. stormy seas; and unnatural events – e.g. horses eating each other in *Macbeth*.

Questions

1 What is the Greek name for the sin of pride of which tragic heroes are often guilty?

2 What is the connection between tragic heroes and goats?

3 Who was Seneca?

4 The word 'comedy' comes from the Greek *komos*. What was this?

5 What do couples usually do at the end of a comedy?

6 Who is the central figure of a history play?

7 What social unit is the basis of order in a romance play?

(Answers on page 146)

How to approach Shakespeare

What we present here is an approach to Shakespeare that you will be able to apply to any of his plays. Of course, you may feel your main difficulty is the use of Elizabethan English, and there are hints on tackling this at the end of the section. However, if you have a broad grasp of what is going on in a play, localised difficulties with individual words or lines will become less of a hindrance.

Telescopic vision

To read Shakespeare you need to be able to zoom in on a single speech and the significance of its individual words, and zoom back out to the structure and meaning of the play as a whole. If you focus only on the detail, you may miss 'the big picture', or become despondent if you can't understand one speech. But if you don't look closely at the speeches, you may see the play simply as its storyline, not appreciating the poetry and how it works within the whole play.

You have already learned about the different genres (types) of play. Luckily, there is a bigger pattern that can be applied to *any* Shakespeare play. This can be summed up as **STAR**.

- **S**ituation
- **T**rigger
- **A**narchy
- **R**esolution

Every Shakespeare play moves from order, to anarchy, and back to order. It begins with a **situation**, e.g. an old king wanting to hand over rulership to his daughters (*King Lear*). There is usually a sense of tension or disorder already developing: *The Tempest* begins with a storm; *Macbeth* starts with Witches stirring up disorder in a storm, on a wild moor, after a battle; *Hamlet* opens with nervous guards on the castle ramparts at night talking about a ghost; *Twelfth Night* begins with a lovesick lord neglecting his duties, while other characters are being cast ashore from a shipwreck.

Next there is a **trigger**. An event, or a human action – usually the result of passion, folly, greed or ambition – unhinges the world and all is thrown into chaos. Of course in practice it may be arguable which event or action this is.

In *Hamlet* the trigger can be seen either as the murder of old Hamlet, which happens before the start of the play, or as his ghost appearing to young Hamlet and urging revenge. In both *Othello* and *Much Ado About Nothing* it is love that causes the initial disturbance. For a military man and confirmed bachelor like Othello, marrying Desdemona is enough to upset the applecart. For Claudio – also a soldier – falling for Hero threatens the social harmony. In both cases embittered villains, like serpents in Paradise, capitalise on this: Iago in *Othello* and Don John in *Much Ado*.

Usually by Act 3 of the play the situation has descended into **anarchy**. In a comedy this will mean that there are multiple confusions, disguises and mistaken identities. Even the characters responsible for these may now get caught up in the chaos.

This happens when Viola in *Twelfth Night* poses as a man – Antonio mistakes her for her brother, whom she thinks dead. In *King Lear*, Act 3 finds Lear, now mad, with his Fool and Edgar (posing as a madman) on a storm-lashed heath at night, ranting at the elements. Gloucester's eyes are gouged out in Act 3 ('Out vile jelly!'). In *A Midsummer Night's Dream*, the instrument of anarchy is Puck, who in Act 3 gives Bottom an ass's head, ensures that Titania falls in love with this man-monster, and then throws the benighted lovers into confusion by misapplying his magic love-juice!

You may find that this 'anarchic' stage of the play reaches a **climax** or **crisis**. For example, in *Macbeth* it is the showdown between Macbeth and Macduff – the

last we see of Macbeth. In *Othello* it is the scene when Othello strangles Desdemona.

Resolution comes at, or near, the end of every play. In a comedy this means marriages, disguises are shed and confusions unravelled. In a history, national stability is restored. A tragedy ends in death – always of the tragic hero, and usually of a few other characters as well – and order is restored only at the cost of blood-letting and sacrifice. Order does not necessarily mean sweetness and light. As the Prince says at the end of *Romeo and Juliet*, 'A glooming peace this morning with it brings;... / some shall be pardon'd, and some punished...'

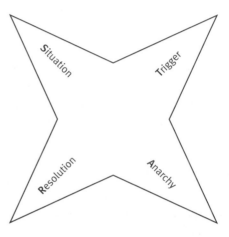

How to study and revise a play

1 Read the play, using 'telescopic vision' to zoom from **detail** to overall **development**. Think about what kind of play it is and how it builds on its genre.

2 Mind Map your **initial impressions** – or new ones if you know the play.

3 After a break of at least a day, reread the first few scenes. Identify signs of developing **disorder** or threat. Highlight lines suggesting this, not forgetting imagery – for example of stormy seas.

4 Focus on a scene from Act 2. Identify how the **action** is **developing** and what **themes** are emerging.

5 Focus on a scene from Act 3 involving the **main character(s)**. Look at character development. For example, Lear begins to show concern for others in Act 3. Pay special attention to soliloquies.

6 Focus on a scene in Act 4. Consider what **outcomes** there could be. Where is the play heading? How does the **language** suggest this?

7 Focus on the final scene. How are problems **resolved**? What is left **unresolved** (e.g. Malvolio's bitterness in *Twelfth Night*)? What **price** is paid for resolution?

Aspects of the play

There are several interrelated aspects on which you should focus. Many exam questions will deal with one of the following aspects.

Plot

The plot of a play is what happens – the action – and how it creates a broad pattern (see the **STAR** approach on page 100). The kind of action and the pattern it makes will depend to a certain extent on the genre (see pages 96–98). In an exam, don't slip into the trap of just regurgitating the plot. You can assume that the examiner already knows it quite well.

Character

This is the aspect concentrated on at GCSE, and there are still plenty of AS and A level exam questions focusing on this. When studying a character, consider:

- what **motivates** them – drives them to act, e.g. Iago's bitterness at being passed over for promotion

- what **tensions** they experience – which may prevent them from acting, e.g. Hamlet

- how they **develop** and learn as the play proceeds, e.g. Macbeth becoming 'bloody, bold and resolute'

- how they reflect the **themes** of the play, e.g. Henry in *Henry IV Part II*, who is sick and 'uneasy', like the nation

- how the **language** they use fits them and the play, e.g. the broken, frantic rhythms of Lear's lines as he descends into madness.

It is valid to look at Shakespeare's characters 'psychologically', but only up to a point. Shakespeare's observation of character is acute. However, don't make the mistake of thinking or writing about his characters as real people. They exist within the play as a whole, and they always have a **dramatic role**. Take Iago in *Othello*. Few people could be as two-faced and consistently villainous as him in real life, but his **role** is to lead Othello to his tragic end.

Themes

Themes are the ideas explored in the play. Common themes in the different genres are given above. In essays, avoid talking in general terms about any theme without referring closely to the text. In particular, you will find that the play's imagery reflects its themes.

For example, *Hamlet* contains numerous images of disease. He sees 'this most excellent canopy the air' as 'a foul and pestilent congregation of vapours' (Act 2, scene 2). We also find images of warfare: 'The slings and arrows of outrageous fortune' (Act 3, scene 1). These reflect the conflict in the state of Denmark, as well as the warring impulses in Hamlet's head and heart.

In *Othello* we find images of monsters and feeding.

> Iago: O, beware, my lord, of jealousy;
> It is the green-ey'd monster which doth mock
> The meat it feeds on.

These images reflect the monster of jealousy that grows within Othello and consumes him, and Iago's intention of feeding on his master Othello.

Remember, it is never enough just to point out images. You must say how they are appropriate to themes of the play. If looking closely at a passage, you should also comment on how the images convey a particular meaning.

Language

We have seen above how imagery reflects themes. But before you can appreciate Shakespeare's language fully, you have to get to grips with it. Here are some hints:

- Most speeches are in blank verse – unrhymed iambic pentameter (i.e. usually containing five pairs of syllables per line, each pair containing a stressed and an unstressed syllable). However, to make sense of them, read them as sentences, without pausing at the end of each line.

- Try to get an overall feeling for what is happening in a scene, and what is being said in a speech; *then* go into detail. A good starting point is to ask yourself what the mood of a speech is. The imagery may help. Also bear in mind the relationships between characters and how this affects what is said.

- Notice the effect of **alliteration** (repetition of sounds at beginnings of words or syllables), e.g. Kent tells Lear *de*-pressing news: 'All's cheerless, dark and deadly:/ Your eldest daughters have fordone themselves,/ And desperately are dead.'

- Notice the effect of rhythm, e.g. Lear's desolate line spoken over Cordelia's corpse: 'Never, never, never, never, never.' This reverses the more usual stress of the paired syllables, because we have to pronounce *ne*-ver, not ne-*ver*. The effect is to make them emphatic but dragged out, fitting the sense.

Individual plays

Hamlet

Even if you are not studying *Hamlet*, we recommend that you read it, or at least some of the scenes mentioned below, as it is probably Shakespeare's finest play. Even if you have not read it, the notes below will show you how the STAR approach works.

The plot is as follows:

> Prince Hamlet is deeply disturbed because his father, Old Hamlet, has died and his mother, Gertrude, has almost immediately married the old king's brother, Claudius. Old Hamlet's ghost appears to Hamlet and announces that Claudius murdered him. He urges Hamlet to avenge his death. Hamlet spends the rest of the play not managing to do this.

> Hamlet has shown some romantic inclinations towards Ophelia, daughter of an old courtier, Polonius. Polonius warns her against Hamlet, but then decides that this has driven Hamlet mad for love. However, they then observe Hamlet harshly rejecting her. Claudius sends for Hamlet's old friends Rosencrantz and Guildenstern to discover his problem. Hamlet hits on the idea of getting some players to perform a play that will imitate Claudius' murder of Old Hamlet.

> Polonius again spies on Hamlet, this time as he upbraids his mother. Polonius cries out from his hiding place and Hamlet stabs him through the curtain, hoping it is Claudius. Ophelia goes mad with grief and Hamlet is sent to England. Laertes, son of Polonius, returns from France furious at his father's murder. He then hears that Ophelia has drowned herself. He confronts Hamlet at her grave, but is persuaded by Claudius to take part in a plot to kill Hamlet using a poisoned foil in a fencing match. The foils get switched, Hamlet and Laertes mortally wound each other, Gertrude is accidentally poisoned, and Hamlet just has time to kill Claudius – at last. Fortinbras of Norway restores order on a stage littered with corpses.

The opening scenes create a sense of unrest. Barnardo challenges Francisco, who is already on guard and therefore should be the one doing the challenging. Already things are disturbed, and talk of a ghost and threatened war adds to the unsettled atmosphere. Horatio says of the Ghost, 'This bodes some strange eruption to our state.' Remember that you should be looking for lines like this that anticipate a breakdown of order.

Scene 2 shows Claudius dealing with affairs of state. All appears well, but we soon discover that this is only on the surface. Hamlet's first line, 'A little more than kin, and less than kind,' is pregnant with meaning. It shows the tension and unhappiness he feels in his enforced relationship with Claudius, his new 'father'. Hamlet deliberately misunderstands his mother's use of the word 'seems', highlighting the themes of appearance and reality – seeming – in the play.

Hamlet is in mourning for his father, but his 'inky cloak' and 'customary suits of solemn black' also identify him as an Elizabethan 'type': the melancholic, whose nature is to brood and agonise over the wrongs of the world. Jaques in *As You Like It* is also a melancholic. Hamlet, however, is given a depth of character far beyond type.

We soon find, when Hamlet is alone on stage, that he is so disillusioned with the world as a result of his mother's hasty marriage to Claudius that he is considering suicide.

> O that this too too sullied flesh would melt,
> Thaw and resolve itself into a dew,
> Or that the Everlasting had not fix'd
> His canon 'gainst self-slaughter. O God! God!
> How weary, stale, flat, and unprofitable
> Seem to me all the uses of this world!
> Fie on't, ah fie, 'tis an unweeded garden
> That grows to seed; things rank and gross in nature
> Possess it merely.

Using our STAR approach, the **situation**, as we understand it so far, is that Old Hamlet has died, and Prince Hamlet seems distraught that his mother has so quickly married Claudius. Some major themes have already been introduced: the meaning of life and whether it is worth living; corruption; the grossness of the flesh and its appetites when ungoverned. Hamlet goes on to voice his disillusion with his mother, which he expresses even more forcefully later in the play as his unhealthy interest in her sexuality surfaces (see Act 3, scene 4).

Continuing with the STAR approach, the main **trigger** to the play's action comes in scene 4 when we discover from the Ghost that Claudius has murdered Old Hamlet in order to get his queen and throne.

In Act 2 we see the theme of appearance and reality developing. Polonius, apparently with good intentions, has Laertes spied on. When Ophelia confides in him that Hamlet has declared his love to her, Polonius insists that Hamlet cannot be trusted. Also in this act, a major issue of the play develops. Hamlet seems to go mad. The big question is whether he is pretending to be mad, or really is mad. If you answer an essay question on this, be particularly careful to relate what you say closely to the text.

Also in this act we see Hamlet agonise over his own apparent inability to avenge his father's death. He goads himself as 'a dull and muddy-mettled rascal' and a coward. But by the end of the act he has found an apparently valid reason for putting off the act – namely that the Ghost may have been a deceiving devil – and embarks on a course of action to secure more evidence – the 'play within a play' that is meant to trap Claudius into admitting his guilt.

Still using the STAR model, Acts 3 and 4 see Hamlet's mind descending into **anarchy**. More than in other plays, the chaos is concentrated in its main character. He upbraids Ophelia, mistakenly kills Polonius, arranges for his old friends Rosencrantz and Guildenstern to be murdered, and pleads with his mother not to sleep with her new husband. However, it is also in Act 3 that Hamlet delivers his famous 'To be, or not to be' speech, considering – and deciding against – suicide. This speech explores the nature of death: 'The undiscover'd country, from whose bourn/No traveller returns.' Even if he is going mad, he still has moments of clarity and perception.

In Act 4 Hamlet continues to procrastinate (put off action), but his self-development continues as he questions the nature of human life (scene 4):

> What is a man
> If his chief good and market of his time
> Be but to sleep and feed? A beast no more.

Remember that this sort of consideration occurs in all the tragedies.

? If you're studying another tragedy, think about where this occurs.

The **resolution** of the play comes only when Hamlet becomes a man of action at last, killing Laertes in a duel, and then the guilty king. He shows that he has resigned himself to death, and his final words express concern for the state – not himself. Order is restored by Fortinbras, but we are left with the uneasy knowledge that now Denmark will be ruled by a Norwegian king. There has been a heavy price to pay for the restoration of order.

Hamlet is not a hero in the traditional role. His own self-recriminations testify to his failure to avenge his father. However, he does struggle heroically with the big questions about human life, and he comes to accept the inevitability of his own death.

We have mentioned the question of whether Hamlet is mad or just feigning madness. The other big question is: Why does he procrastinate in avenging his father? There are several possibilities:

- There are practical difficulties; the right moment evades him. When he finds Claudius praying he decides that to kill him then would be to do him a favour.

- He has religious qualms about murdering a king.

- He is too cowardly, or too much lost in thought, to act decisively.

- He is torn apart by conflicting unconscious impulses based on his unhealthy attachment to his mother. This idea has been championed by the critic Ernest Jones. According to Freud's idea of the 'Oedipus complex', all sons unconsciously want to kill their fathers and sleep with their mothers. By this theory, Claudius has done what Hamlet unconsciously wanted to do. Hamlet either cannot bring himself to kill Claudius for a crime he wished to commit himself, or he feels that if he kills Claudius he must become his mother's new husband and thus commit incest.

? What do you think?

If you consider this issue in an essay, show your awareness of different theories, but try to form a step-by-step argument in favour of your own interpretation. Remember to support it with references to the text, using short quotations where appropriate.

King Lear

The starting **situation** is that the ageing Lear has decided to retire, dividing his kingdom between his daughters, Goneril, Regan and Cordelia.

The **trigger** is easy to spot, and it comes quickly. Lear displays a tragic flaw in his greatness which is to be the source of his downfall: a foolish desire to be praised and flattered by his daughters, a vain willingness to believe the fair words of Goneril and Regan, and a rashness that makes him angrily disinherit Cordelia when she cannot, or will not, flatter him. Ironically, she is actually the only one of the three who loves him.

After this, Lear's world is quickly thrown into chaos and **anarchy**. Goneril and Regan reveal their true lack of love and respect for their father. They first deny him his right to retain his hundred knights as personal followers, causing him to complain bitterly (Act 1, scene 4): 'How sharper than a serpent's tooth it is/ To have a thankless child!' They then bar their doors against him so that he is forced to spend the night on a bare heath while a storm rages overhead. Note the 'serpent's tooth' image, suggesting animal savagery lurking beneath human appearances. Note, too, the storm as a metaphor for the growing chaos of Lear's tormented mind.

An important part of the play's structure, on which an exam question may well be set, is the **subplot**. Gloucester is a loyal and trusted old courtier. Nonetheless he foolishly believes the manipulative lies of his bastard son Edmund and so turns against his loyal 'legitimate' son Edgar. This echoes Lear's readiness to be fooled by his evil daughters and to reject Cordelia. Note, too, the importance of **dramatic irony** in the play, when we, the audience, know things of which a character on stage is ignorant. This is closely linked to the theme of appearance and reality. This in turn is linked to the fact that the two most honest men in the play, Edgar and Kent, assume a series of disguises. This dramatic irony reaches a peak in Act 4, scene 6, when Edgar (as 'Poor Tom') leads Gloucester to what the blind old man thinks is a high cliff, from which he jumps – only to find himself still alive by a 'miracle'.

The anarchy reaches its **climax**, or **crisis**, when Lear and Cordelia are captured in battle by the forces of Regan and Goneril. The **resolution** comes at great cost, with the deaths of Cordelia and Lear, leaving Edgar to restore order.

Themes include the parent–child relationship, old age, madness, and justice – both on a worldly and a cosmic level. Edgar, addressing Edmund (Act 5, scene 3), rather harshly blames his father's extramarital sex for the cruel punishment he suffers:

> The Gods are just, and of our pleasant vices
> Make instruments to plague us;
> The dark and vicious place where thee he got
> Cost him his eyes.

Still on the theme of justice – or the lack of it – Lear, cradling Cordelia's dead body, voices the play's stark, bleak pathos:

> Why should a dog, a horse, a rat, have life,
> And thou no breath at all?

Othello

The **situation** at the start of this play is that Othello, almost against his better judgement, has married Desdemona. Love has got the better of his reluctance to give up his uncomplicated and emotionally independent military life (Act 1, scene 2).

> But that I love the gentle Desdemona,
> I would not my unhoused free condition
> Put into circumscription and confine
> For the seas' worth.

His marriage is the **trigger** that sets events on the road to disorder, but Iago's villainy provides the dramatic **catalyst** that ensures the great man's ruin. Othello is at home on the battlefield, but his innocence, credulity and passion make him easy prey for Iago.

In Act 3, Othello begins to succumb to Iago's manipulation, and by scene 3 he is convinced and swearing revenge. The play is full of water imagery, water being associated both with unreliability and with emotion. Here Othello compares his determination, his 'bloody thoughts', with 'the Pontic sea,/ Whose icy current and compulsive course/ Ne'er feels retiring ebb ...'

By Act 4, scene 1, the **anarchy** that reigns in Othello's heart seems complete. His speech becomes incoherent – 'It is not words that shakes me thus – pish! – noses, ears, and lips. Is't possible? Confess' Handkerchief! O devil!' He falls 'into an epilepsy' at Iago's feet, showing how far he has lost control and fallen into the hands of Iago.

The **resolution** of the play comes with Othello's suicide. We can sense it in the return to a stately, heroic measure in his final speech. Order is sternly restored by Lodovico, but it is hardly harmonious: his final speech concentrates on promising a slow death from torture to the villainous Iago.

Note the prolonged **dramatic irony** in this play. We the audience know what Iago is up to, but everyone else seems to think he is honest and reliable.

A particular issue for you to consider is how Othello and Desdemona complement each other as a couple, and this may contribute to their downfall. Desdemona falls in love with Othello because of his tales of war and bravery. Significantly they make her wish she could be a man. This, and the fact that she is prepared to rebel against her father and marry a Moor in secret, suggests that she has an adventurous, assertive side that seems to be quite lost once she is married. In psychological terms this 'male' energy is now all 'projected' onto Othello. This could explain why she does so little to defend herself against his accusations. He, likewise, is unbalanced by the marriage, listening only to Iago's false reasoning, and not to Emilia's assurances, or to his own intuition.

This is one interpretation of the play. See for yourself whether it is justified, looking closely at the evidence of the text.

Twelfth Night

The **situation** with which this play opens is relatively simple. Orsino is lovesick for Olivia, who is determined to mourn her brother for the next seven years. Both attitudes are equally silly, though we may have slightly more sympathy for Olivia, given the self-indulgent staginess of Orsino's language in the first scene.

The **trigger** that starts all the confusions is a natural event rather than a human act – the shipwreck. In psychological terms we might see Viola and her brother Sebastian as male and female aspects of one person. A kind of secondary trigger is Viola's decision to disguise herself as a man until she feels the time is right for her to reveal herself. Quite why she does this is puzzling, but we have to assume that she feels safer in a strange country doing this. We also have to suspend our disbelief more for the comedies than for other types of play.

The shipwreck is a foreshadowing of the **anarchy** to come, but in fact no one drowns. Viola's disguise leads to complex confusions. Meanwhile, in the **subplot** Sir Toby Belch and Sir Andrew Aguecheek are engaged in their own unruliness and drunken disorder. In fact critics have identified Sir Toby as a 'Lord of Misrule' from a much older tradition of Christmas 'Twelfth Night' celebration related to the Roman festival of Saturnalia. The puritanical killjoy Malvolio, whose name means 'ill will', is a natural target for their trickery.

This anarchy is reflected in the **language** of the play. Wordplay, including deliberate misunderstandings, make chaos out of the linguistic orderliness. Words, like Viola disguised as Cesario, are no longer what they seem. For example, at the start of Act 3:

> Viola: ... Dost thou live by the tabor?
> Feste: No, sir, I live by the church.

In addition, the play abounds with images of war, stormy seas and madness.

Throughout the play there is an enjoyable tension between disorder – particularly that produced by love – and socially acceptable behaviour. Olivia, for example, knows that she is flouting convention and risking her honour by courting a youth, 'Cesario' (Viola). Love turns the world upside down: 'Love's night is noon,' says Olivia. She knows that her love is irrational, but uncontrollable:

I love thee so that, maugre all thy pride,
Nor wit nor reason can my passion hide.
(*maugre*: despite)

This disorder **climaxes** as it threatens to lead to real problems. Antonio, who has succumbed irrationally to the pull of friendship to the extent of risking his life on enemy shores, is arrested. Arch-trickster Toby is himself caught up in the trickery, being wounded by Sebastian, whom he thinks is 'Cesario'.

The **resolution** comes before serious harm can be done. The harmony of love emerges, the three marriages placing its irrational power in a socially acceptable framework.

The Tempest

This romance is possibly the last full play Shakespeare wrote and is unusual in many ways. The **trigger** has already occurred at the start of the play: Antonio has usurped Prospero and set him and Miranda adrift on a rotten boat without mast or sail – perhaps an image indicating the loss of direction into which Prospero has drifted in neglecting his duties for magic and scholarship.

Since the play is set on an enchanted island, 'anything can happen'. This makes it easier for us to accept the reality of its inhabitants: Ariel the spirit, and Caliban the semi-human monster.

The play is also unusual in that the **anarchy** is largely created and stage-managed by Prospero, with his magical powers and the help of Ariel. He creates and calms the storm, casting the courtiers ashore unharmed, to be led around, confused and controlled by magical music.

As in earlier, more straightforward comedies, love is a major theme. Ferdinand and Miranda fall instantly in love, but Prospero wants to test Ferdinand and make him work to secure Miranda. Perhaps an even more important theme, however, is that of power. Prospero has lost his worldly power through seeking magical power. On the island he enslaves and torments Caliban for attempting to rape Miranda. He also makes a bond-servant of Ariel, supposedly in repayment for his freeing the spirit from a pine tree where he has been painfully imprisoned by the witch Sycorax. Prospero wields his magical power over the baffled courtiers for most of the play.

The **resolution** comes when Prospero relinquishes his magical power, is reconciled to his brother, and prepares to return to Naples to resume his dukedom. In keeping with more conventional comedy, too, there is a promised marriage – that of Ferdinand and Miranda – to ensure social continuity.

Henry IV Part II

The **situation** at the outset of the play is already unsettled. Civil war is raging. Nothing is certain, as the bizarre figure of Rumour, in a suit of tongues, makes clear. The unsettled situation has its roots in history – and in an earlier play by Shakespeare, *Richard II*, in which Henry is exiled by Richard, a weak and indecisive king, and then returns to overthrow him. Though he feels justified, his conscience is never easy.

The immediate **trigger** for the action in this later play is Northumberland's receipt of the news that his son, Percy Hotspur, leader of the new set of rebels, has been killed by Prince Hal in battle. Stirred from his sickbed by this news, Northumberland makes a proclamation of disorder, or **anarchy**:

Let heaven kiss earth! How let not Nature's hand
Keep the wild flood confin'd! Let order die!
And let this world no longer be a stage
To feed contention in a ling'ring act;
But let one spirit of the first-born Cain
Reign in all bosoms, that, each heart being set
On bloody courses, the rude scene may end,
And darkness be the burier of the dead!

Good-humoured anarchy reigns in the ample form of Sir John Falstaff, who encourages young Prince Hal to drink, whore and play tennis. The hilarious tavern and brothel scenes, and the gentler but equally silly scenes in rural Gloucestershire with Justice Shallow, are very much in contrast with the serious scenes relating to the threat to the throne. A disorderly, sponging braggard, Falstaff has much in common with Sir Toby Belch (see *Twelfth Night* on page 105). There is no real harm in either of them.

In a key scene (Act 4, scene 5), the Prince, thinking the King asleep on his sickbed, tries on the crown for size. Note the oxymorons (paradoxical, contradictory

images) that suggest the mixed blessing of kingship: 'O polish'd perturbation! golden care!'

Note, too, the play's imagery of animals, sickness and disgust, exemplified by the Archbishop speaking of the general populace:

> So, so, thou common dog, didst thou disgorge
> Thy glutton bosom of the royal Richard;
> And now thou wouldst eat thy dead vomit up,
> And howl'st to find it.

The **resolution** of the play comes when Henry dies and Prince Hal comes to the throne. He surprises everyone by mending his disorderly ways. Most of all he surprises and dismays Falstaff, who has ridden to London at speed expecting royal favours. The new king disowns his old companion and mentor: 'I know thee not, old man.' This may seem harsh, but in fact Falstaff is not exiled – only sent to prison for a short time, thereafter to live away from court until he can show that he deserves promotion. This is what is expected of a king: the nation is now in safe hands.

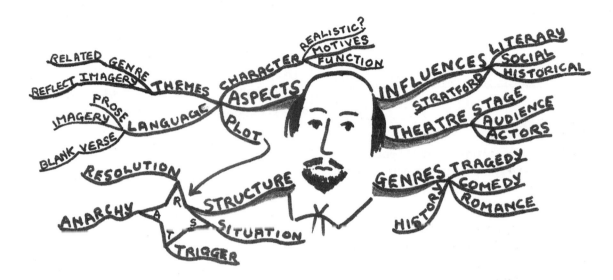

Summary

This chapter has told you the following:

- Shakespeare lived in a relatively *secular* society, but most people believed in *God*. Thinkers debated *fate* and *free will*. International *trade* was important.

- Shakespeare *borrowed* his *plots*. He and other playwrights and poets were influenced by *classical literature*.

- Theatres had a *socially varied* audience, little *scenery* and no electric *light*.

- Shakespeare wrote *tragedies, comedies, histories* and *romances*.

- When analysing plays use the STAR formula – Situation, Trigger, Anarchy, Resolution.

- Pay attention to *plot, characterisation, themes* and *language*.

What is poetry?

You have probably already been studying poetry for so long that it is worth going 'back to basics'. This will help you to appreciate poems and not just see them as comprehension exercises.

The earliest poetry was not written down – it was memorised, and sung or chanted by bards, who usually accompanied themselves on a stringed musical instrument such as a lyre or harp. This early poetry mostly consists of **epic** poems, telling stories about heroic deeds. Metre, rhythm and rhyme (see below) were pleasing in themselves, but they also made the stories easier for the bards to remember.

In these origins we can already see three ingredients that make poetry different from prose:

1 **Form** – shape and structure, in metre, rhyme etc.

2 **Sound** – the musicality of the words when spoken aloud

3 **Theme** – usually an event, idea or feeling that rises above the level of everyday life.

Of course the differences are sometimes blurred. Modern poetry has tended to move away from formal structure. Some poems, if printed running on across the whole page, would be hard to distinguish from prose. Find a poem with no obvious metre, rhyme or imagery and write out a few lines in this way to test this for yourself. Some modern prose, on the other hand, is very poetic. Read, for example, the last paragraph of James Joyce's story, 'The Dead' (in *Dubliners*) or any story by Dylan Thomas.

What makes this kind of prose 'poetic', and what characterises any good poetry, is that the author strives to express an idea not just in the logical

meaning of the words, but through their rhythm, the way the words sound, and imagery. The words appeal to our senses and stir our feelings.

Poetry should never be reduced to a comprehension exercise. Good poetry is never difficult just for the sake of it. Appreciating a poem does not just mean working out what it means. Accept that it may be impossible, even for the poet, to say exactly what it means. It may have several layers of meaning.

The good news is that what *you* think the poem means is valid. You will be given credit for your personal response, providing you justify your opinion with accurately observed evidence.

The purpose of poetry

Like any good writing, a poem has a purpose – or several different purposes. It may:

- **E**ntertain
- **N**arrate (tell a story)
- **P**ersuade
- **E**xpress or explore ideas or emotions
- **C**elebrate or lament.

You could remember this as **ENPEC**.

Most poems entertain in some sense. Some narrate – tell stories. One traditional type of narrative poem is the ballad, which has a vigorous metre and regular rhyme scheme, as seen here in a verse from Coleridge's 'Rime of the Ancient Mariner' (1798).

> The fair breeze blew, the white foam flew,
> The furrow followed free;
> We were the first that ever burst
> Into that silent sea.

A twentieth-century example with which to compare this is 'The Ballad of the Long-Legged Bait', by Dylan Thomas:

> Sails drank the wind, and white as milk
> He sped into the drinking dark;
> The sun shipwrecked west on a pearl
> And the moon swam out of its hulk.

Fewer poems set out to persuade, but there are politically motivated poets, such as Tony Harrison. The majority of poems set out to express and explore an idea or emotion. The poet writes out of a need to express, but if the poem is successful, it strikes a chord with which readers will be able to identify.

Subject, theme and mood

When you begin to read a poem, whether or not you intend to write a critique of it, the first aspect to look at is simply its **subject**. This means what the poem appears to be about. The **theme** is the underlying idea suggested by the subject matter. A long poem may have several themes. The **mood** of the poem usually fits the subject and theme. It will be suggested by the poet's choice of words, any images used, and by rhythm and rhyme. It may for example be mournful, angry, humorous or nostalgic.

Now read the poem on the right, 'The Flea' by John Donne (1572–1631). As you read, consider the subject, theme and mood, and how they relate to each other.

The **subject** of this poem is the flea. However, Donne was not writing a study of the natural history of small bloodsucking insects. The closest we get to an observation of the flea is in the phrase, 'these living walls of Jet'. Jet is a black stone – so the flea is black and hard-cased. The **theme** of the poem is the poet's argument that his girlfriend should sleep with him – based on the idea that they are virtually married already in that their bloods have mingled in the body of the flea who has bitten them both. There are poems, especially animal poems, in which the poet simply tries to capture the essence of the subject, but this is not one of them.

TRY THIS

What do you think is the *mood* of 'The Flea'? How serious is the poet's argument? At the start of the second stanza his beloved is about to kill the flea and he begs her not to, arguing that this would constitute a triple murder. At the start of the final stanza, she has ignored his plea and crushed the flea between her nails. Does his tone of outrage at her 'Cruel and sodaine [sudden, abrupt]' act ring true? Is he a paid-up member of Friends of the Flea?

The Flea

Mark but this flea, and mark in this,
How little that which thou deny'st me is;
Me it sucked first, and now sucks thee,
And in this flea, our two bloods mingled be;
Confess it, this cannot be said
A sin, or shame, or losse of maidenhead,
    Yet this enjoys before it woo,
    And pampered swells with one blood made of two,
    And this, alas, is more than we would do.

Oh stay, three lives in one flea spare,
Where we almost, nay more than married are:
This flea is you and I, and this
Our marriage bed, and marriage temple is;
Though parents grudge, and you, we're met,
And cloistered in these living walls of Jet.
    Though use make thee apt to kill me,
    Let not to this, self murder added be,
    And sacrilege, three sins in killing three.

Cruel and sodaine, hast thou since
Purpled thy nail, in blood of innocence?
In what could this flea guilty be,
Except in that drop which it sucked from thee?
Yet thou triumph'st, and sayst that thou
Find'st not thy self, nor me the weaker now;
    'Tis true, then learn how false, fears be;
    Just so much honour, when thou yield'st to me,
    Will waste, as this flea's death took life from thee.

John Donne

FACTFILE

The Metaphysicals

The term *metaphysical* was invented by John Dryden (1631–1700) and established by Samuel Johnson (1709–84), who criticised the metaphysical poets, saying that their imagery was forced. The best-known metaphysicals are John Donne, Andrew Marvell and George Herbert. Herbert is a religious poet. Donne is most famous for his love poems, but he also wrote poems full of religious fervour.

Metaphysical poems present tightly argued attempts to persuade. They often enter into philosophical debate. Above all, they use ingenious and elaborate conceits – extended comparisons more notable for their cleverness than for their real accuracy.

Speaker and spoken-to

In 'The Flea' the **speaker** – also called the **voice** – was the poet himself, and he was speaking to his beloved. However, poets often adopt a 'persona' other than their own, and write as if they were that person or thing. Here is an example, 'The Man He Killed' by Thomas Hardy (1840–1928).

'Had he and I but met
By some old ancient inn,
We should have sat us down to wet
Right many a nipperkin!

'But ranged as infantry,
And staring face to face,
I shot at him as he at me,
And killed him in his place.

'I shot him dead because –
Because he was my foe,
Just so: my foe of course he was;
That's clear enough; although

'He thought he'd 'list, perhaps,
Off-hand like – just as I –
Was out of work – had sold his traps –
No other reason why.

'Yes; quaint and curious war is!
You shoot a fellow down
You'd treat if met where any bar is,
Or help to half-a-crown.

This poem, written in 1902, hints at the absurdity of war by relating an incident through the eyes of an ordinary soldier. It uses appropriately down-to-earth language and a simple rhyme scheme. There is a deliberate irony in the weakness of the soldier's explanation for killing the man. This is underlined by the internal rhyme and repetition, suggesting a going round in circles – not a real justification:

Because he was my foe,
Just so: my foe of course he was;

Another poem written in a soldier's persona is 'An Irish Airman Foresees His Death' by W.B. Yeats' (1865–1939), in which the speaker asserts that he neither hates those he fights, nor loves those he guards. This is well worth reading.

The 'speaker' or 'voice' of the poem may not even be human, as in Hardy's poem 'The Puzzled Game-Birds'.

They are not those who used to feed us
When we were young – they cannot be –
These shapes that now bereave and bleed us?
They are not those who used to feed us,
For did we then cry, they would heed us.
– If hearts can house such treachery
They are not those who used to feed us
When we were young – they cannot be!

Hardy does not really try to sound like a pheasant here, but the innocent incredulity of the bird does seem to fit the voice, as well as making an ironic comment on human nature.

Many of modern poet Ted Hughes' poems are in the voice of a bird or animal – for example his 'Hawk Roosting'. Even further removed from the human 'voice' is a poem by his wife, Sylvia Plath, 'Mushrooms', which turns mushrooms into something sinister, taking over the world by stealth. To return for a moment to our discussion of subject and theme, in Plath's poem the subject is mushrooms, but the theme is the poet's sense of the menace lurking behind everyday reality.

If you are asked to comment on a poem which adopts a persona in this way, consider:

- how far the poet is simply trying to capture the essence of the person or thing speaking, or is using this persona to represent an idea

- how the language of the poem fits the persona

- how far the poet's own ideas or feelings are ascribed to this persona

- what the poet gains by writing in this way rather than writing in the third person.

Metre and rhythm

Many poems, especially older poems, are written in a particular **metre**. This means a set number and pattern of stressed (/) and unstressed (–) syllables occur in each line.

This can be explained in an example from 'Song', by Aphra Benn (1640–89):

> How strongly does my passion flow,
> Divided equally 'twixt two?

If you speak these lines aloud you will find that the stressed and unstressed syllables divide naturally into **feet**, which in this case are in pairs of one unstressed followed by one stressed syllable. These feet can be marked as shown in another two lines of the poem:

> – / – / – / – /
> One gol den-poin ted dart take back:
> – / – / – / – /
> But which, O Cu pid, wilt thou take?

The feet in these two lines are the commonest feet found in English poetry, called **iams** or **iambic** feet (– /).

Some English verse uses a foot called a **trochee** (adjective **trochaic**). This consists of a stressed followed by an unstressed syllable (/ –):

> / – / – / – /
> Go and catch a falling star,
> / – / – / – /
> Get with child a mandrake root,
> / – / – / – /
> Tell me where all past years are,
> / – / – / – /
> Or who cleft the Devil's foot,
>
> John Donne, 'Song'

The other two-syllabled foot is the **spondee** (adjective **spondaic**), which consists of equally stressed syllables (/ /). This is used very sparingly because it suggests a plodding slowness and heaviness. In Thomas Hardy's poem 'The Voice', the poet remembers his dead wife, and in the final verse pictures himself old and alone:

> / / / – – / /
> Thus I; faltering forward,
> / – / – / /
> Leaves around me falling,

Next we have the three-syllabled **anapaest** (adjective **anapaestic**):

> – – / – – / – – / – – /
> Like the galloping horses the anapest runs

The **dactyl** (adjective **dactylic**) is the foot widely used in Anglo-Saxon (Old English) poetry. In modern times W.H. Auden has used it well. The dactyl consists of one stressed and two unstressed syllables (/ – –). A dactylic line has a strong rhythm, but carries a hint of sadness, as in the opening lines from Hardy's poem quoted above.

> / – – / – – / – – / –
> Woman much missed, how you call to me, call to
> –
> me,
> / – – / – – / – – /
> Saying that now you are not as you were

There is one more foot, less often used, the **amphibrach** (adjective **amphibrachic**), consisting of unstressed, stressed, unstressed (–/–).

> – / – – / – – / – – /
> The amphibrach ambles and shambles along
> – / – – / – – / – – /
> And often appears in the words of a song.

When you understand what 'metrical feet' are, read aloud the lines below and mark stressed and unstressed syllables. Then divide up the lines into feet. Finally, identify each metre.

a) Slowly the bridegroom walked up to the bride and said,

b) As he kissed her on the forehead,

c) 'My love, the world is far too wide

d) For me even to think of the things inside your head.'

e) But he tried.

(Answers on page 146)

Feet in a line

The next important aspect of metre is the number of feet in a line.

You may know that **blank verse**, as used by Shakespeare (see page 95), is also called **unrhymed iambic pentameter**. The word 'iambic' you should now understand: the lines are made up of 'iams' (see page 111). 'Pentameter' means a metre made up of *five* iambic feet (Greek *pent* = five, as in *pent*agon – a five-sided building).

Many other poets have used iambic pentameter. Milton's epic poem *Paradise Lost* is in the unrhymed form (blank verse). Alexander Pope (1688–1784) uses a rhymed form in his satirical *Rape of the Lock*:

The hungry judges soon the sentence sign,
And wretches hang that jury-men may dine;

Try counting the feet in these lines and you should find there are five in each. This will normally mean ten syllables (five pairs). However, you need to realise that in English poetry the important thing is the number of feet, and not always the number of syllables, since poets do sometimes vary this. Spot the extra syllable in Pope's next couplet:

The merchant from the Exchange returns in peace,
And the long labours of the toilet cease.

Read this aloud to see how it should be spoken to keep the metre.

You may also come across:

- **tetrameter** (four feet – as in Donne's 'Song', opposite)

- **hexameter** (six feet).

Sometimes the number of syllables in each line varies in a set sequence through each verse. A very obvious example is to be found in limericks. A more elevated example is found in the following Donne poem an extract of which was quoted earlier. Notice especially the extra length of lines 5 and 6 in each verse, building up to the two short, two-footed lines (7 and 8), which pull us up short before the 'punchline'. Notice, too, how the rhyme scheme and the way the poem is set out emphasise this.

'Song'
Go and catch a falling star,
   Get with child a mandrake root,
Tell me where all past years are,
   Or who cleft the Devil's foot,
Teach me to hear Mermaids singing,
   Or to keep off envy's stinging,
      And find
      What wind
Serves to advance an honest mind.

If thou beest borne to strange sights,
   Things invisible to see,
Ride ten thousand days and nights,
   Till age snow white hairs on thee,
Thou, when thou return'st, wilt tell me
All strange wonders that befell thee,
      And swear
      No where
Lives a woman true and fair.

If thou find'st one, let me know,
   Such a Pilgrimage were sweet;
Yet do not, I would not go,
   Though at next door we might meet,
Though she were true when you met her,
And last till you write your letter,
      Yet she
      Will be
False, ere I come, to two, or three.

The uses of metre and rhythm

Some metres are used conventionally for particular purposes. For example Pope wrote 'The Rape of the Lock' in rhymed iambic pentameter couplets (also called **heroic couplets**) because this was the convention for heroic narrative verse, and it suited his satirical purpose. Some metres are chosen because they help to convey a certain mood, as does Hardy's poem 'The Voice' ('Woman much missed, how you call to me, call to me…'). Anapaestic metre has been used in several poems to suggest horses galloping.

At other times there may be no special significance in the choice of metre. However, in good poetry any rhythmical departure from the metre is always significant . This is normally used to reinforce the sense of the words. Even in a poem with no regular metre – as in many modern poems – the changing rhythms should match the sense of the words. For example, in Hardy's lines:

> Thus I; faltering forward,
> The leaves around me falling,

The rhythm in the second line seems to 'falter'; the second line's regularity suggests falling leaves, as does the way the line ends with an unstressed syllable, and therefore on a 'falling' note.

> ### HINT
>
> **Even if you never learn the names of the metres, try to become aware of the rhythms in any poetry you read, and of how they match the meaning of the words. You will get more marks in an exam for pointing out the way a metre or rhythm works than for just naming it.**

Sound effects

Poets use a number of sound effects in their choice of words. The main ones are **rhyme**, **alliteration** and **assonance**.

Rhyme

Some people think that poetry has to rhyme, or that if two lines rhyme, that makes them poetry. Both ideas, of course, are wrong.

Rhyme is used for a variety of reasons:

- it is pleasing to the ear
- to emphasise a meaning
- to give a sense of completion
- to make a special connection between two words.

In Donne's 'Song' (see page 112), the rhyming of the short lines helps to pull us up short. In Hardy's 'The Voice' (see above), there is a special mournfulness conveyed by the focus of the rhymes usually falling before the end of a line, so that the rhyme is drawn out in a way that suggests the poet's memory is drawn out in time.

The following poem by Gerard Manley Hopkins (1844–89) achieves something of the same effect. Read it aloud, noting the effect of the rhymes and how they relate to the sense. The poem begins in rhyming couplets; then there is a rhyming triplet, the first line

of which includes an internal rhyme ('By and by …'); the poem finishes with three rhyming couplets.

> 'Spring and Fall: to a young child'
> Margaret, are you grieving
> Over Goldengrove unleaving?
> Leaves like the things of man, you
> With your fresh thoughts care for, can you?
> Ah! as the heart grows older
> It will come to such sights colder
> By and by, nor spare a sigh
> Though worlds of wanwood leafmeal lie;
> And yet you will weep and know why.
> Now no matter, child, the name:
> Sorrow's springs are the same.
> Nor mouth had, no nor mind, expressed
> What heart heard of, ghost guessed:
> It is the blight man was born for,
> It is Margaret you mourn for.

The internal rhyme (by… sigh… lie… why) slows us up, and the three rhyming lines which include it draw the first half of the poem to a close. The short phrases 'By and by, nor spare a sigh' contrast with the long, lingering 'Though worlds of wanwood leafmeal lie', suggesting great stretches of sad, dead leaves.

The change of metre in the next line (to an anapaest) combines with the extra rhyme to bring the first half of the poem to a close. In the first part of the poem the poet wonders that the girl can be sad about dead leaves. He says that she will become hardened by worse sorrows, so that she no longer weeps for dead leaves. In the second part of the poem, after the rhyming triplet, he explains the real source of her sorrow over the leaves – namely, the sorrow that is part of the human condition.

This poem also provides a good example of something you should look out for: **enjambement**. This means the continuation of the sense without pause from one line to the next:

> Leaves like the things of man, you
> With your fresh thoughts care for, can you?

> ### FACTFILE
>
> **Poetic techniques**
> *(from W.H. Auden, 'The Nature of Poets')*
> **'Rhymes, metres, stanza forms etc., are like servants. If the master is fair enough to win their affection and firm enough to command their respect, the result is an orderly happy household. If he is too tyrannical, they give notice; if he lacks authority, they become slovenly, impertinent, drunk and dishonest.'**

The term is normally only used where you absolutely have to read on to make sense of the first line, as you do here. Bear in mind, though, that even in less clear-cut cases, you should always follow sense, and not pause mechanically at the end of each line.

A **rhyme scheme** is a pattern of rhymes. Older poetry, especially, is likely to keep to a rhyme scheme. The convention for marking rhyme schemes is to call the first pair of rhyming words A, the second B, and so on. Thus the rhyme scheme in the Hopkins poem on page 113 is AA, BB, CC, DDD, EE, FF, GG.

Alliteration

This is the repetition of consonant sounds at the beginnings of words or syllables. Like rhyming, it is sometimes used simply because it is pleasing to the ear. It is also memorable – which is why it is used in advertising slogans: 'Guinness is good for you.'

A more subtle use of alliteration is to draw two or more words together in sense. This is done in Hopkins' poem:

Margaret, are you grieving
Over Goldengrove unleaving?

and:

Though worlds of wanwood leafmeal lie;
And yet you will weep and know why.

Sometimes, too, a repeated sound has a particular emotional effect. There is something sad in the repetition of the w sounds above. Think of woe, wail, whinge and whine. A similar effect is found in the climax of Milton's *Paradise Lost* (Book IX), when Eve has eaten the forbidden apple:

Earth felt the wound, and Nature from her seat
Sighing through all her Works gave signs of woe,
That all was lost. Back to the Thicket slunk
The guilty Serpent...

FACTFILE

Milton
(*from Samuel Johnson, Lives of the English Poets*)
'He was naturally a thinker for himself, confident of his own abilities, and disdainful of help or hindrance: he did not refuse admission to the thoughts or images of his predecessors, but he did not seek them. From his contemporaries he neither courted nor received support; there is in his writings nothing by which the pride of other authors might be gratified, or favour gained; no exchange of praise, nor solicitation of support.

We have here the woeful w sound, and the sighing s sounds that become the slithery sounds of the slinking serpent. The slithery s is also an example of **onomatopoeia**, the use of words whose sound imitates the thing they describe.

? See what alliteration you can spot in these lines that follow soon after those above, and consider its effect:

Adam shall share with me in bliss or woe:
So dear I love him, that with him all deaths
I could endure, without him live no life.

Assonance

This is the repetition of vowel sounds in words. It is an essential part of rhyming, but two or more words can be assonant without rhyming – for example *fearful* and *weary*, or *cat* and *dagger*. In the following lines from 'February, A Thaw', by John Clare (1793–1864), the open o sounds suggest an opening up of winter's icy grip, and an innocent enjoyment of the thaw. Note Clare uses 'icles' for 'icicles'.

The snow is gone from cottage tops
The thatch moss glows in brighter green
And eves in quick succession drops
Where grinning icles once hath been
Pit patting with a pleasant noise
In tubs set by the cottage door
And ducks and geese with happy joys
Douse in the yard pond brimming o'er

CHECKLIST

You should now understand the following:

✓ *Metre* refers to a pattern of *feet* in lines of verse, each foot consisting of a combination of 1–3 syllables, in combinations of stressed (/) and unstressed (–).

✓ The main feet are: *iams (– /)*; *trochees (/ –)*; *spondees (/)*; *dactyls (/ / – –)*; and *anapaests (– – /)*.

✓ The adjectives from these are *iambic*, *trochaic*, *spondaic*, *dactylic* and *anapaestic*.

✓ A metre has a set number of feet in each line – usually four (*tetrameter*), five (*pentameter*) or six (*hexameter*).

✓ Always read poems aloud to see how *rhythmic variations* help to express sense.

✓ *Rhyme* is pleasing to the ear and can enhance the sense.

✓ *Enjambement* continues the sense of a line without pause onto the next line.

✓ *Alliteration* and *assonance* are the repetition, for effect, of consonant and vowel sounds.

Verse forms

Now that you know about metre and sound effects – especially rhyme – you should easily understand this section on **verse forms**. A verse form is a style of poem with a particular metrical pattern and rhyme scheme. Sometimes it is used for a particular purpose; for example, the sonnet forms (see below) are often used for love poetry.

We have already looked at blank verse (unrhymed iambic pentameter), as used by Shakespeare and Milton. We have also looked at 'heroic couplets': lines of iambic pentameter rhyming in pairs. These were used by Dryden, Pope and other eighteenth-century poets.

The **sonnet** comes in two varieties, both composed of fourteen lines of iambic pentameter:

- Petrarchan (after the fourteenth-century Italian poet Petrarch)

- Shakespearean (Shakespeare wrote the most famous sonnets)

In the **Petrarchan sonnet** there is one rhyme scheme for the first eight lines (the octave) and another for the remaining six (the sestet). A typical rhyme scheme for the octave is ABBAABBA (easy enough to remember if you happen to be a fan of a certain 1970s Swedish singing foursome!). The sestet normally rhymes CDCDCD. The theme of the sonnet is presented in the octave, and this is commented on in the sestet. See how this works in the following example from an insomniac William Wordsworth (1770–1850).

> 'To Sleep'
> A flock of sheep that leisurely pass by,
> One after one; the sound of rain, and bees
> Murmuring; the fall of rivers, winds and seas,
> Smooth fields, white sheets of water, and pure sky;
> I have though of all by turns, and yet do lie
> Sleepless! and soon the small birds' melodies
> Must hear, first uttered from my orchard trees;
> And the first cuckoo's melancholy cry.
> Even thus last night, and two nights more, I lay
> And could not win thee, Sleep! by any stealth:
> So do not let me wear tonight away:
> Without Thee what is all the morning's wealth?
> Come, blessed barrier between day and day,
> Dear mother of fresh thoughts and joyous health!

Compare this with one more example of the Petrarchan sonnet, by Elizabeth Barrett Browning (from *Sonnets from the Portuguese*, 1850). Its theme is traditional – love – but the movement of ideas from octave to sestet is less so: the change comes halfway into line 9, and is less clear-cut than in the Wordsworth sonnet.

> If thou must love me, let it be for naught
> Except for love's sake only. Do not say,
> 'I love her for her smile – her look – her way
> Of speaking gently, – for a trick of thought
> That falls in well with mine, and certes brought
> A sense of pleasant ease on such a day' –
> For these things in themselves, Beloved, may
> Be changed, or change for thee – and love, so
> wrought,
> May be unwrought so. Neither love me for
> Thine own dear pity's wiping my cheeks dry:
> A creature might forget to weep, who bore
> Thy comfort long, and lose they love thereby!
> But love me for love's sake, that evermore
> Thou mayst love on, through love's eternity.

? What stylistic differences and similarities can you find in these two sonnets? Look, for example, at the sound effects, and at the use of enjambement (refer back to these notes if you don't remember what this is!).

In the **Shakespearean sonnet** the theme is stated in the first twelve lines. These lines may be divided into three groups of four lines (quatrains), and typically rhyme ABABCDCDEFEF. A conclusion is drawn in a final rhyming couplet (GG). In the following sonnet, Shakespeare dismisses more conventional love poetry's insistence on idealising the beloved's appearance as if she were a goddess – but look for the twist in the final couplet. (Note that *dun* means brown; also that a pale skin and blonde hair were fashionable.)

> My mistress' eyes are nothing like the sun;
> Coral is far more red than her lips' red;
> If snow be white, why then her breasts are dun;
> If hairs be wires, black wires grow on her head.
> I have seen roses damask'd, red and white,
> But no such roses see I in her cheeks;
> And in some perfumes is there more delight
> Than in the breath that from my mistress reeks.
> I love to hear her speak, yet well I know
> That music hath a far more pleasing sound;
> I grant I never saw a goddess go –
> My mistress when she walks treads on the ground.
> And yet, by heaven, I think my love as rare
> As any she belied with false compare.

Another verse form is the **Spenserian stanza**, after Edmund Spenser (1552–99), author of 'The Faerie Queen', which probably had an influence on Shakespeare. This has eight lines of iambic pentameter followed by one of iambic hexameter (six feet). It rhymes ABABBCBCC. The hexameter line acts like the final couplet in a Shakespearean sonnet, concluding the stanza. John Keats (1795–1821) uses this form in his long poem *The Eve of St Agnes*.

Diction

This refers to the poet's choice of words (vocabulary), and to their arrangement (grammar and syntax). For example, we saw earlier how in 'The Man He Killed' (see page 110), Hardy chose words and grammar that might have been used by an ordinary soldier.

Sometimes a word stands out, perhaps because the poet has invented it, as in Hopkins' use of 'wanwood': *wan* is an old word, usually applied to someone's appearance, meaning pale and exhausted. Hopkins also takes some liberties with conventional word order:

> Leaves like the things of man, you
> With your fresh thoughts care for, can you?

He might have written:

> With your fresh thoughts you can
> Care for leaves like the things of man, can you?

Which do you prefer, and why?

Now read two stanzas by Alfred Lord Tennyson (1809–92), taken from 'The Lotos-Eaters'. This poem is based on an episode from Homer's *Odyssey* in which Odysseus and his men land on an island where people eat Lotos (or Lotus), a plant that drugs them into a blissful, dreamlike lethargy. In this state they give up all ambitions and endeavours, and are merely enjoying their surroundings. Notice the differences between the two stanzas.

> There is sweet music here that softer falls
> Than petals from blown roses on the grass,
> Or night-dews on still waters between walls
> Of shadowy granite, in a gleaming pass;
> Music that gentlier on the spirit lies,
> Than tired eyelids upon tired eyes;
> Music that brings sweet sleep down from the
>   blissful skies.

> Here are cool mosses deep,
> And through the moss the ivies creep,
> And in the stream the long-leaved flowers weep,
> And from the craggy ledge the poppy hangs in
>   sleep.

> Why are we weighed upon with heaviness,
> And utterly consumed with sharp distress,
> While all things else have rest from weariness?
> All things have rest: why should we toil alone,
> We only toil, who are the first of things,
> And make perpetual moan,
> Still from one sorrow to another thrown:
> Nor ever fold our wings,
> And cease from wanderings,
> Nor steep our brows in slumber's holy balm;
> Nor harken what the inner spirit sings,
> 'There is no joy but calm!'
> Why should we only toil, the roof and crown of
>   things?

Look at the contrast between the two stanzas. Almost all the words in the first contribute to a mood of calm and tranquillity. The 'sweet music', the 'petals from blown roses' contrasting pleasingly with the 'still waters between walls/ Of shadowy granite', the 'blissful skies' and 'cool mosses' – all this suggests the delights of a new Garden of Eden. Above all, the language appeals to the senses.

Notice, too, the lulling repetition of 'music', the suggestion of sleep in the 'tired eyelids upon tired eyes', and the poppy that 'hangs in sleep' – Victorian readers would associate the poppy with opium. The only hint of anything less than blissful comes with the word 'weep' in the penultimate line of the stanza.

What do you make of this?

TRY THIS

1 **What kind of feet are used in the Tennyson stanzas quoted above?**

2 **Read both stanzas aloud, tapping out the rhythm. Count the feet in each line.**

3 **Mark the feet in the two stanzas and write down the number of feet in each line.**

4 **What are the names for lines with these different numbers of feet? (Check above if you need to.)**

5 **Suggest how the numbers of feet in each line complement the sense of the lines.**

HINT

Look for any build-up in length, and any matching development in sense.

6 **Look for *alliteration* and *assonance* in the first stanza. What effects do they create?**

7 **Mark the rhyme scheme in the second stanza. How is rhyming used here to make connections between words or punctuate the sense?**

8 **Mind Map the stylistic features used in this poem and their effects.**

The second stanza has none of this gentle appeal to sensuality. Instead it is full of unappealing, intellectually demanding abstract nouns: 'heaviness', 'distress', 'weariness' and 'sorrow'. Note, too, 'utterly consumed', 'toil' (repeated), and 'perpetual moan' rhyming with 'thrown' – suggesting a life of turmoil and torment. The choice of words creates a temporary mood of grimness and misery – which the Lotos-Eaters present as the alternative to joining them.

Imagery

Images can be briefly defined as 'word pictures', but there are some variations on this. First, images can appeal to senses other than that of sight. John Clare appeals to our sense of hearing in the following lines describing cranes flying:

> Cranking their jarring melancholy cry
> Through the long journey of the cheerless cry

The following two lines from Ben Jonson, Shakespeare's friend, present an image of softness:

> Have you felt the wool of beaver
> Or swan's down ever?

FACTFILE

The Romantic Poets

The Romantic Movement in poetry was part of a wider movement in the arts. It emphasised the individual's spirit, imagination, emotions and feelings about the world. Romantic poets often championed individual liberty, and were inspired by nature – perhaps stirred by the grim urbanisation of the Industrial Revolution. Blake, arguably an early Romantic, wrote of 'these dark Satanic mills'.

In part, Romanticism was a reaction against the classical intellectualism of the Augustans. It also contributed to, and was fuelled by, the French Revolution of 1789. Romantic poets tended to sympathise (at least theoretically) with the common man, and to be anti-authoritarian. Shelley, for example, wrote 'The Masque of Anarchy', bitterly satirising the reactionary right-wing government of his day. Wordsworth and Coleridge made a conscious effort to write in the language of 'the common man', rather than the self-consciously rhetorically poetic language of the Augustans.

John Keats is perhaps the Romantic poet who most cultivated the movement's sensuality and surrender to feeling. He also fits the popular image of the Romantic poet in that he died tragically young, of consumption.

In addition, some people use the term 'imagery' for any kind of word picture or use of words appealing to the senses; for example, 'a host of golden daffodils'. Others limit the term to figures of speech that appeal to the senses and compare one thing with another. The Clare lines above include an image by this definition: 'Cranking their jarring melancholy cry'. Cranking, strictly speaking, is done by something mechanical, such as a water pump; therefore Clare is saying that the cranes sound as if they produce their cry by operating a crank. (This image is a **metaphor** – see below.)

Twentieth-century poet Cecil Day Lewis suggests that an image is 'a word-picture charged with emotion or passion'.

Imagery can be used in prose, but it is more often used in poetry. The main types are outlined below.

Simile

This is the easiest kind of image to describe. Similes almost always include 'like' or 'as', and they compare one thing with another. Shelley (1792–1822) in his poem 'Ode to a Skylark' uses several similes. Here are two stanzas, each containing a simile. Note that in the first, 'even' means 'evening'; in the second, the 'sphere' is the moon.

> The pale purple even
>   Melts around thy flight;
> Like a star of heaven,
>   In the broad daylight
> Thou art unseen, but yet I hear thy shrill delight –
>
> Keen as are the arrows
>   Of that silver sphere
> Whose intense lamp narrows
>   In the white dawn clear,
> Until we hardly see, we feel that it is there.

The second simile is of the kind which compares something in *degree*: 'Keen as...' We often use this kind of simile in everyday speech: 'as white as a sheet', 'as big as a house'.

Metaphors

Metaphors are less obvious than similes. You may not have noticed that there is one in the second line of the first stanza above: 'Melts....' Since the evening is not made of chocolate or ice, it does not really melt; it does so only metaphorically. Moreover, although 'melting' is often used to describe something disappearing, Shelley's use is more original and beautiful: he describes the evening melting around the skylark, rather than the more obvious image of the skylark melting into the evening.

A metaphor, then, is a compressed simile. It describes something as if it were something else. If I say, 'The sea clawed at the cliff-edge', this is a metaphor. If I say, instead, 'The sea was like an animal clawing at the cliff-edge,' this is a simile.

Personification

This means speaking of something abstract, such as love, death or sleep, as if it were a person or a god. Wordsworth **personifies** sleep in the sonnet quoted on page 115.

> Come, blessed barrier between day and day,
> Dear mother of fresh thoughts and joyous health!

Personification is used less often in modern poetry. However, it has still been used to great effect, for example by W.H. Auden in 'As I Walked Out One Evening':

> But all the clocks in the city
>   Began to whirr and chime:
> 'O let not Time deceive you,
>   You cannot conquer Time.
> 'In the burrows of the Nightmare
>   Where Justice naked is,
> Time watches from the shadow
>   And coughs when you would kiss.
>
> 'In headaches and in worry
>   Vaguely life leaks away,
> And Time will have his fancy
>   To-morrow or to-day.'

? How many things are personified here? How effective is Auden's use of personification?

Oxymorons

One other type of image worth mentioning here – although used relatively rarely – is the colourfully named **oxymoron**. This combines opposite, paradoxical ideas. Romeo uses these in *Romeo and Juliet*, indicating his confusion and mixed feelings. Thomas Gray (1716–71) uses one in his 'Ode on a Distant Prospect of Eton College':

> Still as they run they look behind,
> They hear a voice in every wind,
> And snatch a fearful joy.

Questions

1 What are 'heroic couplets'?

2 How many feet are there in a line of blank verse?

3 How many lines are there in a sonnet?

4 What are the two types of sonnet?

5 Which of the two types starts with the rhyme scheme ABBAABBA?

6 What kind of image contains the words 'like' or 'as'?

7 'Close bosom-friend of the maturing sun' (Keats, 'Autumn'). What type of image is this?

8 'Swift haste, cold fire' – what kind of images are these?

9 Which type of image is like a compressed simile?

10 Why is it slightly limiting to define an images as a 'word picture'?

(Answers on page 146)

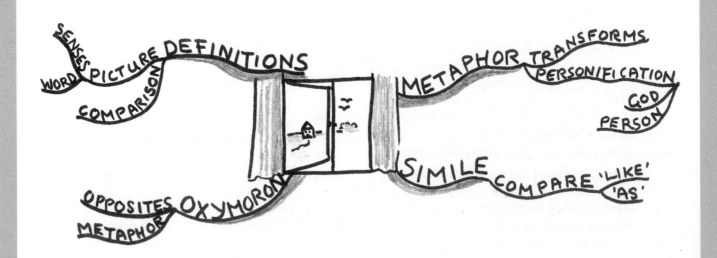

Getting to grips with a poem

If you've read this chapter carefully so far, you should now have a good idea of **what** to look for in a poem. This section suggests **how** you can look, and what to do with what you find.

One useful technique is to photocopy the poem, preferably blowing it up to twice its original size. If you do not have access to an enlarging photocopier, stick or staple a copy onto a large sheet of plain paper. This will enable you to underline, circle or highlight features of interest, and to write notes in the margins. It is also helpful to have the whole poem on a single sheet, rather than having to turn a page.

How you **read** the poem is important. You may find it helpful to skim-read the whole poem first to gain an overall impression of its arrangement and of what kind of poem it seems to be. Also look out for the **subject** of the poem.

After this you will need to read the poem more slowly. Reading aloud, whether 'in your head' or literally out loud, will help you to sense the rhythm and appreciate the sounds of words. At this stage, don't try too hard to analyse the poem.

Now read the poem more slowly still. Allow yourself to flit backwards and forwards, rereading anything that is unclear, or that you particularly like. Don't feel that you always have to go from beginning to end.

Start to highlight any words or phrases that interest you, looking for the features described so far in this chapter. At this stage it is acceptable to notice features – for example alliteration or metaphors – without fully appreciating how they work.

Also allow yourself time to imagine any details or images that appeal to the senses. If the poet describes crowds as 'fields of harvest wheat', try to picture this 'in your mind's eye'; if laughter is compared to the 'tinkling of bells', imagine that sound.

Now move on to exploring the **theme(s)**. Mind Map how this relates to the subject, and how the poetic features contribute to the poem's meaning and effect. For some poems you may want to make separate Mind Maps for particular features, such as imagery.

Finally, 'stand back' from the poem to appreciate its structure. How does it develop? How does the meaning unfold, and how does this relate to the poetic features? At this point you may need to read the poem quickly again, to take it in as a whole.

Below is a poem annotated in the way suggested, together with a Mind Map on page 120 exploring it. Read the poem and add any comments of your own.

What verse form is it written in? (Refer to page 115 if you're not sure.)

'The Silken Tent'

She is **as** in a field a **silken tent** ——————— simile; silk-luxury, softness, strength

At midday when a sunny summer breeze ——————— sounds carefree; onomatopoeia – s – breeze

Has **d**ried the **d**ew and all its **r**opes **r**elent, ——————— paired alliteration – sense of harmony and balance

So that in guys it gently sways at ease,

And its supporting central **cedar** pole, ——————— Exotic – Cedars of Lebanon?

That is its **pinnacle** to heavenward ——————— slightly unusual word – stands out

And signifies the sureness of the soul,

Seems to owe **naught** to any single cord,

But strictly held by none, is loosely bound

By countless **silken** ties of love and thought ——————— repetition for emphasis

To everything on earth the compass round,

And only by **one's** going slightly taut ——————— Who?

In the **capriciousness** of summer air ——————— pronunciation necessitates slight change in rhythm – echoing sense

Is of the slightest bondage made aware.

Robert Frost

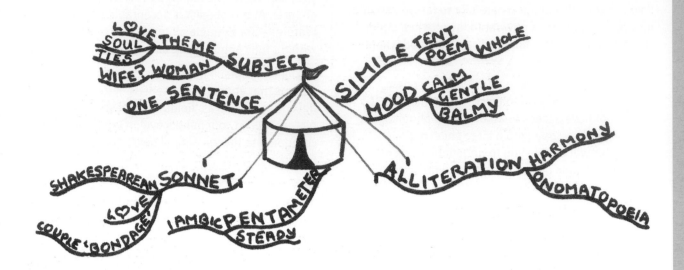

Writing about poems

Most exam questions on poetry fall into one of three broad categories:

1 **Unseen** poetry: you will be asked to comment on a poem which you will probably not have read before.

2 A **comparison** of two poems, usually unseen, often widely separated in period.

3 Questions on a **set** poet.

If writing about an **unseen** poem, read it, annotate it and Mind Map it. Instructions may be loose, e.g. 'Comment on what you find interesting'. Sometimes hints will be given. If the question is more specific, stick to what it asks you to do.

If **comparing** two poems, begin by comparing the obvious similarities and differences in subject and theme. These will usually be the basis of their similarity, and the reason for the examiner choosing them. Then analyse each poem in turn, looking at the features described in this chapter. Finally, summarise the main similarities and differences. If asked to say which you prefer, be sure to explain your preference.

Questions on a **set** poet may focus on one poem and ask you how typical it is of the poet. In this case you must use the poem to anchor your comments, but you have a wide scope within which to discuss other poems, always referring back to the given poem. If asked to comment on one feature, such as imagery, or a particular theme, do not just focus on whatever you know most about. However, you would usually earn credit by suggesting how the main feature was enhanced by other poetic devices, such as rhythm.

TRY THIS

1 **Write a critique of Robert Frost's 'The Silken Tent' (see page 119) using the notes given, together with your own observations.**

2 **Choose a short poem that you are studying. Photocopy, annotate and read it as suggested, then Mind Map its subject, theme(s), metre and rhythms, rhymes and imagery.**

3 **Test yourself on the whole chapter by copying the main branches of the Mind Map opposite, and then adding to them from memory.**

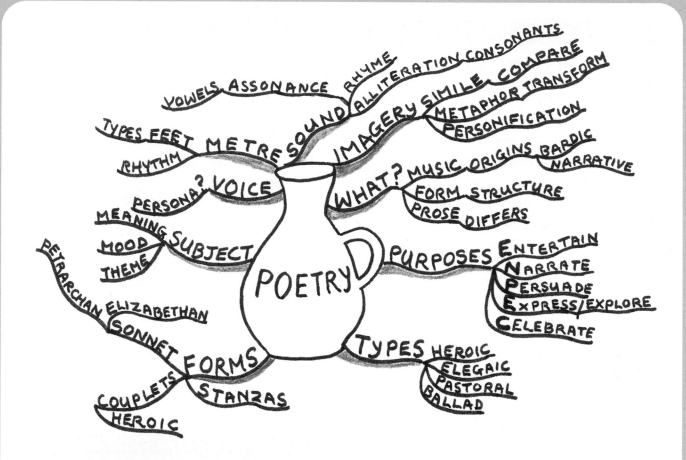

Summary

This chapter has told you the following:

- Poetry emphasises *form*, *sound* and *theme*.

- Poetic purposes can be summed up as *ENPEC*.

- A poem's *theme*, stemming from its *subject*, is its underlying idea; its *mood* is its emotional effect.

- A poem's *voice* is the persona in which it is presented.

- *Metre* refers to a pattern of *feet*. A metre has a set number of feet in each line.

- *Rhythmic variations* help to express sense.

- *Rhyme*, *alliteration* and *assonance* please the ear and enhance sense.

- *Verse forms* (e.g. the sonnet) may suit a particular purpose.

- *Diction* (choice of words) and *imagery* (*metaphors*, *similes*, *personification*) help to express the poet's meaning.

- Certain *movements* in poetry emphasise particular approaches and preoccupations; e.g. the *Metaphysicals* (conceits, closely argued), the *Augustans* (heroic couplets, intellect), and the *Romantics* (the individual, feelings, nature).

Start a Mind Map similar to the one shown below. As you work through the chapter add your own points and ideas, with particular reference to the text you are studying.

Chaucer's life

Knowing something about the kind of person Chaucer was and the kind of life he led will help you to understand his work. Remember the **TAT** technique – consider the relationship between:

Text
Author
Time or period.

The Canterbury Tales

The Canterbury Tales is a group of stories told by pilgrims travelling from the Tabard Inn in London to Canterbury Cathedral, the shrine of St Thomas à Becket. In 'The General Prologue' to the stories, Chaucer describes the individual pilgrims, and sets out the framework for the tales. The host suggests that each pilgrim tells a story on the way to

Canterbury and one on the way back, and the person who tells the story that is voted best will be treated to a dinner at the others' cost. It is likely that the text you are studying is 'The General Prologue', and/or one of the tales.

HINT

Even if 'The General Prologue' is not specifically set for study, it's a good idea to read it and become familiar with the characters. It will help you to understand the context in which the tale you are studying is told, and will give you an idea of the storyteller's immediate audience. It will also give you greater understanding of the interaction between the pilgrims as the tale is told. For example, the Franklin refers to the Squire's tale, the Pardoner interrupts the prologue to the Wife of Bath's tale, the Merchant tells his story in response to the Clerk's tale, and the Host comments throughout and uses his authority to maintain peace and harmony.

It is absolutely essential to read the description of the pilgrim who tells the tale you are studying. (You will probably find the description in your edition of the particular tale.) You will find out about the pilgrim's appearance, ideas and behaviour, and you will also get an idea of what Chaucer thinks about the individual. A key aspect of studying *The Canterbury Tales* is linking the tale and its teller, and 'The General Prologue' is the best place to start.

TRY THIS

1   Make a rough drawing or diagram of the pilgrims as they might appear when they are travelling. Use the order given in 'The General Prologue'. Highlight the character who tells the story you are studying, and use arrows, captions and/or speech bubbles to show the pilgrims with whom he or she travels and interacts.

2   Make your own Mind Map or list of present-day 'pilgrims'. What kinds of people would you include as representatives of modern society? What virtues and what failings would you want to illustrate?

    Divide the characters in your finished list into categories of class and occupation, and compare them with Chaucer's group of pilgrims.

3   How does the description of the teller of the tale you are studying help your understanding of the story? Make a Mind Map of your ideas.

Chaucer's range

Geoffrey Chaucer was an educated and cultured man, sophisticated and socially aware. Through his position as a court member and his work as a civil servant he gained knowledge and understanding of a variety of subjects – trade, money, the law, the structure and hierarchy of society. He was interested in medicine, astronomy and astrology; he was familiar with classical, French and Italian literature. Chaucer's life experience and learning is reflected in his poetry, where you will find references to all the above topics and more, including philosophy, religion, morality and marriage.

TRY THIS

Skim the text you are studying. Which of the topics in the above paragraph are mentioned or explored in detail? Make a Mind Map of your text's subject matter. You could include short quotations and the relevant line or page references. You could finish this Mind Map of the topics in the 'The General Prologue'.

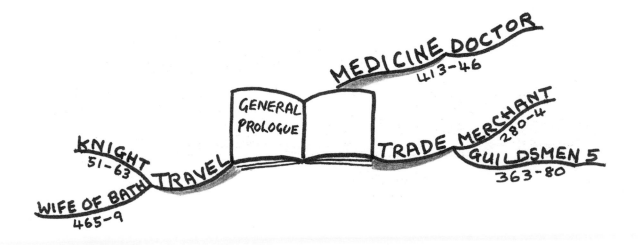

Social and historical background

An overall view of the social and historical context within which Chaucer wrote and which produced such a distinguished poet will help you to study your text with greater confidence and understanding. The first thing you should realise is that medieval society was much more rigid and structured than contemporary society. Attitudes and behaviour were governed by a fixed framework of beliefs, and a person's position in society was seen as an ordained part of an ordered social structure. There was little emphasis on individual fulfilment and achievement. When you read Chaucer, don't try to apply modern values and judge his characters and ideas according to contemporary views of people and society, but do look for how Chaucer presents characters who in their attitudes or behaviour challenge the established order.

Social structure

The structure of medieval society was feudal, that is, it was based on a social and political system in which the poor and illiterate peasant class worked on the land and were more or less owned by the masters they worked for. The social groupings of the characters in 'The General Prologue' to *The Canterbury Tales* give some idea of the position of different classes. The Knight with his family group heads the pilgrimage, reflecting his noble status; the middle

Questions

Draw a pyramid to represent medieval society. Mark in the position of the King and the position of the peasants, or *cherls*. Where do the characters from the text you are studying fit in? Draw or write them in. When you have finished, read the suggestions and comments in the answers on page 146.

classes are well represented by characters such as the Merchant, an overseas trader, and the Wife of Bath, a successful weaver; characters such as the Plowman and the Miller represent the lower orders.

Changing times

During Chaucer's lifetime rapid social change and political upheaval challenged the accepted order. Two important events affected the nature of society:

The Black Death, or bubonic plague

The Plague, brought into England by black rats, wiped out between 30 and 50 per cent of the population. This led to a shortage of labour, which meant that agricultural workers could ask for higher wages, and could also seek to be released from their feudal servitude.

Questions

1 The timeline below shows some important dates. Fill in any other events that you think are significant.

2 What kinds of disruptive, antisocial or rebellious behaviour appear in the text you are studying? Look for attitudes and behaviour that go against accepted ideas of what is morally and socially acceptable. What is Chaucer's attitude to this behaviour? Make notes or a Mind Map of your ideas, then read the suggestions in the answers on page 146.

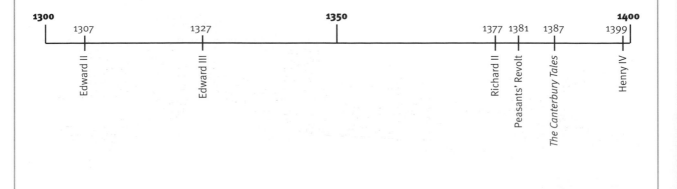

The Peasants' Revolt

This rebellion of 1381, led by Wat Tyler and Jack Straw and sparked by the introduction of a poll tax, reflected the peasants' desire for freedom and justice. Chaucer's apartment in the City of London overlooked the road on which the group of rebels marched to London, and he may have seen the twenty headless bodies in the London streets described by a contemporary account of Wat Tyler's attack on the Flemish weavers! In 'The Nun's Priest's Tale', Chaucer refers to this event:

> Certes, he Jakke Straw and his meynee*
> Ne made nevere shoutes half so shrille
> Whan that they wolden any Fleming kille
>   ('The Nun's Priest's Tale', lines 628–30)
> *followers

Religious background

The Church

The Church, that is the English branch of the Roman Catholic Church, was central to medieval society. It was a huge, complex organisation with enormous influence and significance. The Church owned about one-fifth of England's land, and employed about one-tenth of England's work force. Many were involved in the spiritual work of the Church, dedicating their lives to the service of God through ministry and prayer. Chaucer's Nun, Parson, Monk and Friar are among this number. Others, like the Summoner and the Pardoner, served the Church's legal and financial interests. Think of the Church as a major employer, offering viable careers not only to those with religious vocations but to those with skills in a range of areas – financial, medical, managerial. Chaucer's inclusion of nine professional Church men and women in his group of thirty pilgrims gives you some idea of the Church's dominance.

Corruption

Like any powerful institution with huge assets in cash, land and property, the medieval Church had within its ranks those who were corrupt and dishonest. Among Chaucer's pilgrims there are characters, such as the Pardoner, who for his own gain unscrupulously exploits the faith of the congregations to whom he preaches:

> I preche of no thing but for coveitise*
>   ('The Pardoner's Prologue and Tale', line 138)
> *covetousness, greed

The Monk is less morally deplorable than the Pardoner, but his love of worldly pleasures falls far short of the monastic ideal:

> This ilke Monk leet olde thinges pace,*
> And heeld after the newe world the space.
>   ('The General Prologue', lines 175–6)
> *pass away

> **TRY THIS**
>
> **What characteristics should the religious figures possess? How does Chaucer portray them? Make notes or a Mind Map to show how far the characters live up to the ideals of behaviour that would be expected of them. An example has been started for you below.**

Important concepts and ideas

Some of the ideas and concepts that are central to Chaucer's poetry are specific to the period in which he wrote and are difficult to translate into modern English. The ideas described on the following pages are crucial to a number of texts including 'The General Prologue', 'The Merchant's Tale', 'The Wife of Bath's Prologue and Tale', 'The Franklin's Tale', 'The Clerk's Tale', and 'The Knight's Tale'.

Gentillesse (noun); gentil (adjective)

This word refers to the kind of behaviour – courteous, generous, refined, morally correct – that would be expected of people of noble birth. It was supposed that birth and virtue were linked, and that the quality of 'gentillesse' was inherited by those high on the social scale.

> **HINT**
>
> Chaucer presents the concept of 'gentillesse' in different ways, and challenges the accepted view. When you come across the idea of 'gentillesse', ask yourself what is Chaucer's attitude and what point he is making about birth and virtuous behaviour.

Vileynie

This word sounds like the modern 'villain', and its meaning in Chaucer's work has some similarities to its modern application. 'Vileynie' describes the kind of behaviour, uneducated, coarse or even sinful, that would be associated with a 'villein' or 'cherl', a person of the lowest class.

> **HINT**
>
> Look out for the contexts in which Chaucer presents the concept of 'vileynie', and consider how far he associates types of behaviour with social status.

Courtly love

This idea is part of a literary tradition that sees love as a formal, elegant game played by people of high birth. The rules of the game were set down in a thirteenth-century poem called *The Romance of the Rose*, which Chaucer knew very well. Medieval courtly love involved a triangle: a woman, her husband, and another man who was in love with the woman. It may sound like the staple diet of soap opera story lines; the difference is in the 'high tone' and strict formality of the proceedings, which elevated the art of love to something like religion. The rules were that the lovesick suitor would suffer as from an illness or injury. He would suffer in silence and in secret, feeling that he would die if the lady did not take pity on him, and would reveal his feelings only in the form of poems and songs written to his loved one, who was raised almost to the status of a goddess. When the lady eventually showed pity and generosity, as a reward for his devotion and loyalty, the lover was elevated and ennobled by the experience, acquiring virtue through the playing out of the ritual. What about the husband, you might think? Well, the tradition of courtly love developed in a period when marriage wasn't based on love but on issues of land, money and dynasty. Did people really behave like this? It's possible that in courtly and high society, life imitated art in the way that in our society television and films can influence behaviour and attitudes. However, it is highly unlikely that the art of courtly love was practised among the lower social classes.

Ask yourself how Chaucer presents courtly love in the text you are studying. Is his attitude critical, mocking, exploratory?

Humours

No, this isn't about being funny – it's a term to do with medicine and science. It was believed that human beings were made up of parts of the four elements – air, water, earth and fire – and that each element corresponded to one of the four *humours*, or vital juices. People's character and personality depended on which humour was predominant in their make-up; the ideal was to have a balance of all four humours. The diagram shows the relationship between the elements, humours and personality types.

Element	Humour	Complexion (temperament)
Air	Blood	Sanguine
Fire	Choler	Choleric
Earth	Melancholy or bile	Melancholy
Water	Phlegm	Phlegmatic

> **CHECKLIST**
>
> The words used to describe medieval humours are still in use today. Learn them and practise using them – you will find them a useful addition to your vocabulary when you are discussing characters from Chaucer – and characters in texts by other writers.
>
> ✓ **Sanguine** – hopeful, confident
> ✓ **Choleric** – angry, quick-tempered
> ✓ **Melancholy** – depressed, miserable, dejected
> ✓ **Phlegmatic** – cold, sluggish, not easily moved
>
> Put another tick next to each word when you have learnt it and used it.

1 What word means behaviour that is the opposite of 'vileynie'?

2 What modern English word, deriving from 'cherl', describes rude, surly behaviour? (Use a dictionary to find a word that sounds like 'cherl' but is spelt differently.)

3 Name the four humours or types of character.

(Answers on page 146)

Chaucer's language

Chaucer's language is known as Middle English, so called because it comes between Old English and Modern English. The grammar and vocabulary of Chaucer's English are influenced by a number of languages – French, Latin, and Anglo-Saxon (Old English). Chaucer could have written *The Canterbury Tales* in French, the language of the court, but he chose to write in his native dialect, reflecting and contributing to the emergence of English as the main language. Chaucer wrote in an East Midland dialect, with some London elements. Modern Standard English derives from this dialect, so to some extent Chaucer's language is easy to understand, or at least looks vaguely familiar. However, there are some important differences to bear in mind.

Wordy matters

Some words that Chaucer uses have no equivalent in Modern English. Some 'job titles' have disappeared, such as 'limitour' (a friar licensed to beg within certain limits) and 'summoner' (an official whose job was to summon or order wrongdoers to attend the ecclesiastical court). Unfamiliar words such as these present few problems, because you will look up their meaning and become familiar with them. You need to be more careful with words that look just like modern English, but whose meaning is different or has changed. For example, some characters' 'job titles' look as if they refer to modern occupations, but they need more interpretation than a straightforward modern application. For example:

word	modern meaning	Chaucer's meaning
merchant	shopkeeper, seller of goods	overseas trader, financier, money dealer
clerk	office worker	scholar, professional academic

TRY THIS

1 Add more examples to the chart.

2 What is the profession and position of each of the pilgrims referred to in the illustration?

You could find out what kind of experience (a) the churchgoers (b) the guests are likely to have!

Watch out for these

If you assume that a word in Chaucer will have the same meaning as the modern English word it looks like, you will miss some of the meaning and subtlety of his work, and your answers may show limited understanding and response.

For example, The Friar is described as 'a ful solempne man' ('The General Prologue', line 209). You might think of 'solempne' as 'solemn'. However, it means dignified, impressive, important – words far more applicable to the Friar, who isn't in the least bit solemn! What about 'Tho rowned she a pistel in his ere' ('The Wife of Bath's Tale', line 1021)? You might think that the line describes the old lady thrusting a pistol in the knight's ear (you might also think that is what he deserves). However, 'pistel' means 'message', which of course makes much more sense in the context.

> **HINT**
>
> **Always see words in their context and consider the overall meaning and tone of the passage.**

> **CHECKLIST**
>
> **Use the following process to acquire a sound understanding of your text's meaning:**
>
> ✓ **Skim through the text to get a general idea of what it's about.**
>
> ✓ **Jot down, or explain to a friend, the impression you have of the characters and what happens.**
>
> ✓ **Read the text again, and use the Glossary and notes in your edition to help you form an accurate picture.**
>
> ✓ **Remember to look up words which seem familiar.**
>
> ✓ **Make a list or Mind Map of unfamiliar vocabulary.**
>
> ✓ **Practise using the words – turn them into a chant or a song, or have a mock Middle English conversation with a friend.**
>
> ✓ **Don't use a modern English translation – it's a much better idea to become familiar with the original.**

> **TRY THIS**
>
> **Make a list or Mind Map of words in the text you are studying that have changed their meaning. Make another one of words that no longer exist.**

> **Questions**
>
> What do the following words (frequently used in 'The Canterbury Tales') mean?
>
> **a)** er **b)** eke or eek **c)** honest **d)** swich
>
> (Answers on page 146)

Getting grammatical

The best way to become familiar with the grammatical structure and syntax (order of words) in Chaucer's English is to read the poem out loud and concentrate on the rhythm and meaning. You will become used to some grammatical forms that we no longer use. For example:

- *es* is used to show possession: 'That womman is for mannes helpe ywroght' ('The Merchant's Tale', line 112); *es* also shows a plural.

- *y* is added to the beginning of a word to make a past participle: 'And many a maid yslain hirself, allas!' ('The Franklin's Tale', line 693).

- some pronouns have different forms: 'its' can mean 'his' or 'hers'; 'hem' means 'them; 'hire' means 'their'.

- word order can be different, with the subject of the sentence not coming at the beginning, as is usual in Modern English. Chaucer says 'A marchant was ther with a forked berd' ('The General Prologue', line 272), whereas Modern English would say 'There was a merchant…'.

> **HINT**
>
> **If you are having difficulties, decide first on the subject of the sentence.**

Style focus

Poetry

Chaucer's work is poetry, written to be read aloud and listened to by an audience in an age which had no printing press and in which books were scarce. *The Canterbury Tales* is written in rhyming couplets, also known as **heroic couplets**. The main metre of the poem is **iambic pentameter**. Each line has five groups of syllables with the stress falling on the second syllable. This sounds more complicated than it is – just try reading some lines out loud, following a sound pattern like 'de-dum'. Use the following lines as an example:

> Whan that Aprille with his shoures soote
> The droghte of March hath perced to the roote

CHECKLIST

Follow these tips for getting to grips with the sound of Chaucer's poetry.

✓ On the whole, pronounce all letters, including the final *e* and the *k* at the beginning of words like 'knight'.

✓ Don't pronounce the final *e* if the next word begins with a vowel or an *h*.

✓ Read the lines out loud. You could try whispering, shouting, singing, marching in time to them. (Give appropriate warnings to anyone nearby.)

✓ Read passages aloud with or to a friend.

✓ Listen to a tape recording of a professional reading – try your school or local library or bookshop for a copy.

✓ Make your own tape recording of selected passages from the text you are studying.

Questions

Choose the best answer to the following questions. Add your own words and ideas.

1 What is the effect of the rhythm in this description of the Squire?
'He was as fresshe* as is the month of May.'
('The General Prologue', line 92)
*lively, energetic
The rhythm suggests that the Squire is:

a) lazy **b)** lighthearted **c)** slow **d)** tired
e) youthful.

2 What is emphasised by the rhythm in this description of the Parson?
'A bettre prest I trowe that nowher noon is.'
('The General Prologue', line 526)

a) the Parson's love of gambling

b) Chaucer's admiration of the Parson

c) the parson's good qualities

3 What is the effect of this rhyming couplet?
   'She wende* nevere han come in swich a trappe.
'Allas,' quod she, 'that evere this sholde happe!' ' ('The Franklin's Tale', lines 670–1)
*imagined
The rhyming sound of 'trappe' and 'happe' creates a feeling of:

a) running away **b)** a trap snapping shut
c) the speaker's despair **d)** happiness.

(Answers on page 146)

TRY THIS

Choose a passage from the text you are studying and make notes on the effect of the rhyme and rhythm of the verse.

And namely when a man is old and hoor; Thanne is syf athe fruit of his tresor.

The rhyming words really emphasise January's age and the way he sees marriage as a financial contract.

HINT

Your exam answer will be improved if you can discuss the effect of rhyme and rhythm. Always listen for the effect of the rhythm, and how it affects the meaning and your response to the verse.

Sound effects and imagery

Chaucer's use of alliteration, simile and metaphor is an integral part of his poetry, adding to and creating its effect.

Alliteration

Chaucer chooses alliterative words to increase the effectiveness of his lines, enhancing the meaning of phrases through the repetition of sounds. For example, note the repetition of the *b* sound in this description of the Miller:

Ful big he was of brawn, and eek of bones.
   ('The General Prologue', line 548)

This emphasises the Miller's brutal strength.

Similes

Chaucer chooses comparisons that enliven and add to his descriptions. The simile that describes the hairs on the Miller's wart suggests something of his animalistic, unpleasant nature.

> Reed as the brustles of a sowes eris
> ('The General Prologue', line 558).

In contrast, the sincerity of Dorigen's love for her husband is movingly expressed in the comparison:

> That loveth hire housbounde as hire hertes lyf
> ('The Franklin's Tale', line 143).

Metaphors

Poetic images heighten Chaucer's description and narrative. Some images are woven into the text and gain their effect from allusion and repetition, such as the presentation of the Parson as a shepherd and his parishioners as his flock in 'The General Prologue', or the image of the prison in 'The Knight's Tale'. The image of the garden is central to 'The Merchant's Tale' and to 'The Franklin's Tale'; the black rocks in 'The Franklin's Tale' have metaphorical force and acquire various levels of symbolic meaning, as, for example, when Dorigen turns them into symbols of her anxiety and the focal point of her misgivings about the divine ordering of the universe. In 'The Wife of Bath's Prologue', the thread of commercial imagery suggests something about her view of marriage. Other images vividly evoke the essence of an aspect of character, such as the description of the Franklin: 'It snewed in his hous of mete and drinke' ('The General Prologue', line 347). The image suggests abundance and generosity, adding to the picture of the Franklin's hospitable nature.

TRY THIS

1   **From the text you are studying, choose a few short passages to illustrate Chaucer's use of alliteration and simile. Make some notes to help you discuss the effect of each passage.**

2   **Make a Mind Map of the central images in the text you are studying.**

HINT

Your exam answer will be improved if you not only identify imagery but also discuss its effect.

Conversational or colloquial tone

Another feature of Chaucer's style is the colloquial tone that captures the flow and rhythm of conversational speech. The conversational style of *The Canterbury Tales* is achieved through a number of techniques, including the use of little phrases characteristic of colloquial speech, such as 'sikerly' (certainly, truly) and 'pardee' (by God, certainly). In 'The General Prologue', the use of such expressions reinforce the link between the reader and Chaucer the poet-narrator. In the tales, an effect of realism is gained as the storytellers use these little tags to punctuate their narratives, providing us with a constant reminder of the tales' audience and context. For example, the Franklin refers to 'the knight of which I speke of thus' ('The Franklin's Tale', line 35), and the Merchant says of a married man, 'He may not be decyved, as I gesse' ('The Merchant's Tale', line 44). The Knight refers to the length of his story: 'I have, God woot, a large feeld to ere' ('The Knight's Tale', line 28).

? Find some examples of colloquial tone from the text you are studying. What do they add to the effect?

Irony

Chaucer's tone is characterised by his use of irony. You will find examples of this technique in many of his descriptions of the pilgrims, particularly those whose moral weaknesses Chaucer wishes to expose. Chaucer does not always openly condemn the characters he criticises, but uses a variety of ironic statements and devices to indicate his disapproval – or in some cases, his amusement.

You will find good examples of Chaucer's irony in his description of the Monk in 'The General Prologue'. The Monk's ideas are presented through reported speech:

> 'What[1] sholde he studie and make himselven wood[2],
> Upon a book in cloistre alwey to poure,
> Or swinken[3] with his handes, and laboure,
> As Austin[4] bit?
>   ('The General Prologue', lines 184–7)
> [1]why   [2]mad   [3]work   [4]St Augustine

Chaucer repeats the Monk's words, allowing him to condemn himself as he declares his rejection of the monastic ideal, seeing no contradiction in the way of life he has vowed to uphold and the kind of life he actually lives. The irony is clear as Chaucer pretends to agree with him:

> And I seyde his opinion was good
>   ('The General Prologue', line 183)

Read aloud the passage quoted on page 130 ('The General Prologue', lines 184–7). Try different tones of voice. Which tone most effectively conveys the meaning of the lines?

Hint: Imagine a present-day Chaucer saying of a doctor (for example): 'Why should he spend his time caring for his patients? He's off to play golf! And do you know, I think he's got a good point.'

You may well have chosen a sarcastic tone of voice as the most effective. Irony is like a written form of sarcasm – but it is more subtle, using a wider range of linguistic techniques and creating a broader spectrum of effects.

Irony in the tales

Look for the ironic presentation of character and theme in the tales.

You will find irony in the presentation of characters where there is a difference between Chaucer's and our own perception of characters and the way they see themselves. In 'The Merchant's Tale', for example, January sees himself as a vigorous young lover like Paris, the lover of Helen of Troy.

> . . . he that night in armes wolde hire streyne
> Harder than evere Paris dide Eleyne.
> 'The Merchant's Tale', lines 541–2)

In fact, January is old and feeble and much more like Helen's deceived husband.

Themes are sometimes treated ironically. For example, Chaucer's treatment of love, marriage and the courtly tradition can be ironic. In 'The Miller's Tale' courtly love is effectively debunked through the ironic way in which Chaucer presents the characters as part of this tradition, then shows them behaving in a way quite contrary to it.

TRY THIS

What is Chaucer's attitude to the characters and the themes in the text you are studying? Is it admiring, gently mocking, critical, amused? Does it vary throughout the tale? What is Chaucer's intention in the tale? Make notes or a Mind Map of how irony is used to create particular effects.

Chaucer's humour

Irony and humour combine in much of Chaucer's work. (Don't confuse this meaning of humour with the medieval meaning! Look up **humours** (see page 126) if you are not sure.) Humour is created through tone, exaggeration, contrasts, through the treatment of themes such as the courtly love tradition and the fabliau genre. (A 'fabliau' is a short story displaying broad, sexually explicit humour. 'The Miller's Tale' reflects this genre.)

? What humorous effects does Chaucer create in the text you are studying? How are these effects created?

Chaucer's rhetoric

An important aspect of Chaucer's style is his use of the poetic art of rhetoric. Poets in the Middle Ages were not expected to be original, but to use certain rhetorical techniques to embellish old stories and give them new life. Examples of Chaucer's use of rhetoric include:

- **Apostrophe or exclamatio** – an address to a person or concept, as in 'The Merchant's Tale': 'O perilous fyr, that in the bedstraw bredeth' (Merchant's Tale, line 571).

- **Exemplum** – a story that gives an 'example' of a moral point. The Wife of Bath, the Franklin and the Pardoner are among the pilgrims who make use of this technique to strengthen their tales.

- **Sententia** – a general truth about life, often beginning with a comment such as: 'Ful sooth is seyde'.

FACTFILE

In 'The Franklin's Tale', Dorigen gives 21 consecutive 'exempla', all examples of women who killed themselves rather than suffer dishonour.

HINT

Your exam answer will be improved if you discuss the effect of Chaucer's use of rhetorical techniques. Think about what the storytellers' use of rhetoric suggests about their characters and how it contributes to the tales' particular characteristics, such as humour and irony.

'The Wife of Bath's Tale'
Who tells the story?

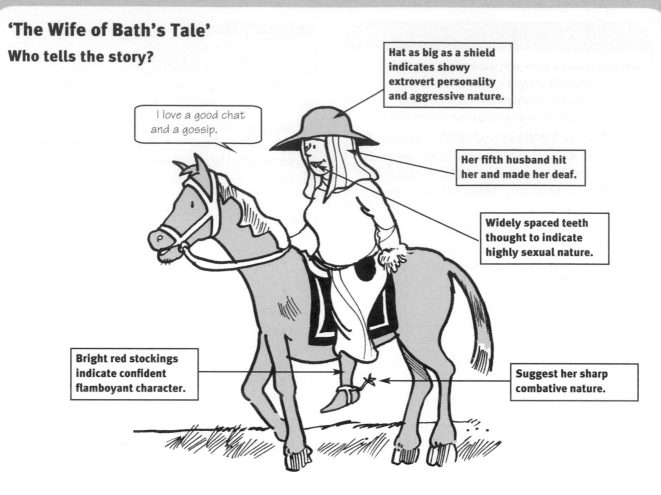

I love a good chat and a gossip.

Hat as big as a shield indicates showy extrovert personality and aggressive nature.

Her fifth husband hit her and made her deaf.

Widely spaced teeth thought to indicate highly sexual nature.

Bright red stockings indicate confident flamboyant character.

Suggest her sharp combative nature.

Tales and tellers

Although you are studying only one or two tales for examination purposes, you will find it helpful to see *The Canterbury Tales* as a whole, with the characters and their stories presenting an entertaining, complex, interwoven structure in which personalities and themes relate to and reflect each other. Part of the realism of the poem comes from the way the characters react to each other and each other's stories, such as the Franklin's somewhat fawning compliments to the Squire, and the Friar's laughing comment about the Wife's preamble to her tale (for which she pays him back with her derogatory references to friars in her tale!).

What is the story about?

The prologue

Before Alison gets to her story, she takes nearly 900 lines to tell us about herself and her married life. She challenges the Church's authority to criticise women like her for marrying more than once, and she argues in favour of marriage and sexual activity. Her first three husbands were rich and old and she could take their land and money from them. Her fourth husband wasn't so easy to handle – he was unfaithful to her, and she tried to pay him back by making him jealous.

When he died she married Jankyn, who mistreated her and, as an anti-feminist, was determined to dominate her. They had a bitter struggle for supremacy which she eventually won.

The tale

In the days of King Arthur, a knight rapes a woman, and the Queen spares his life on the condition that he finds the answer to the question: what do women most desire? An old woman gives him the answer, that women most desire supremacy, but in return for the answer the knight must marry her. He is reluctant to do so because she is old, ugly and of low birth. After lecturing him on these matters, the woman gives him the choice: an old, ugly wife who will be faithful to him, or a young, beautiful one of whom he could never be sure. The knight asks the woman to choose, so conceding dominance to her, and is rewarded by her turning into a young, beautiful woman.

Main character

Alison, the Wife of Bath

Alison is a complex character, who has been described as both comic and tragic. In some ways she is like a conventional comic figure, reminiscent of characters in allegorical plays, with her outrageous opinions and larger-than-life personality exaggerated for comic effect. However, she is a far more fully developed character than such a description suggests. Her clamorous insistence on 'maistrye' and her triumphant attack on male textual authority may be seen in a different light when we consider the nature of her much-vaunted experience. She was married at 12 years of age, had a succession of elderly husbands, and was beaten by one of them. Her tale begins with a rape.

Themes and key ideas

'Maistrye', love, marriage, gentillesse

Critical approaches and interpretations

You will come across different critical interpretations of the Wife's character and tale, many of which are reflected in examination questions. You could prepare your response to these points:

- Issues of power and authority in the prologue and tale – what does the text say about money and property? What does it say about textual authorities such as the Bible and the writings of saints?

- Allegorical readings of the prologue and tale – could the text present a comment on the ruling style of Richard II?

- Feminist ideas in the prologue and tale – does the text represent the Wife as a 'feminist' figure? Is her desire for 'maistrye' seen as an unacceptable illustration of aggression and coarseness, or is it an admirable response to male domination?

'The Merchant's Tale'
Who tells the story? What's it about?

A sixty-year-old knight decides to get married, because of the pleasure, comfort and security of the married state. He asks his friends to find him a wife, who must be young and pliable, and finally chooses the young and beautiful May. Damian, a squire in January's household, loves May and longs for her to take pity on him (look under **courtly love** on page 126). He writes May a secret letter, which she reads and throws in a cesspit, determining that she will show him her favour. January has a private garden built for himself and his wife.

January suddenly goes blind, and becomes very possessive of May, insisting always on having her in his grasp. May, longing for an opportunity to show her favour to Damian, makes him a copy of the garden key. As January and May converse in the garden, Damian slips in and climbs a pear

I will now tell you about my business profit.

tree. May tells January that she has a craving for pears and asks him if she can stand on his back to reach them. January obliges and May shins up the tree, where she and Damian consummate their love.

The King of the Underworld, Pluto, and his wife Proserpina have seen the whole thing. Pluto, supporting the deceived January, restores his sight at that very moment. Proserpina, supporting all women against male accusers, gives May a ready answer. May tells January that she was told that this was the way to cure his blindness. January is reassured.

Characters

January

January wants sexual pleasure and spiritual salvation, and in his moral blindness and self-delusion thinks that marriage to May will secure him both.

What is he like?

The following words may be used to describe January. Add your own ideas to the list. Illustrate each word with an example and short quotation from the text.

> naive, hypocritical, lustful, insensitive, gullible, self-deluding, vulnerable, touching, possessive

The lovers

May and Damian are presented as stock characters in the courtly love tradition. May fulfils the role of the adored lady who graciously takes 'pitee' on Damian; Damian feels 'peyne' that can be cured only by May's generosity ('franchise'). As characters, they are types rather than individuals.

Themes and key ideas

Courtly love, marriage, deception, battle between the sexes.

HINT

Look for irony in tone and visual images. For example, the constant references to May as 'gentil' and 'fresshe' are juxtaposed with comic images of surreptitious and overwhelming sexual desire – secret notes being read in the privy, Damian crouching in the pear tree.

HINT

You might admire January's thoughtful behaviour to his squire Damian, and feel sympathy for the way he is deceived by a servant he likes and trusts. This approach reflects humanist criticism, which discusses characters in terms of psychological realism. A different approach would see January's attitude to Damian as admirable, but as an expression of his lord's role.

TRY THIS

1 **What view of marriage do you find in 'The Merchant's Tale'? Make notes or a Mind Map to prepare an answer.**

Hint: You could look at the marriage of January and May in terms of their motives for marrying and their treatment of each other; the debate between Justinus and Placebo (lines 265–363); the intervention of Pluto and Proserpina; the treatment of adultery as part of the courtly love tradition and through Biblical parallels.

2 **Choose three passages from the text that illustrate Chaucer's use of irony. Explain your choices to a friend.**

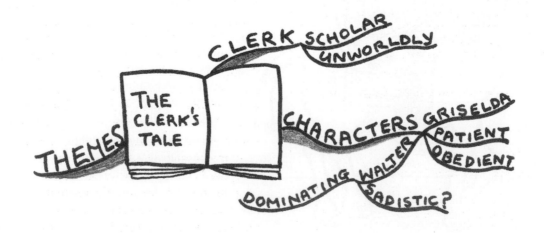

Critical approaches and interpretations

Most critical comment focuses on the presentation of marriage and courtly love in the tale. You could prepare your response to these points:

- How and to what extent does the tale mock or undermine the convention of courtly love?

- Do you have any sympathy for January?

More about marriage

'The Clerk's Tale' and 'The Franklin's Tale' address similar themes to the tales discussed above. You could complete these Mind Maps of the Clerk's and Franklin's stories, or make one of your own.

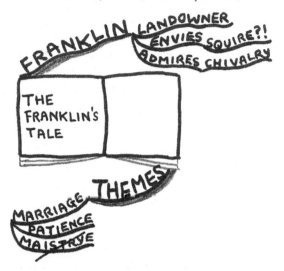

Writing about Chaucer

You will get a good grade for your Chaucer essay if it is relevant, clearly expressed, well structured and makes appropriate use of quotation and reference.

CHECKLIST

You could follow some of these suggestions for preparing your text.

✓ **Make a Mind Map of the content of the text.**

✓ **Make a Mind Map of characters and themes.**

✓ **Select short passages that illustrate key aspects of the text – theme, character, imagery.**

✓ **Select short quotations to illustrate your comments.**

✓ **Plan answers to questions that have been previously set.**

✓ **Make up your own short questions on the text.**

✓ **Make up your own essay titles on the text.**

TRY THIS

The opening lines of 'The General Prologue' suggest an optimistic view of the world. To what extent is this impression confirmed in the rest of the prologue or in the tale you are studying?

CHECKLIST

✓ **Refer to the text as poetry.**

✓ **Discuss the effect of poetic techniques.**

✓ **Show your awareness of Chaucer's humour.**

✓ **Demonstrate your awareness of Chaucer's use of irony.**

✓ **Integrate short quotations into your answer.**

✓ **Use the form of the word that is correct in the context (e.g. gentil/gentillesse: someone is 'gentil'; someone shows 'gentillesse'.)**

Writing the essay

The following checklists will remind you of points that have been made in this chapter. You are more likely to get a good grade if you discuss your Chaucer text appropriately and accurately.

Before you read the following answer, decide how you would approach this question. Make notes or a mini Mind Map. If you like, you could write the introductory paragraph or more of the essay. Remember that there is no specific 'right' answer – any valid response showing knowledge and understanding of the text, supported by reference and quotation, is acceptable. The answer reproduced here is one response; yours may be entirely different.

Suggested answer

'The General Prologue' opens with a lively evocation of spring and the natural impulses that stir the whole of nature at this time of year. The combination of the 'shoures soote', the warm west wind and the blossoming flowers[1] creates an optimistic impression of the power of nature to renew and regenerate. Chaucer suggests that human beings too respond to the rhythmic pull of nature and are filled with the desire to go on pilgrimages. The idea of the pilgrims making their way to Canterbury to give thanks at the shrine of Thomas à Becket offers an image of people as fundamentally good, harnessing the animal vitality awakened by the coming of spring to their sense of religious duty.[2] However,[3] the presentation of the Pardoner and his tale seems to contradict this optimistic view of the world, focusing as it does on the cynical selfishness of an amoral character who exploits the simple religious faith of church congregations in order to line his own pocket.

In the prologue to his tale, the Pardoner shocks his audience with his confession of the tricks of his trade.[4] He describes how he displays his documents and the 'cloutes' and 'bones' that he passes off as saints' relics, and makes the outrageous claim that he has the power and authority to absolve people from their sins if they make offerings to these 'relics'.[5] The Pardoner openly declares his viciousness and his lack of concern for the 'lewed people' who are taken in by his histrionic performance.

'I rekke nevere, whan that they be beryed,
Though that hir soules goon a-blakeberyed!'[6]

The feeling of warmth and renewal experienced at the beginning of 'The General Prologue'[7] is replaced by a sense of the depravity of which people are capable. The Pardoner is motivated solely by avarice.

'For myn entente is nat but for to winne,
And nothing for correcioun o sinne'

... and yet this is the very sin he preaches against. Such hypocrisy surely displays human nature at its worst, evil, irresponsible and self-centred, and leads us towards a far from optimistic view of a world in which vice seems to flourish.

At the same time,[8] it is true to say that although Chaucer's Pardoner does present an accurate, realistic picture of many corrupt pardoners in the fourteenth century, he also belongs to a conventional literary tradition of morality figures. In some ways[9] he is a personification of False Seeming or Misleading Appearance, an allegorical figure from *The Romance of the Rose* who openly confessed his inner motives and boasted of his power to deceive. To a certain extent the Pardoner is placed in a framework of morality. While his confession is undoubtedly shocking and appalling, it could be argued that it is not entirely realistic and that its conventional aspect lessens the impact of its evil, so that we can on one level enjoy his blatant self-revelations knowing that eventually a more moral, optimistic[10] world view will be re-established.

The Pardoner's story and sermon may be seen as a celebration of the art of preaching. Although the Pardoner perverts the spiritual purpose of the sermon, he presents a powerful piece of rhetoric that evokes a sense of the horror of sin. He makes effective use of rhetorical devices[11] such as exclamatio as when he

declares 'O wombe! O bely! O stinking cod', and illustrates his attack on gluttony with strong exempla and references to textual authority. The Pardoner holds the attention of the congregation and indeed the audience of pilgrims with his range of tone and methods, one minute delivering harrowing biblical stories, the next jokingly mimicking the sound of a drunk man's breathing: 'Sampsoun, Sampsoun!' He is a masterly storyteller, enhancing the gripping tale of the three revellers with dialogue and description, moving from their encounter with the haunting figure of the old man to their brutally casual deaths with practised aplomb.

At the end of his story the Pardoner strikes a sober, moving note with his prayer:

'And Jhesu Christ, that is our soules leche,
So graunte yow his pardoun to receive,
For that is best; I wol yow nat deceive.'

These lines engender a feeling of optimism. They focus on the possibility of redemption, perhaps even for a figure as evil as the Pardoner. It is true that doubt is immediately cast on the Pardoner's sincerity at this point, as he goes on to invite the pilgrims to pay 'Nobles or pens' to kiss the false relics and receive his false pardon, so enraging the Host. However, at the Knight's intervention the Host and Pardoner make peace and order is established. Although the Pardoner's prologue and tale hardly reflects the warm optimism of 'The General Prologue', it offers a celebration of human nature at its most depraved and its most brilliant, and an exhilarating, dramatic experience.[12]

Good points about the essay:

1 textual detail

2 relates to question

3 introduces argument

4 develops argument

5 integrated quotation

6 illustrative quotation

7 focus on question

8 links paragraphs

9 literary and historical context

10 focus on question

11 style/language

12 clear conclusion

Questions

1 In what century did Chaucer write *The Canterbury Tales*?

2 *The Canterbury Tales* is:
   a) a drama b) a story c) a poem.

3 *The Canterbury Tales* is written in:
   a) a mixture of French and English
   b) Old English
   c) Middle English
   d) Anglo-Saxon.

4 The main rhythm of *The Canterbury Tales* is…

5 The characters in the text I am studying are:

6 The themes in the text I am studying are:

7 An effective use of the rhyming couplet in my text is:

8 It is effective because…

(Answers on page 146)

Summary

This chapter has told you about:

- **aspects of Chaucer's life and work**

- **aspects of medieval society**

- **concepts and ideas such as 'gentillesse' and courtly love**

- **Chaucer's language: vocabulary and grammar**

- **Chaucer's poetic style, including imagery and rhetoric**

- **irony in Chaucer's work**

- **outlines of various tales**

- **how to write about Chaucer**

PREVIEW

This chapter focuses on improving written work by drafting and proofreading. It deals with:

- **drafting**
- **sequencing and paragraphing**
- **proofreading**
- **punctuation**
- **common errors**

Drafting and proofreading

Drafting refers to the process of writing a 'first draft', then putting it aside for a while, then finally rereading it with a fresh perspective and making improvements. At this stage the kind of improvements you make may be on a fairly broad scale.

- You may feel that you need to change the sequencing of ideas. It may be possible to do this simply by switching around paragraphs, but it may be necessary to rewrite the beginnings and endings of the paragraphs in order to retain the flow of ideas.

- You may discover that you have left out something important. Again, if you insert a new sentence or paragraph, make sure that the new version still flows grammatically and in terms of ideas.

- Some sentences may now seem unclear and need to be reworded. If it seems that your reader will be unclear of your meaning and have to backtrack, even for a moment, you need to reword.

- Some sentences may seem awkward, perhaps because you were working out your ideas as you wrote. If you have to keep pausing in mid-sentence in order to grasp a number of interrelated clauses, check whether you can make the sentence more streamlined by re-ordering it. This is most easily done on a computer; on paper, use arrows, or rewrite between lines in a different colour.

- You may need to check the meanings or spellings of some words, or to check details or quotations given as evidence.

You may feel that all this is a waste of time, and that you can get it right first time. Almost certainly, you will in fact be able to improve on your first effort. If, on the other hand, you find yourself getting bogged down in major revisions of your first draft, or writing several quite different drafts and never quite managing to say what you mean, this is a sign of inadequate planning. Next time Mind Map and sequence your ideas more

thoroughly, and have your evidence in order ready to insert where appropriate.

In exams you won't have time to draft and redraft a whole essay, although you may find it worth drafting the first and last paragraphs. Again, swift Mind Mapping will help you to develop your ideas and get them in order before you start.

Proofreading is what you do at the stage when you know you've got your paragraphs in order, arguments (or events) linked, and quotations in place. You should now be looking for errors in spelling, punctuation and grammar. In coursework, or in the exam, you will lose marks for these, however good your work is as a whole. In particular, if you make simple mistakes, it does make a bad impression that may dispose a reader to underestimate your other strengths. If you suspect that you are dyslexic, however, it may be possible to have this taken into account if you have taken a test that proves this.

If it seems that you may have to mark a lot of corrections, you could mark them with a coloured pen, so that they stand out. If you think that there will only be a few, and that you will be able to hand in this copy, use pencil, then the pen that you used for the draft.

To identify your weaknesses, check at least ten pages of your *marked* written work. Whenever you find a mistake of the kind listed in the grid opposite, make a mark in pencil (so you can reuse it). Then total your mistakes to see where you need to focus.

Punctuation

A major exam board has identified inadequate control of punctuation as one of the biggest causes for concern in candidates' continuous writing. The commonest error is the use of the comma as an all-purpose pause indicator. In particular it is used where in fact a new sentence should be started, with a full stop and capital letter. If you have any doubts about what constitutes a sentence refer to Chapter 2.

Another common error cited is the over-use of the dash. Students sometimes use it for a variety of purposes, rather than for its quite specific correct use (see page 139). Apostrophes also continue to cause problems for some students. Perhaps as a result of teachers trying to prevent their indiscriminate use, some candidates now leave them out altogether. The rules are given on page 140.

Mistakes made	How often	Total
misuse of quotation marks (e.g. in dialogue)		
failure to start a new sentence		
apostrophe used unnecessarily (e.g. 'Feel it's fur')		
apostrophes of ownership (e.g. girl's/girls')		
contractions (e.g. can't, didn't)		
word confusions (e.g. their/there; accept/except)		
misuse of -ible/-able/-uble (e.g. possible/impassable)		
single/double letter spellings (e.g. assess)		
plurals misspelt (e.g. potatoes, pansies)		
other spelling mistakes		
tautology (e.g. 'an unexpected surprise')		
awkward word order		

Commas and full stops

The commonest punctuation mistake is using a comma in place of a full stop and capital. Look at these words:

Raj ran towards the door

This is a sentence. It has a subject (Raj) and a verb (ran). 'Raj ran' is a sentence, but 'towards the door' is not. Try another one:

Raj ran towards the door, it swung open as he reached it.

This is wrong. You could write: 'Raj ran towards the door. It swung open as he reached it.' For a smoother effect, you could write: 'Raj ran towards the door, which swung open as he reached it.'

Commas, dashes and clauses

A **comma** is useful in dividing up clauses to make the sense clear:

I invited Kate, who works from home.

Without the comma, this could mean 'Kate who works from home, not Kate the doctor.' A separate clause in the middle of a sentence can also be divided off by commas:

The lorry, which had been teetering on the cliff-edge, fell at that moment.

Reading aloud is a good guide. Try reading the sentence above, first with the commas, then without. What's the difference?

Dashes can be used where a slightly more dramatic effect is required. They can also be used to make a deliberate break in the flow of sense:

The young man – he might have been 18 – turned towards me.

Capitals

A useful guide is that giving something a capital makes it more *specific*. The word 'cat' doesn't need a capital, any more than any other species of animal, but your pet Siamese Mimi does! Likewise, it's 'My **mum** hates housework,' but 'I think **Mum** needs a break.'

Question and exclamation marks

A question mark goes at the end of a question. Is the following correct?

He asked if I wanted it with knobs on.

This is correct. There's no question mark, because the question is reported. On the other hand, you would write, 'Do you want it with knobs on?'

Normally an exclamation mark only goes after an exclamation – usually a few words spoken with feeling, often an order.

Stop that! You fool! Oi! Keep out!

However, rhetorical 'questions', which aren't really questions, get an exclamation mark too:

Who do you think you are!

Colons (:) and semicolons (;)

A major exam board has commented on how refreshing it is to find candidates who not only use commas and full stops correctly but also know how to use semicolons.

A **semicolon** is stronger than a comma, but not as strong as a full stop. It's particularly useful to divide two balanced halves of a sentence, in place of 'but':

> Some people hate work; personally I can't get enough of it.

A **colon** gives the sense that something is about to follow on as a direct consequence of what's gone before:

> It turned out I'd wasted my time: she'd already left.

It can also be used to introduce a list:

> For the sponge, you will need: eggs, flour, jam...

Apostrophes

Here are some correct uses:

> she's, you'd, I'd, didn't, couldn't, wouldn't, can't (to show contraction)

> The teacher's face fell. The students' work had gone. (one teacher, two or more students)

Never insert an apostrophe just because a word is plural: tomatoes, potatoes, etc.

Dialogue

Dialogue can help to bring a piece of writing to life. Here's how to punctuate it:

> 'Don't give me that!' he snarled.
> 'I'm not giving you anything,' sneered Emma.

For complicated cases, see how it's done in any good novel.

Quotations

Long quotations are best presented as a separate block of text without quote marks; shorter ones like this:

> Romeo's line, 'O brawling love!' shows his confused feelings.

For quotations within a quotation, used double quote marks.

Spelling rules

Some spellings can be remembered by rhymes, or by using mental pictures. These memory techniques are called **mnemonics** (see opposite).

Pronunciation is also helpful, often providing the key to whether or not a word has a double letter in the middle:

> tinny/tiny, spinner/spiny, dinner/diner, bitter/biter, winner/winer

It can also help you tell whether a word has an *e* on the end or not:

> dot/dote, spat/spate, tot/tote, writ/write, mat/mate

A lot of these words turn into 'ing' words in a consistent way. Those without the *e* usually double their last letter, those with an *e* don't:

> dotting/doting, totting/toting, matting/mating, winning/wining

Mnemonics

Mnemonics (from Mnemosyne, the Greek goddess of memory) are useful in spelling, particularly if you make up your own. The best-known is:

> I before E, except after C, but only when the sound is EE.

Examples:

> brief, belief, chief, thief, mischief, siege

> receipt, receive, deceive, ceiling (after C)

> weir, seize, their, weight, height (no *ee* sound)

Mental pictures can also be useful, especially if they're striking, absurd or funny. You might combine them with a sentence. For example you might remember 'assessment' by saying 'I mustn't make an *ass* of myself in my *ass*essment,' and picturing someone with an ass's head. Your own will work best.

-able, -ible, -uble

This refers to a group of commonly confused word endings:

> comfortable, suitable, forgivable, fashionable, believable, passable

> inedible, indelible, incredible, horrible, indefensible, forcible, possible, contemptible

> soluble, voluble

Groupings

When you look at spelling corrected in your written work, see if they fit into categories, such as:

> bought, brought, drought, throughout

> caught, fraught, haughty

> rough, tough, enough

These can also be turned into mnemonics.

Spellchecks

If you have a computer your spellcheck will help you, but you won't be able to use it in the exam, and there are lots of other occasions in life when you'll have to rely on memory. Get to know exactly what your spellcheck does. It won't catch simple word confusions (such as bought and brought), and it will probably offer you silly alternatives to names – such as 'Huge' for 'Hugh'.

Commonly confused words

Most of these words sound similar to each other – though if you listen carefully there is often a slight difference. Study the list and examples below. Then test yourself.

accept/except	I accept your offer – except that I insist on paying.
access/excess	There's no access to anyone with excess baggage.
adverse/averse	I am averse to working in adverse conditions.
affect/effect	The rain won't affect us indoors. You'll spoil the effect.
alternate/alternative	I go on alternate Sundays; there's no alternative.
ambiguous/ambivalent	'Children free' is ambiguous. Does it mean no children, or no charge for children? I'm ambivalent – I have mixed feelings.
aural/oral	My hearing's poor – I need an aural test; my dentist says my oral hygiene is fine.
complement/compliment	The flavours complement each other: my compliments to the chef!
continual/continuous	We were continually arguing. Old printers use continuous paper.
councillor/counsellor	The Labour councillor needed a marriage counsellor.
delusion/illusion	He has delusions of grandeur. The conjuror created an illusion.
dependant/dependent	I'm not dependent on anyone, and I have no dependants.
deprecate/depreciate	I don't wish to deprecate your judgement, but I think your car will rapidly depreciate (lose value).
discreet/discrete	Diplomats are discreet. Wales isn't England – it has a discrete identity.
economic/economical	You may be interested in economic affairs, but your new car is hardly economical.
flaunt/flout	She flouted the rules and flaunted her jewellery.
imply/infer	I infer from your tone that you wish to imply that I am lying.
knew/new	I knew you'd found someone new.
lead/led	You now lead me where I once led you.
licence/license	A driving licence (noun) doesn't license (verb) you to kill.
lose/loose	I'd hate to lose my loose change.
passed/past	I passed (verb) a ghost from my past (noun) on the way here.
practise/practice	Try to practise (verb) every day – practice (noun) makes perfect.
principal/principle	The new school principal has no principles.
quiet/quite	Do be quiet – you're making me quite ill.
stationary/stationery	The train is stationary. A stationery shop sells paper.
there/their/they're	Over there you'll see their clothes: they're swimming.
thorough/through	The police were thorough in going through my drawers.
to/too/two	Thanks to you it's too late to find a room with two beds.
uninterested/disinterested	You seem uninterested in my conversation. I have nothing to gain – I'm a disinterested observer.
who's/whose	Who's the culprit? Whose muddy boots are these?
your/you're	Your brother's a criminal, and you're almost as bad.

Common errors

between	Avoid 'Between you and I'; use 'you and me'.
bored	Use 'bored with/by', not 'bored of'.
comprised	In 'comprised of', the 'of' is unnecessary.
equally	'Equally as good (etc.)' is wrong.
fed up	Use 'fed up with', not 'of'.
literally	Use only when strictly true. 'I'm literally gutted' is wrong.
reason	'The reason . . . is because . . .' is wrong. Use 'The reason is that . . .'

Tautology

This is a very common type of error, in which an idea is unnecessarily duplicated.

> He had an easy facility with words.
> I hope we can co-operate together.
> This is an entirely new and innovative technique.
> He sprinted quickly towards the goal.

Closely related is the use of 'less', 'more', 'completely' etc., with words that are already absolutes.

> This is completely perfect.
> I'm rather devastated.
> The town's absolutely dead tonight.
> They're less equal than they were.

Dangling prepositions

Prepositions (to, at, by, from etc.) left 'dangling' at the end of a sentence or clause often sound clumsy, especially in written form. Here are some examples, together with improved versions:

> This is a plan I give my full support to.
> This is a plan to which I give my full support.

> We talked about the party we'd met at.
> We talked abouty the party at which we'd met.

> This is the talent I make my living by.
> This is the talent by which I make my living.

> The man I gave my life to...
> The man to whom I gave my life...

Split infinitives

Sometimes a split infinitive sounds clumsy and should be reworded:

> We do not want to unthinkingly condemn him.
> We do not want to condemn him unthinkingly.

At other times, especially with only a short word between 'to' and the verb, it is acceptable:

> I decided to quickly run to the shop.

TRY THIS

Test yourself on the commonly confused words given earlier by covering the right-hand column and trying to make up sentences using the words correctly. Better still, get a friend to test you.

Summary

This chapter has told you about:

- what you need to check at 'draft' level
- what you need to check at 'proofreading' level
- how to use paragraphing
- when to use commas and full stops
- when to use semicolons, colons and dashes
- when to use question and exclamation marks
- how to punctuate dialogue and quotations
- what spellings you need to learn
- what your computer spellcheck will and won't do
- the correct use of commonly confused words

PREVIEW

This short chapter focuses on how to revise, and on exam technique. It covers:

- using **Mind Maps**
- making the most of your time before the exam
- making the most of your time in the exam
- examiners hints on how to succeed, and pitfalls to avoid

Revision

Throughout this book we have encouraged the use of Mind Maps for exploring your ideas, planning essays and keeping track of your learning. They can also be used for revising and testing yourself.

One great advantage of Mind Maps in revision is that you can see the whole of a topic at a glance, as well as how its different aspects interconnect. In addition, if you realise that you've left something out, you can usually fit in another branch to include it.

To test yourself using a Mind Map, just cover up the outer branches and try to fill them in from memory. You could even cover them with a piece of paper with a hole cut in the middle, so that you can draw your branches straight on.

Timing

Whether or not you use Mind Maps, you should not leave your revision to the last minute. No doubt you have been told that, and you may have ignored this advice or agreed in theory and yet not made any plans to revise in advance. If there is still time, work out a revision timetable. If you revise a subject several times, leaving increasing intervals of time in between (see Introduction), the memory will be 'stamped in', and you will remember what you have learned for life. Moreover, you will develop a better understanding of the subject before the exam, so that you can apply yourself to answering any question, not just the ones you have learned by heart.

If you are reading this at the last minute, and have not yet revised very much, at least make sure that you have read the relevant texts and made some quick Mind Maps of your initial impressions of them. There should still be some time to try some Mind Map essay plans for old exam question as well. If there's time, talk the texts over with a friend doing the same course.

And remember the **PAL** formula:
Purpose + Audience → Language

Give yourself a break

Allow yourself breaks during revision. Give yourself things to look forward to, both in the short term ('OK, cup of cocoa after this chapter!') and in the longer term ('Club Loco on Saturday night!'). Revising with friends can also help to take the pressure off. So can a change of scene, and getting bursts of exercise.

Directed revision

Just reading through pages of notes will probably not get you very far, and will quickly become dull. Looking at Mind Maps will be better, especially if you have used colours and images. Ideally you should make yourself think afresh as well as going over the old ground. Making Mind Map essay plans for questions on old exam papers will be more useful than reading old notes. Don't try to learn answers to these questions. There are too many possible questions, and you may be tempted to write an answer that you've learned, when you should be addressing yourself to the precise question that is asked.

The exam

Here's some advice based on what examiners say about candidates.

English language continuous writing

- Choose your question carefully.
- Plan, and use your time well.
- Organise and structure your writing according to the task set.
- Demonstrate basic writing skills and grasp of vocabulary.
- Offer a developed and relevant response to the set task.

Unseen comprehension and analysis

- Demonstrate your understanding of the material.
- Identify and evaluate the use of syntax and diction.
- Demonstrate an understanding of intention and any bias present.
- Analyse how the writer attempts to achieve a purpose. Be precise: don't just say something 'is effective', is used 'for effect', 'creates impact' etc. Say what the effect or impact is.
- Give personal responses, backed up by evidence.

- Make correct, precise use of technical terms where appropriate.
- Avoid vague language and cliché.

Unseen poetry

- Show an understanding of the poem.
- Use technical terminology where appropriate, but only if you can use it correctly.
- Don't just point out a technical feature – say how it is used to achieve an effect, what that effect is, and how it adds to the poem as a whole.
- If a particular feature does not seem to be of key importance, e.g. alliteration as 'word music', or a more standard rhyme scheme – do not dwell on it or try to read more significance into it than there is.
- Keep quotes short.
- Try to tackle the poem as a whole, not just line by line.

Shakespeare and other drama

Unseen extracts require close analysis of language, with *some* placing in context. You will lose marks if you spend too much time on the context and too little on the given extract itself.

For other questions on set texts:

- maintain an awareness of the text as theatre
- be prepared to comment on the language, and how it reflects the themes of the play – remember STAR (see page 100)
- use quotations selectively and appropriately
- develop a clear line of argument
- be prepared to write about themes, plot or character, in response to the precise question chosen.

Novels

- Don't retell the whole plot just because you know it.
- Don't talk about characters as if they were real people.
- Don't indulge in speculation about information that is not in the novel: 'Perhaps Miss Haversham had frightened her lover off, or perhaps…'
- Use the present tense ('Miss Haversham *is* a bitter and disappointed woman…')
- Show an awareness of setting and atmosphere, and of narrative stance.

Exam technique

Avoid late-night cramming the night before: try to relax instead. Treat the exam as an opportunity to show off what you know. You may even enjoy the exam – it has been known! There is little to be gained by last-minute cramming. At most, scan your Mind Maps or keyword notes. Get someone else to ask you a few questions if that helps. Then switch off!

In the exam itself, take your time.

- Read the exam paper thoroughly – don't start frantically scribbling as soon as you have the slightest idea of what you're doing. Ignore anyone else who does this.
- Be sure you understand how many questions you need to answer, and from which sections.
- Spend a few minutes considering your choice. You might even do a Mini Mind Map of one or two options to see what you might make of them, before deciding.
- *Read the question* and be sure that you understand what is required. If you don't, choose another question.
- Plan your time. If the marks allocated for each question are given, plan your time accordingly. Whatever happens, avoid spending almost all your time on one answer when you have to write two or three. However good your one answer is, it can only earn you a certain number of marks.
- If you still find that the clock has caught you out, you may get some credit for notes explaining where your essay would have gone had there been time!
- Allow time to proofread your work.
- Take a break before you start revising for the next exam.

> ### Summary
>
> **This chapter has told you to:**
>
> - **plan and start your revision well in advance**
> - **use Mind Maps**
> - **read questions carefully**
> - **write answers which are strictly relevant**
> - **relax – but not too much**

Answers

Page 20

1 **a)** S, V, DO **b)** S, V, C **c)** S, V, IO, DO **d)** S, V

2 **a)** compound **b)** simple **c)** complex **d)** simple

Page 37

a) letter – Dorothy Wordsworth to William Wordsworth (1808)

b) sermon – John Donne (1624)

c) autobiography – Maya Angelou (1969)

d) travel – Redmond O'Hanlon (1984)

e) essay – Raymond Williams (1961)

f) biography – Philip Norman (1984)

Page 38

1 Make those people easy with whom we converse (make people we talk to feel comfortable).

2 reason, good sense

3 pride, ill nature, lack of good sense

4 Swift seems to have a poor opinion of human beings; he says 'very few among mankind' have good sense.

5 They have agreed upon fixing some rules about how people should behave.

Page 49

1 **i)** b **ii)** f **iii)** a, d **iv)** a, e **v)** c

2 **a)** Emily, Charlotte and Anne Brontë

  b) George Eliot

Page 58

1 F 2 F 3 F 4 F 5 F 6 F 7 F 8 T 9 T

Page 67

Charles Darwin; Sigmund Freud

Page 70

1 eighteenth century

2 late eighteenth, early nineteenth century

3 letters

4 story, structure, design

5 themes

6 false

7 stream of consciousness

8 **a)** *Frankenstein* by Mary Shelley, 1818

  b) *Mansfield Park* by Jane Austen, 1814

  c) *The Garrick Year* by Margaret Drabble, 1964

  d) *Joseph Andrews* by Henry Fielding, 1742

  e) *Middlemarch* by George Eliot, 1871

Page 73

You should have ticked 1, 4 and 6.

Page 79

You should have ticked 3, 6, 7 and 8.

Page 83

1 He is annoyed because the previous evening Millament refused to see him.

2 He thinks they are idle fools.

3 She doesn't like being reprimanded, being told what to do and being told her faults.

Page 85

1 Mrs Malaprop disapproves of Lydia's romance; Mrs Malaprop is in love with Sir Lucius and has written him love letters under a false name; Lydia dislikes Acres; Lydia has provoked a quarrel with Beverley.

2 Lydia appears to be emotional and posturing. She wants to have a quarrel with Beverley because she feels that is the way lovers should behave. Lydia seems to live in a world of romantic fantasy. If you included here (or in your plot points) the idea that the resolution of the play will show that Lydia has developed a more clear-sighted and realistic approach to love, give yourself a pat on the back!

Page 87

1 The dialogue is the most striking characteristic. The characters are not clearly differentiated – they are like mouthpieces for the dialogue. Even the servant speaks in the same way as the two men.

2 b, d, f, g, i

Page 89

1 F 2 F 3 T 4 T 5 T 6 F 7 T 8 T 9 F 10 F
11 T 12 T 13 T 14 F

Page 92

1 You could have included costume, lighting, music, stage directions, scenery, costume

2 acts and scenes

3 resolution

4 subplot

5 the words spoken between characters in plays

6 *Everyman*

7 because it refers to the restoration of the monarchy when Charles II came to the throne.

8 George Bernard Shaw, Oscar Wilde

9 e.g. Henrik Ibsen, Bertolt Brecht

10 *Look Back in Anger*

11 **a)** *The Way of the World*, 1700

  b) *A Taste of Honey*, 1958

  c) *The Duchess of Malfi*, 1612

Page 96

1 1564

2 non-religious

3 Fate

4 (b)

5 To Christians, money-lending was a sin, and Jews were banned from professions.

6 Elizabeth I

7 They ruled 'by Divine Right', so it was a crime against God.

8 plague

9 James VI of Scotland, who became James I of England

10 Edmund

11 bodies

12 there was no curtain

Page 99

1 *hubris*

2 'Tragedy' comes from a Greek word for goat; a tragic hero was a *scapegoat*.

3 a Roman dramatist who influenced Shakespeare

4 a village festival to honour Dionysus, god of wine and fertility

5 marry

6 the king

7 the family

Page 112

a) dactylic b) trochaic c) iambic d) anapestic
e) spondaic.

Page 118

1 paired rhyming lines of iambic pentameter

2 five

3 fourteen

4 Petrarchan and Shakespearean

5 Petrarchan

6 simile

7 personification

8 oxymoron

9 metaphor

10 Images can appeal to senses other than that of sight.

Page 124

Your pyramid should show the King, appointed by God, at the top. The Knight, who owes duty to the king, should be next below him. The landless peasants, the *cherls*, are at the bottom. You may have assessed the wealth and status of the middle class pilgrims and placed them accordingly. Notice that Chaucer's group of pilgrims doesn't include the very top or the very bottom layers of society – there is no top-ranking bishop in the church group, and the Plowman, though humble, is a tenant farmer.

Page 124

You might have considered the characters in 'The General Prologue' who behave in an amoral or antisocial way, or who abuse their position of trust, such as the Summoner, Pardoner, Friar, Miller, Manciple, Reeve. Chaucer condemns these characters with varying degrees of intensity. You may have thought about Chaucer's attitude to the Wife of Bath's provocative claim to the right to bigamy and 'maistrye' (dominance) in marriage, or to May's deception of her husband in The Merchant's Tale. You might have considered Chaucer's view of institutions such as the Church and the law, and to what extent you feel he promotes reform of such bodies. Your answer could refer to Chaucer's mixture of condemnation and admiration for some characters. You could go on to think about how Chaucer reveals his attitude, for example, through his use of irony as a weapon of criticism. (Look under **Style** for more about this.)

Page 127

a) gentillesse b) churlish c) sanguine, choleric, phlegmatic, melancholy

Page 128

a) before b) also c) honourable or respectable
d) such

Page 129

1 b and e   2 b and c   3 b and c

Page 137

1 14th century   2 b and c   3 c   4 iambic pentameter

Words printed in **bold italic** in an explanation have their own entries.

abstract nouns *nouns* labelling intangible things; e.g. 'love'.

accent the characteristic modulation of speech found in a particular region.

active (verb/sentence) verb form, or sentence containing it, in which the *subject* does what the *verb* indicates; e.g. 'The fish eats the worm.' (See also *passive*.)

adjective a word describing a thing.

adverb a word modifying a *verb*, *adjective* or another adverb; as in, e.g. 'laugh *loudly*', '*quietly* confident', '*surprisingly* slowly'.

adverb of frequency one indicating how often something is done; e.g. rarely, always.

allegory an extended metaphor in which events symbolise other events.

alliteration the repetition, for effect, of consonant sounds.

allusion the use of literary, cultural and historical references.

anapaest a *foot* of two unstressed syllables and one stressed (– – /).

aside in drama, a short speech spoken by one character as if thinking aloud, not meant to be heard by others on the stage.

assonance the repetition, for effect, of vowel sounds.

audience the readers of a text, as well as those who watch a play, etc.

bias an understanding or reporting of facts that misrepresents them in favour of one view rather than another.

bibliography list of works referred to in the process of writing essays, etc.

blank verse unrhymed *iambic pentameter* (each line having five pairs of syllables, the first of each pair unstressed, the second stressed).

broadsheet large-format newspaper aimed at the more educated reader.

catalyst in drama, the key circumstance or event which determines the direction of the plot.

catharsis in tragedy, the purging of an audience's dangerous emotions achieved by the hero's death and the resolution of conflict.

clause part of a sentence (which may itself form a *simple sentence*) containing a *subject* and a *finite verb*.

comedy (Shakespearean) type of play featuring: characters who flout social conventions; confusions of rank; disguises; women dressed as men; trickery; and happy endings with marriages.

comedy of manners genre ridiculing the manners and customs of a fashionable social class.

complement word giving information about a *subject* when used with an *intransitive verb*. e.g. 'She *seems* puzzled.'

complex sentence one with two or more clauses, one independent and the other(s) dependent on it; e.g. 'I came top, which was nice.'

compound sentence one with two clauses linked by a conjunction: 'I like ducks but not geese.'

conceit extended comparison more notable for cleverness than accuracy.

concrete noun a word denoting a tangible thing.

conjunction word joining phrases or clauses; e.g. 'and', 'beneath'.

connotation whatever is suggested by a word beyond its basic sense, determined by the contexts in which it is normally used.

co-ordinating conjunction word simply linking clauses; e.g. 'and', 'but', 'or'.

couplet pair of lines, usually rhyming.

courtly love medieval literary tradition in which a knight, a lady and her husband form a love triangle and behave according to certain rules.

dactyl a *foot* of one stressed and two unstressed syllables (/ – –).

declarative (sentence) one making a statement.

determiner word modifying a *noun* and specifying its significance or quantity; e.g. the *articles* and 'this', 'that', etc.

dialect any systematic variation of English based on region or social group, differing from standard English in *grammar*, *lexis* and *idioms*.

diction choice and arrangement of words.

direct object the thing or person in a sentence to which something is done; as in e.g. 'She tore *her dress*.'

discursive presenting a logical argument, step by step.

dramatic irony when a play's audience knows something of which a character on stage is ignorant.

dynamic verb one which describes what a subject does.

emotive language language which manipulates its audience's emotions.

enjambement continuation of the sense of a line without pause onto the next line.

epic poems, telling stories about heroic deeds.

epigram short, witty statement; e.g. 'Hunting is the pursuit of the inedible by the unspeakable.' (Oscar Wilde)

epistolary novel genre of fiction in which the plot unfolds through letters.

exclamatory sentence one consisting of an exclamation; e.g. 'Phew!'

fact any state of affairs generally thought to be true.

faction novel which is a mixture of fact and fiction; e.g *In Cold Blood* by Truman Capote.

feminist criticism critical approach developed in the 1960s, based on assessing the role of gender in the production of texts. A particular issue is the subordination of women in a patriarchal society.

finite verb verb form which can occur alone in a main clause, attributed to a *subject*; as in e.g. 'Jo coughed.'

foot in verse, a group of syllables constituting a metrical unit.

free indirect speech technique of blending a character's words and thoughts with those of the narrator.

genre type of literary work conforming to certain expectations; e.g. tragedy.

Gothic novel genre of fiction popular in the eighteenth century, in which eerie and supernatural events take place in sinister settings.

grammar system of rules for organising words to make mutually agreed sense.

heroic couplet pair of rhyming lines of *iambic pentameter*.

hexameter pattern of verse with six *feet* in a line.

history type of Shakespeare play based on history, especially on kingship; similar in some ways to *tragedy*.

iam a *foot* of one unstressed and one stressed syllable (– /).

iambic pentameter *metre* in which each line contains five *iams*.

idiom a characteristic expression of a language or *dialect*.

image a word picture bringing an idea to life by appealing to the senses.

imperative a command.

industrial novel novel dealing with the issues of the Industrial Revolution, often set in the north of England e.g. *North and South* by Elizabeth Gaskell.

interrogative sentence asking a question.

intransitive verb one used with no object; e.g. 'The gerbil plays.' (See also *transitive verb*.)

irony a style of writing in which one thing is said and another is meant, used for a variety of effects, such as criticism or ridicule.

lexis vocabulary, or choice of words.

magical realism a fiction style which combines mythical elements, bizarre events and a strong sense of cultural tradition; e.g. *Midnight's Children* by Salman Rushdie.

main clause one making full sense in itself, containing a subject and finite verb; e.g. in the sentence, 'The kitten, which was only three days old, purred loudly,' the main clause is 'The kitten purred loudly.' (See also *subordinate clause*.)

Marxist criticism critical approach which sees literature in relation to class struggle, and assesses the way texts present social realities.

media the various forms of mass communication; usually television, radio, newspapers, magazines and the Internet.

metaphor a compressed *simile* describing something as if it were something else.

Metaphysicals group of poets whose poems are characterised by argument, philosophical debate and elaborate *conceits*.

metre the pattern of *feet* in verse, each foot consisting of 1–3 syllables, in combinations of stressed (/) and unstressed (–).

monologue a solo spoken performance; e.g. Alan Bennett's *Talking Heads*.

morphemes the smallest units of language in terms of meaning, in some cases smaller than a *syllable*; e.g. 's' when used to make a plural.

morphology the study or composition of *morphemes*.

narrator in a novel, a character who tells the story. An *omniscient* narrator has complete knowledge of everything that takes place in the narrative; an *unreliable* narrator is one whose knowledge and judgements are limited and biased.

non-finite verb verb form which cannot function as a clause's main verb; i.e. the infinitive (e.g. 'to eat') and the present and past participles (e.g. 'eating' and 'eaten').

noun word denoting a thing.

object the thing to which a *subject* is doing something.

onomatopoeia use of words whose sound imitates the thing they describe.

opinion a subjective view or interpretation of facts.

oxymoron an *image* which combines opposite, paradoxical ideas.

paradox an apparently contradictory statement which contains some truth; e.g. 'I hear her hair has turned quite gold from grief' (*The Importance of Being Earnest*).

parody a copy of a writer's style made for humorous effect.

passive (verb/sentence) verb form, or sentence containing it, in which the sentence *subject* has done to it whatever the verb indicates; e.g. 'The worm is eaten by the fish.' (See also *active*.)

pentameter pattern of verse with five *feet* in a line.

persona an assumed identity.

personification an *image* speaking of something abstract, such as love, death or sleep, as if it were a person or a god.

Petrarchan sonnet verse form usually with the first eight lines (the octave) rhyming ABBAABBA, the remaining six (the sestet) CDCDCD.

phonetics the sounds of words, and how those sounds are made.

phrase any group of words not containing a subject and verb.

picaresque type of novel popular in the eighteenth century, featuring the adventures of a wandering rogue; e.g. *Tom Jones* by Henry Fielding.

Pidgin an extreme variant of English evolved by originally non-native speakers of English with diverse linguistic backgrounds in order to communicate with one another.

plot the story; the events that take place and how they are arranged.

polysyllabic composed of several syllables.

possessive pronoun word denoting ownership; e.g. 'my', 'mine'.

post-modification the use of a phrase *after* another word or phrase to qualify it; e.g. 'The sound, *strangely compelling* ...'

pre-modification the use of a phrase *before* another word or phrase to qualify it; e.g. 'The *already exhausted* child ...'

predicate the part of a sentence excluding the *subject*; e.g. in 'Laura looks great,' the predicate is 'looks great'.

prefix a unit of meaning coming at the beginning of a word; e.g. '*pre*decessor'.

preposition word relating one thing or action to another; e.g. 'beside'.

pronoun word replacing a noun; e.g. 'she'.

proper noun word used to name people, places, etc.

Received Pronunciation (RP) the standardised accent used by many public speakers.

register the style and form of English used, determined by the situation, or context – in turn determined by intended audience and purpose.

relative pronoun word replacing a noun and used to ask a question or introduce a relative *clause*; e.g. 'which'.

Restoration comedy type of drama produced between the restoration of the monarchy, in 1660, to the end of the century; e.g. *The Way of the World* by William Wycherley.

revenge tragedy type of play popular in early seventeenth century, in which plot hinges on revenge; featuring real or feigned madness, and deaths.

rhetoric in medieval times, the art of embellishing literary expression according to certain rules; in modern times, eloquence, particularly in speech-making.

romance type of Shakespearean comedy featuring exotic settings, mysterious magical events, strong moral and spiritual messages, and characters learning through suffering.

Romantic Movement late eighteenth- and early nineteenth-century arts movement emphasising the individual's spirit, imagination, emotions and feelings about the world.

satire literature which humorously exposes and ridicules vice and folly.

semantic field a broad area of meaning including a range of related words.

semantics meaning of words, including their *connotations* and *subtext*.

sentence a group of words including a *subject* and a *predicate* – what the subject is, or is doing.

Shakespearean sonnet verse form in which a theme is stated in the first twelve lines, typically rhyming ABABCDCDEFEF, and a conclusion is drawn in a final rhyming couplet (GG).

simile an *image* comparing two things similar in some way but different in others, normally using 'like' or 'as'.

simple sentence one with one subject and one verb: 'I like ducks.' This is one clause.

sonnet see *Petrarchan sonnet* and *Shakespearean sonnet*.

Spenserian stanza verse form with eight lines of iambic pentameter followed by one of iambic hexameter (six feet); rhymes ABABBCBCC.

spondee a *foot* of two stressed syllables (//).

standard English the particular form of English, originally based on East Midlands dialect, most often used by educated speakers in formal situations.

stative verb one describing a *state* of being or becoming; e.g. 'I *appear* (happy ...)'.

stream of consciousness technique exploring the thought processes and unconscious minds of characters; used by writers such as Virginia Woolf and James Joyce.

structure the organisation of a text; e.g. narrative, plot, repeated images and symbols.

style the form and expression of a text.

subject in a sentence, the person or thing governing the *verb*.

subordinate clause one which only makes sense in relation to a *main clause*.

subordinating conjunction word establishing a relationship between ideas; e.g. 'if'.

subplot subsidiary plot coinciding with the main plot and often reflecting aspects of it.

subtext what a speaker or writer is suggesting beneath the obvious, literal sense.

suffix unit of meaning coming at the end of a word; e.g. 'ornith*ology*', 'the*ology*'.

syllable unit of pronunciation uttered without interruption, having one vowel sound and usually with a consonant or consonant before and/or after.

syntax the aspect of grammar focusing on word order within a sentence.

tabloid a small-format newspaper aimed at a less educated readership.

tense the form of a verb determining *when* an event takes place.

tetrameter pattern of verse with four *feet* in a line.

tone the mood created by a writer's choice and organisation of words; e.g. angry, persuasive.

tragedy play focusing on a hero whose nobility or achievement we admire, and whose downfall and death through a weakness or error, coupled with fate, wins our sympathy.

transitive verb one used with an object; e.g. 'The gerbil plays poker.' (See also *Intransitive verb*.)

trochee a *foot* of one stressed and one unstressed syllable (/ –).

verb a word denoting doing or being.

verse form style of poem with a particular metrical pattern and rhyme scheme, sometimes used for a particular purpose; e.g. *sonnet* for love poetry.

viewpoint the way a narrator approaches the material and the audience.

word classes categories of word, determined by function; e.g. *noun*.